Gender Locales and Local Genders in Archaeology

Edited by

Tove Hjørungdal

BAR International Series 1425
2005

Published in 2016 by
BAR Publishing, Oxford

BAR International Series 1425

Gender Locales and Local Genders in Archaeology

ISBN 978 1 84171 864 4

BAR Publishing is the trading name of British Archaeological Reports (Oxford) Ltd.
British Archaeological Reports was first incorporated in 1974 to publish the BAR
Series, International and British. In 1992 Hadrian Books Ltd became part of the BAR
group. This volume was originally published by Archaeopress in conjunction with
British Archaeological Reports (Oxford) Ltd / Hadrian Books Ltd, the Series principal
publisher, in 2005. This present volume is published by BAR Publishing, 2016.

Printed in England

BAR
PUBLISHING

BAR titles are available from:

BAR Publishing
122 Banbury Rd, Oxford, OX2 7BP, UK
EMAIL   info@barpublishing.com
PHONE   +44 (0)1865 310431
FAX   +44 (0)1865 316916
www.barpublishing.com

For Raimond Thörn

Contents

List of Contributors

László Reményi,   PhD, Budapest History Museum, Hungary

Sophie Bergerbrant,   PhD student, Stockholm University, Sweden

Sabine Reinhold,   Dr., Feodor Lynen research fellow, Alexander-von-Humboldt foundation, Institute of Archaeology, RAS (Russian Academy of Sciences), Moscow, Russia

Marie Svedin,   PhD student, Gothenburg University, Sweden

Anita Synnestvedt,   PhD student, Gothenburg University, Sweden

Lillian Rathje,   Dr., Västerbottens Museum, Umeå, Sweden

Per Cornell,   Dr., Associate Professor, Gothenburg University, Sweden

Linda Lövkvist,   PhD student, Gothenburg University, Sweden

Tove Hjørungdal,   Dr., Associate Professor, Gothenburg University, Sweden

Figures & Tables

Introduction

Tove Hjørungdal

Gothenburg University, Sweden

The present volume, *Gender Locales and Locale Genders in Archaeology*, has its initial point of departure in an EAA session in Thessalonica, Greece in September 2002. Four of the Thessalonica papers are included, which are Cornell, Rathje, Svedin, and Synnestvedt. The other four papers have joined us later on, and are represented by the contributions of Reményi, Bergerbrant, Reinhold, together with a co-written paper by Lövkvist & Hjørungdal.

The 2002 EAA session was planned to cover chosen issues of social theory and gender in Archaeology. So it did in a range of aspects, and so does this book intend to do as well.

It is predominantly Swedish colleagues and Swedish graduate students who have written the papers. But there are also contributions from colleagues in Germany and Hungary. The concept of this volume, are case studies, and the papers give examples of such from a rather wide geographical area within Eurasia; Sweden; Norway; Denmark; Germany; Hungary; Kaukasia; and from as far away as Argentina on the other side of the World. The volume is as such represented by contexts from three continents. Most of the papers give cases with reference to the relationships between materiality, aspects of social conditions, and with a focus on gender. Two of the papers cover historical and present times, while the majority among them analyse prehistoric contexts. One paper is on gender in the professional education of Archaeologists.

The papers are as far as possible arranged according to chronology, with the earliest contexts first and present examples to close the volume.

The papers

László Reményi writes on *The Golden Age of the Carpathian basin and the Beautiful Warrior,* and looks at relations of the Middle Bronze Age social history in the Carpathian basin. His paper takes up social issues on a more general level, but includes as well a discussion of the construction of gender identity in the development of a warrior elite in the Bronze Age. Reményi draws on Paul Treherne's paper (1995) that gives a broad analysis and discussion of the issue in question. The first half of 2nd Millenium BC is interpreted as the golden age of the Carpatian Basin. Economic and social changes are met with in this period, and material changes appear as fortified settlements - two level settlement-structure -, rich graves with weapons and gold, as well as bronze depots and imports. The paper discusses the reasons behind the changes following the *Koszider* period, from a new point of view in Hungarian archaeology. In this context the new warrior elite raised. The power of the elite and defence of the community was protected by the gendered warrior aristocracy found in graves with weapons. The Bronze Age growth culminated in the *Koszider* period. The cultures of the Carpathian basin organized most-extended exchange system in this period. After the *Koszider* period due to various reasons the instable system of the Middle Bronze Age chiefdoms crashed. This crisis caused demographical decrease, so the permeation of the *Tumulus* culture ran quickly. At the beginning of the Late Bronze Age mixed groups of the T*umulus* culture and the earlier population lived in the Carpathian basin.

Sophie Bergerbrant takes up the question of female interaction during the Early and Middle Bronze Age in Europe, with special focus on bronze tubes on dress. Bronze tubes have traditionally rather been overlooked as a source of information about social conditions. Bergerbrant makes a research into the sources, and looks at the occurrence of the bronze tubes in chosen geographical regions of Europe. Bronze tubes are traditionally associated with the string end of the female skirt.

The present study does however point to the fact that bronze tubes were worn in many different ways on the dress. And, it was as well an object worn by men and children. There are interesting local and regional differences observed in the ways of using bronze tubes on dress. Persons (women) as well as ideas moved in the case of bronze tubes. Both women and men travelled, which might have given them special status as they had knowledge of other places. Among the conclusions drawn, is that bronze tubes seem to have been used by specific people in the society, as there seems to have been only one wearer of bronze tubes in a generation. The questions of how these possible exclusive statuses were constructed and on which bases, will be followed up in Bergerbrant's further research.

Sabine Reinhold discusses the engendering of communication networks, and analyses gender related exchange systems of North Caucasian Iron Age societies in the geographical areas between high mountains, piedmonts, and the steppe. Here the so called *Koban* culture took shape amid the larger cultural networks of Eurasia and the Near East. The base of this study is made up of about 340 inhumation burials of the pre-Scythian period, i.e. from the 10th to the end of the 8th century

BC. The main endeavour of this paper is to present a review of the social organisation of these societies with a focus on gender related communication networks. Mainly two different gender groups are defined, a male and a female one, but each of them with an internal ranking system. Three cultural networks can however be defined by the support of artefact distribution, and similarities in costume, armour, fighting techniques. Two of them involve the male sphere – armour and prestige goods exchange, and one of them shows female aspects like costumes and costume elements. The female network, geographically link the two male circles, which otherwise stand rather against each other. Alternative explanations to the differences in male and female networks are tried, but the two gendered network systems were however not impermeable of interaction with each other.

Marie Svedin analyses the significance of children, animals and teeth in life and death, and relates her investigations to kin- and gender negotiations at Styrmansberget in Gotland, during the period between AD 100 and 550, i.e. a time span roughly covering the Roman Iron Ages and the Migration Period. By placing the child-adult graves at Styrmansberget an individual's position in the kin, relations between different genders, ages and relations between adult and children in life and death, could be negotiated. Attention is given to the relationship between different animals, especially between birds, humans and children. The significance of teeth, life course and kin is focused as well. As an assessment, the graves from Styrmansberget are compared to 6 other child burials from Gotland. The author throws light at the statement that in the life course transformation gender identity of individuals is created as well as it represents an understanding of society. The socialization of persons takes place through playing, expectations, self-apprehension, inhibitions, upbringing and changes of both social and biological kind, and becomes important for the person's whole life cycle. In the discussion arguments from a microarcheological perspective are used. The paper is closed by a preliminary interpretation of some general aspects of gender relations in Gotland during the Roman Iron Age and the Migration period.

Anita Synnestvedt aims to look at material culture from a different kind of view, in her paper titled *Making People Visible. Tapestries from Viking Age Norway.* Her departure is in Margaret Conkey's method of Context of action/contexts for power (Conkey 1991), while the case study includes the tapestries from two Viking ship burials in Norway, the Oseberg and Haugen ships. The use of Conkey's model of analysis presented through a discussion of possible scenarios in the material culture, and through a search for chains of associations between these scenarios. Gender relations are as such regarded as historical forces.

It is the production of textiles that is analysed more in detail. Conclusions are that textile production seems to

have had a high social status. It has also been possible to identify powerful and might roles and positions among women in Viking Age contexts. These are positions related to the production of art and crafts. Synnestvedt also advocates the use and contextual usefulness of Conkey's model. It presents us with a great challenge as it has such a great potential to be adjusted to context.

Lillian Rathje explores folk belief and society in a Northern Swedish context. She works with the method of relational analysis, especially on notions of folk belief, and discusses how they can be used in our endeavours to interpret and understand prehistoric societies. The models concern in particular models for gendered action, and gendered division of labour. The case study chosen is the contexts of Late Iron Ages and Early medieval periods, North Sweden. This might be approximately what is pointed out as The Land of the Amazons in the map drawn by Adam of Bremen on the Nordic countries about AD 1080.

By the analysis of material structures, folk belief on sexuality and on folk medicine, Rathje draws conclusions on more flexible gender roles, and less strictly norms on gender and sexuality in North Sweden compared to the Southern parts of the country. Women in the North seem also to have had a more powerful position within farm economy, as compared to Southern parts of Sweden.

The use of models developed within historical contexts must however be used with caution if transmitted to prehistoric contexts. Rathje makes us highly aware of this fact through her critical evaluation. Relational analogies make it however possible to build a ground for discussions on gender systems, gender norms, and issues like division of labour.

Per Cornell explores aspects of early 21st century popular cult in Argentina. The paper has a two fold aim. First, it is to demonstrate the existence of the cult of popular saints. Second, and on a theoretical and methodological level, it is to discuss the possibilities for a future archaeological contribution to the study of this type of social practice.

Focus is on chosen representatives of popular saints, more exactly on two female saints, *Santa Gilda* and *Difunta Correa*, their altars, and offerings. Male saints, like *Gaucho Gil*, are represented as well. Cult places for the saints are constructed by the way of altars, in geographical locations that have been of importance to the lives of, or to the legends about the saints. People bring flowers and material things of various kinds into the cult locales with the aim to honour the saint, and also to obtain something. Personal observations made by the author himself through several visits to Argentina from 1987 to 2004, build the sources for reflection on the phenomenon in question. Important conclusions are that the popular saints are given different material things according to their area of relation. This case study then, illustrates clearly some significant aspects of the potential of archaeological studies of the recent past and the present, an archaeology of the *"contemporaneity"*, as well as it relates to a discussion of social materiality in a specific context of practice.

Linda Lövkvist & Tove Hjørungdal present a co-authored paper on the role of gender in tertiary, professional education of Archaeologists. Both students and teachers are encompassed by the discussion set off. The starting point is as such learning, and chosen aspects of learning are discussed with references in pedagogical literature. Our objective is that this huge matter needs much more discussion in Archaeology, and as such we sketch some points for a discussion in this vein.

The first draft of the text was written some years ago, and has been thoroughly changed, and partly rewritten, since. When we wrote the first draft, we were dreaming of the possibilities to perform the programme we sketch in the paper. Now, we partly can perform it! Our department has become more money, not least thanks to the fact that we were given a developmental project from the *Council for the Renewal of Higher Education*, in many respects advocating the same policy as we proposed in earlier drafts of this paper. The pedagogical project, named *From receiving to performing. Learning field archaeology,* aims at developing new working methods in our field courses for undergraduates. Methods developed are expected to be transmittable to other and more theoretical courses, and to other contexts of education (For a presentation, see Hjørungdal et al. forthcoming).

So, things have changed, indeed. But we still wanted to present our initial thoughts and their background, although they are somewhat modified if not completely altered. A general background to this paper is the fact that the present overwhelming problem in academia is the permanent unstable economic situation, along with the lack of time for university teachers to develop their skills, and to do good research. These, as 10-15% of our weekly working time, i.e. 4-6 hours a week are reserved for research, indeed!

This paper contents consequently, a range of interrelated problems and issues in tertiary education that warrant light in many aspects. We look at the educational and pedagogical situation in a Gothenburgian, and a Swedish context, and do as well relate to the general European context. Hence we also had the opportunity to become aware of other analyses and discussions of pedagogy and its contemporary context, recently published by Yannis Hamilakis (2004), and that shows sceneries appearing portentous familiar to us.

Gender and feminism

Two different main types of discourses on gender and feminism are represented in this volume. The one type, represented by most papers, namely those written by Reményi, Reinhold, Bergerbrant, Svedin, Synnestvedt, Rathje, and Cornell, refer to how material things, bodies and structures can be involved in, and are active in, the processes of making and negotiating gender. Another type of discourse is come within reach of by Lövkvist & Hjørungdal who refer to education, and the practice of feminist pedagogy. They have found a point of inspiration in an article by Conkey & Tringham (1996), who discuss the professors' own experiments in their teaching of archaeology – experiments which have been motivated and informed by various aspects of feminist thought. Among the points is found how to scrutinize explicitly the links between their feminist thinking and scholarship, and their classroom practices.

The eight papers of the present volume do also contribute to different discourses on gender and feminism, through diversity in theoretical approaches to gender. Feminism is an underlying theory in many aspects, and in some of the papers, but the choices of focus and of theoretical characteristics, represent a mixture of nuances.

Theory is as such found to be explicit as well as implicit, in the papers. In other aspects the papers also show a more implicit stance as theories of gender and of other social relationships are not explicated. Conclusions drawn on gender are however informed with theory, anyway. One example is Reinhold who draws conclusions about complementary male and female genders in her case study. She does anyway find fine distinctions within her definitions of male and female networks that show the way to a problematiziation of a complementary and static, model of gender. The same is the case with Reményi's study that does not explicit on gender theoretically, but still has the capacity of showing the relevance of a more inherent gender construct. Treherne's warrior's beauty has emanated much interest and launched a problematization of elite masculinity in prehistory.

A difference-within perspective on gender groups or categories (Moore 1994), is as well found throughout the papers collected here. This is illustrated by people who distinguish themselves from many other people of their kinds, like the people (women) wearing bronze tube skirts, or the warriors grooming their appearances, or as well by the children buried with adults in Gotland.

The question of the construction of male and female gender through, and in relation to, materiality, is has taken a predominant position, but in a range of ways. All together, the capacity to problematize male and female gender, and to open up to new approaches and interpretations of social contexts, are found to be important aspects and aims of the papers in this volume.

Gender Locales and Local Genders in Archaeology

All of the papers give local or regional contexts for gender negotiations and constructions. Therefore, the title of this volume was chosen as *Gender Locales and Locale*

Genders in Archaeology. All of the contexts under analysis represent, in some way, locales for the negotiations of gender, an issue that has been extended on in archaeology since some years ago (cf. Sørensen 2000). Thus, the papers show a wide variety in how gender can be constructed, negotiated, performed, and mediated. All of them give overt local, or at least, regional examples of how gender and social theories are at work. The approach of many of the papers, and consequently the choice of title to the volume, has a more general background, however. This is found in discussions on gender in archaeology, that have shown a development of context-related processes of gender, and with a stress on the many facetted role of materiality in these processes of action and of cooperation among people (e.g. Arwill-Nordbladh 1998; Chapman 2000; Derevenski 2002). Examples are given of a life course perspective, and the construction and changes of gender as continuous processes throughout human life, and in death as well.

An aspect of gender, setting off widely in archaeology, is the matter of how gender intersects with other categories and traits, like age, ethnicity, class, language and religion, to mention a few important issues (e.g. Derevenski op.cit.). Svedin's and Cornell's papers give various, but clear examples of approaches within this cluster of perspectives, although they are touched upon in other papers, too, however not always apparent.

The interest in local scales in archaeology (cf. Cornell & Fahlander 2002 with references) is due to a post colonial influence, directly, or, more often, indirectly. This concerns not least current theories of gender and feminism in archaeology, are thus getting noticeable through the directions taken in some of the present gender studies, seeking to intersect processes of gender with age and geographic locations (post colonial theorists would here be represented by not least Spivak (1993), Mohanty (1985) and Bhabha (1994); for an instructive overview see Childs & Williams 1997). Post colonial influences are more explicit in fields of archaeology like Classics (e.g. Gosden 2004), but have with few exceptions so far left faint features in other contexts of archaeology, too. Thus the most prominent example of an explicit post colonial approach from a Scandinavian context is represented by Lise Nordenborg Myhre (2004; a thesis on Norwegian contexts, but examined in Cambridge, UK).

There is also currently an extension on the possibilities of material studies and social theory in archaeology in general. The extension concerns as well the time aspect, as a scope of studies have a propensity to encompass époques of modern and current times, too.

There is by and large a consciousness about the role and potentials of materiality in the processes of negotiating and transforming gender, a consciousness shared by a range of scholars presently. Issues in current feminist theories, and in other aspects of social theory, along with a general trend in the direction of materiality, and in the temporal perspective, are thus, more or less visible in the papers presented in this volume, however not yet all through taken up in general. They give examples of gender alone, and gender together with intersecting, and co-working processes in history. Of importance is then, that for the moment being, several approaches to gender in archaeology tend to co-exist. Thus they actually bring in to loosen some of the discipline's built in categorizations, and also to explore the processes of gender and intersecting components in local perspectives.

References

Arwill-Nordbladh, E. 1998. *Genuskonstruktioner i nordisk vikingatid: förr och nu.*GOTARC; Series B; Gothenburg Archaeological Theses 9. Gothenburg.

Bhabha, H. 1994. *The location of cultures.* London: Routledge.

Chapman, J. 2000. Tensions at burials. In: Dobres, A. M. & Robb, J. eds. *Agency in Archaeology.* New York: Routledge.

Childs, P. & Williams, P. *An Introduction to Post-Colonial Theory.* Prentice Hall. Harvester Wheatsheaf.

Conkey, M. W. 1991. Context of action/contexts for power. In: Conkey, M. W. & Gero, J. eds. *Engendering Archaeology: Women and Prehistory.* Oxford: Basil Blackwell.

Conkey, M. W. & Tringham, R. 1996. Cultivating Thinking/Challenging Authority: Some Experiments in Feminist Pedagogy in Archaeology. In: Wright, Rita P. (ed) *Gender and Archaeology.* PENN. University of Pennsylvania Press. Philadelphia. Ch. 8.

Cornell, P. & Fahlander, F. 2002. Microarchaeology, Materiality and Social practice. *Current Swedish Archaeology Vol. 10,* pp. 21-38.

Derevenski, J. Sofaer 2002. Engendering Context. Context as Gendered Practice in the Early Bronze Age of the Upper Thames Valley, UK. *European Journal of Archaeology Vol. 5(2),* pp. 191-211.

Gosden, C. 2004. *Archaeology and colonialism: cultural contact from 5000 B.C. to the present.* Cambridge University Press.

Hamilakis, Y. 2004. Archaeology and the politics of pedagogy. *World Archaeology Vol. 36(2),* pp. 287-309.

Hjørungdal, T.; Cornell, P.; Gillberg, Å.; Gustafsson, A.; Karlsson, H.; Nyqvist, R. & Bille, U. forthcoming: *Students as searchers, creators, and critics of knowledge. On the development of methods that aim to integrate students in their education.* Manuscript edited by Marquet, J. C. & Barker-Pathy, C.

Mohanty, C 1985. Under Western Eyes: Feminist Scholarship and Colonial Discourse. *Boundary.* Spring/Fall 1985.

Moore, H. L. 1994. *A passion for difference: essays in*

anthropology and gender. Cambridge, Polity.Nordenborg Myhre, L. 2004. *Trialectic Archaeology. Monuments and Space in Southwest Norway 1700-500 BC*. AmS-Skrifter 18. Arkeologisk Museum i Stavanger.

Spivak, G. C. 1993. Can the Subaltern speak? In: Williams, P. & Chrisman, L. (eds.). *Colonial Discourse and Post-Colonial Theory*. Hemel Hempsted: Harvester Wheatsheaf.

Sørensen, M. L. S. 2000. *Gender Archaeology*. Polity Press.

Treherne, P.1995. The warrior's beauty: the masculine body and self-identity in Bronze-Age Europe. *Journal of European Archaeology 3.1*, pp. 105-144.

Acknowledgement

Each one of the contributors is thanked warmly for good cooperation and for showing an immense amount of patience. As most of the editorial work has had to be carried out off ordinary office hours, the process has been excruciating long. I am grateful to Dr. David Davison for the opportunity to publish in B.A.R., and for his help and support all the way through. My most sincere thanks also to Alice Doyle for her help with the manuscript. In the winter of 2004-2005 many weekend hours were spent in the office with the manuscript instead of with my husband, Raimond Thörn. By dedicating this volume to him, I thank him for not only accepting the circumstances, but for supporting my work as well.

Gothenburg March 2005
Tove Hjørungdal

The Golden Age of the Carpathian basin and the Beautiful Warrior

László Reményi

Budapest History Museum Hungary

Abstract

The first half of 2nd Millenium BC is interpreted as the golden age of the Carpatian Basin. In this paper I will take a look at the economic and social changes in this period, retrospecting to 3rd millennium events as well. The material changes appear as fortified settlements— two level settlement-structure—rich graves with weapons, gold and bronze depots and import artifacts. The paper issues the reasons for changes following the Koszider period from a new point of view in the Hungarian research. In this context the new warrior elite emerged.

Introduction

The relative framework of the Bronze Age in the Carpathian basin is different from other parts of Europe. Traditionally the beginning of the Bronze Age is reckoned from the dissolution of the great cultural unit of the Late Copper Age and the emergence of the *Vučedol* culture, which is known for the new metal works and the relationship with the Balkan region. These events must have taken place in the first third of the third millennium BC, based on radiocarbon analysis, while the Middle Bronze Age, regarded as the "golden era", lasted from about 2000 to 1500 BC.

Despite the fact that most of the processes in the Middle Bronze Age were closely linked to the development of the earlier period, the Middle Bronze Age is not only a chronological unit: it brought numerous social and economic changes, and created a different lifestyle, which distinguishes it from other periods. Some of these changes, for example regarding the settlement histories, can be detected also in other parts of Middle Europe in the late phase of the Early Bronze Age (Shennan 1993a:130-135; Shennan 1993b). The characteristics of the period in the Carpathian basin are listed by Tibor Kovács: "permanency of the territory of a people demarcated by research; formation of layered settlements, so-called *Tells*, showing long sedentary lifestyle (in some cases settlements that had been built earlier were re-inhabited); economy capable of producing surplus for exchange; and last but not least, the emergence of metal workshops that provided the necessary tools and weapons (supplied by raw material from the exchange of goods; Kovács 1995a:19).

In this paper I will discuss the era of the Middle Bronze Age by examining these characteristics, in order to find out what factors contributed to the rise of the "golden age" and to its downfall.

The Economic Development

In the period before the formation of the *Tells*, the Carpathian basin – except for the area of the *Vučedol* culture – could be described as an area sparsely inhabited by small communities (Szathmári 1999). Judging from the settlement structures, we must suppose that communities in the region had an exploitative (extensive) economic strategy, who after using up all the resources in their environment, moved on. This kind of subsistence strategy was possible in the Carpathian basin as it was sparsely inhabited by small groups at this time. Moreover, according to the general observations of historical demography, in sparsely populated areas with sufficient raw material extensive economic methods were more beneficial and even necessary because small population size did not allow the application of intensive, more labour demanding methods.

However the population of communities, who used extensive methods and had ample raw material at hand, grew relatively fast. This demographic growth can be traced in the settlement histories from the middle of the Early Bronze Age: the formation of the first *Tells* dates from this time.

As a consequence of demographic expansion, the natural resources – earlier available without limit – became scarce. There was less and less land to be occupied, and thereby the possibility to move on also decreased. Due to increased population size, communities had to start cultivating more fields, thus they had to cultivate land further from the settlement and land of inferior quality. This required new methods and new tools, but new procedures were also needed for a better exploitation of local resources, once the more distant and less productive lands were used up as well. The innovation that managed the challenges, seems to have been the plough.

The utilisation of animal force for ploughing was one stage in a long development process that led to the secondary products' revolution, and the more extensive exploitation of animals (Sheratt 1983, 1997; Shennan 1986:132). After the introduction of the plough at the end of the Copper Age, another important phase in agricultural development begun in the Carpathian basin in the Early Bronze Age: the use of the horse became widespread.

1

Relative Chronology	Absolute Chronology (BC)	Southwest Hungary	Northwest Hungary	Middle Hungary (Danube Valley)	Northeast Hungary	North Great Hungarian Plain	South Great Hungarian Plain	East Hungary
Reinecke B2 / Late Bronze Age 1	1500	Tumulus Culture	Tumulus Culture	Tumulus Culture	Piliny	Tuulus Culture (Rákóczifalva Group)	Tumulus Culture (Csorva)	Tumulus Culture
Reinecke B1 / Middle Bronze Age 3	1700	Koszider Period; Transdanubian Incrusted Pottery	Koszider / Koszider; Gáta-Wieselberg; T. D. Incrusted	Koszider Period; Vatya 3	Koszider Period; Hatvan, Füzesabony (Ottomány)	Koszider Perood; Vatya 3	Koszider-Szeremle / Koszi-der; Vatya 3 / Maros Perjámos	Koszider; Ottomány (Gyulavarsánd); Ko szi der / Hat-van
Reinecke A2 / Middle Bronze		(Transdanubian Incrusted Pottery)	(T. D. Incrusted)	Vatya 2	(Hatvan, Füzesabony (Ottomány))	Hatvan/Vatya	Vatya 2	Hat-van / Ottomány
Reinecke A2 / Middle Bronze	2000			Vatya 1	Hatvan	Hatvan	Vatya 1 / Nagy-	
Reinecke A1 / Early Bronze Age 3	2300	Kisapostag	"P tt" Kisapostag	Nagyrév (Kulcs) / Nagyrév (Classic)	Hatvan	Hatvan / Nagyrév / Nagyrév (Classic)	Nagyrév	
Vučedol C / Early Bronze Age 2	2500, 2700/2800	Somogyvár-Vinkovci	Somogyvár-Vinkovci	Bell Beaker- / Bell Beaker-	Makó 2	Early Nagyrév (Ökörhalom) / Makó 2 (?)	Proto-Nagyrév, Ada / MarosPitvaros	Nyírség
Vučedol B / Early Bronze Age 1		Vučedol B	Makó 1	Makó 1	Makó 1	Makó 1	Makó 1	Makó 1

Figure 1.1. Chronological Framework of Early, Middle and Late (1) Bronze Age of Carpathian Basin.

Domesticated horse became widely used in the cultures of the Eastern European steppes in the 4th millennium BC, whereas the horse appeared in Central Europe at the end of the 4th millennium, and in Western Europe at the middle of the 3rd millennium (Sheratt 1997:212 ff). The horse however did not play a great role in the Carpathian basin until the middle of the Early Bronze Age. The number of horses in the settlements of the *Bell beaker Csepel* group was so considerable that supposedly it was a central place for horse breeding. This centre might have been the starting point from where the horse expanded into Europe in the middle of the 3rd millennium BC, which was possible by the network of *Bell beaker* settlements along the great rivers of Europe (Sheratt 1997:219).

With the intensified exploitation of animals, and the widespread use of the plough, a radical and complex transition took place in farming. To provide the necessary animal force, larger fields were needed for grazing, when at the same time the size of available land grew due to intensive cultivating methods. Lands that had been impossible to cultivate earlier with the old methods, became cultivated. The forest could not conquer back the worn out, fallow lands, because animals grazed there, while their manure helped the regeneration of these fields (Shennan 1986:132). That there is a correlation between intensive farming strategies and animal husbandry is proven by the fact that in the temperate forests of Europe the diffusion of the horse and the increase in domesticated animals happened parallel to the spreading of the plough (Sheratt 1997:219).

The production of significant amounts of agricultural surplus was made easier not by intensive farming methods, but also by some advantageous environmental changes. According to paleo-climatolocigal research (Birks 1981; McGhee 1981; Gyulai 2001:89), the cold period of the early sub-boreal climate-phase ended around 2000 BC, and at the turn of the millennium the middle sub-boreal phase started. The climate became considerably warmer, which caused an increase in precipitation (Shennan 1993a:123 ff).

Since climatic changes are the result of long processes, the climate change detected at the end of the 3rd millennium supposedly also contributed to the changes in farming and lifestyle that were under way already in the second half of the Early Bronze Age. However, in the Middle Bronze Age the clearly detected positive climatic changes, surely could be a reason behind the good harvest, and thus contributed to the further economic and demographic developments.

The Metallurgic Expansion

Following the antecedents of the early Bronze Age, a great increase in metallurgy (both in quality and in quantity) can be observed in the cultures of the Carpathian basin and the surrounding cultures of Eastern Europe from the end of the Early Bronze Age, and especially from the Middle Bronze Age (e.g. Schubert 1973; Novotna 1980; Shennan 1986, 1993a, 1993b, 1999).

The metallurgy centre in the Alps region had been greatly impacting the cultures of the Western Carpathian basin since the end of the Early Bronze Age. More and more metal objects from Central Europe appeared in the Dunántúl region (Transdanubia) and across the area of the *Vatya* culture (Kovács 1995b:38; Honti & Kiss 2000; Reményi 2002). According to metal moulds found in the region, these objects were being cast also on the premises. Then with the development of some local variations in metal items, the western part of the Carpathian basin developed its own, characteristic metallurgy, which relied on imported raw material due to the lack of local ore quarries.

Another centre of metal workshops started to develop in the Eastern Carpathians (Transylvania, Tisza region) shortly after. The characteristic, very high quality products of this centre spread across the Carpathian basin and even reached different places of Europe starting from the middle phase of the Middle Bronze Age (Kovács 1995b:38 f).

The rise of the metallurgy centre in the Alps region can be dated to the end of the third millennium. The products of these metal workshops not only reached the neighbouring Western European cultures, but they also appeared in the Aegean region and Anatolia, transmitted by the late *Nagyrév* culture, then later by the *Vatya* culture through the *Perjamos* culture. At the same time the relations with areas to the north became closer as well: the Baltic region also became part of the trade system with the transmission of the *Aunjetitz* culture (Sheratt 1993:22 ff). The trade relations formed with the Baltic region are supposed to reveal itself through the amber beads that travelled in the opposite direction to the metal works (Harding 1990; Sheratt 1993:22 ff, *Figure 1.6*).

During the next period, the second half of the Middle Bronze Age, the trade system of the Bronze Age changed somewhat. Maybe due to the exhaustion of the copper mines in the Harz mountain, the eastern Carpathian metal workshops started to play a more and more important role. The cultures of *Wietenberg*, *Ottomány* and *Füzesabony* got in touch with the northern areas across the valleys of Nyitra and Vág (Sheratt 1993:24-29, *Figure 1.7*; 1998, *Figure 1.6*).

Social Differences and Material Culture

If we examine the distribution of metal objects – either produced locally or imported – and that of amber, we can get an idea of the social relations in this era. The unequal distribution of such prestige objects is most apparent in the burials. The existence of unusually rich graves have been known in the *Aunjetitz* culture for a long time, but similar inequalities between graves are also evident in the surrounding cultures (Shennan 1986:125 ff; 1993a:151 ff). The social differences can be best observed in the cemeteries of the *Füzesabony* culture (Kovács 1977:54f). The communities living in the Great Hungarian Plain and the Transdanubia had less spectacular graves, which is connected to the lack of ore quarries there (Shennan 1986: 128, 139).

The increasing social differences were indicated by the change in settlement structures, the appearance of a two level settlement hierarchy (Shennan 1993:151). In the Middle Bronze Age in the Central and Eastern European regions – thus in the Carpathians as well – it became a practice to surround the best situated settlements with trenches or mounds. The fortified settlements appear in the *Hatvan, Füzesabony, Ottomány, Vatya, Incrusted Pottery, Tokod* cultures.

As a result of the fast demographic expansion that set off in the Early Bronze Age, resources became limited and this increased the tension between communities. The leaders of the larger and therefore more complex communities could keep their power only by ensuring the necessary resources for their people and by protecting the land owned by them. Thus they surrounded the central settlements that lay on defendable ground with mounds and/or trenches. Besides their practical function, such fortifications were also symbolic expressions of land ownership. This was similar to the visible demarcation of graves, which were for example piled up in several areas of Central Europe, or marked by stones in the *Vatya* culture. The fortified settlement may not only have had symbolic meaning for the foreign communities, but they may also have signified the social differences between the people living inside and those living outside the fort within the same community.

There is much evidence that the fortified settlements were important economic and social centres: they can be regarded centres for the production and redistribution of many strategically important objects (bronze objects, carved bone tools) (Bandi-Petres 1969; Novotna 1983; Shennan 1986:120, 139, *Figure 1.4*; Shennan 1993a:151 f). The fact that the bronze (occasionally gold) treasures hidden in the *Koszider* period were almost always found in or right next to these fortified settlements implies that the inhabitants of these fortifications must have had a decisive role in the making and distribution of metal objects (Kovács 1984a: 223). The peculiarly decorated bone ornaments of horse bits are of special attention. These were mostly found in fortified settlements, which indicate the connection between horseback riding and high social status (Shennan 1986:120 f).

Social Dynamics – A Discussion

The social organisation of the Bronze Age can be generally interpreted as a chiefdom-society based on the archaeological findings, despite some still open questions (Harding 2000:390). Chiefdom can be defined as a social

unit, in which the social elite – due to its inherited social and economic power – has central control over a few thousand people living in one area, and over the economy, society, and religious life, while maintaining the socio-economic status quo (see Harding 2000:388 f).

The co-ordination of the economy was possible by redistribution. At the same time the chiefdoms in the Bronze Age used new methods to control the society and to maintain the social status quo. The significant growth in community size required the re-organisation of power based on territory (Fried 1967).

The archaeological cultures and the social units – A Discussion

It is a long debated issue whether we can draw a connection between the archaeologically defined cultures and the social units. Archaeological cultures are characterised by having (usually) the same burial rituals, similar settlement structure, and more or less a standard material culture. Based on these characteristics however, such a cultural unit cannot be equated with social or political units. The above discussed chiefdoms in the Bronze Age, which supposedly constituted the largest political units at that time, could only control a few narrow stretches along a river-valley. Thus one archaeological culture was composed of such small communities, all of which had their own burial rituals, and produced and used approximately the same kind of tools.

We must interpret the "permanency of the territory of a people demarcated by research" in the Middle Bronze Age as the increasing economic and political power of the Bronze Age chiefdoms. Similarly, the transformation of cultures was also due to the expansion, collapse and other changes of the small ruling units.

The beautiful warrior in this context

In this new social structure a new means to exercise power appeared: armed men, who had increasingly high social status, protected the power of the elite. This change can be archaeologically detected in Central European graves, where more and more weapons were buried (e.g. Kovács 1977:61 ff; Shennan 1986:127 ff; 139 f; Treherne 1995:108 f), but for example the appearance of different relief-like weapon images in the late period of the *Vatya* culture can also be connected to this (Kovács 1973).

As the warriors – raised from the society – got significant economical and ideological power their appearance brought ideological and ritual changes. The rising warrior aristocracy introduced new casualities, new lifestyle and created a new common heritage. In this ideology the balance shifted from the community and common place – that played major role in the Neolothic and Copper Age – toward the personality. As the members of the warrior communities were males, not the person but the male played the central role in the ideology.

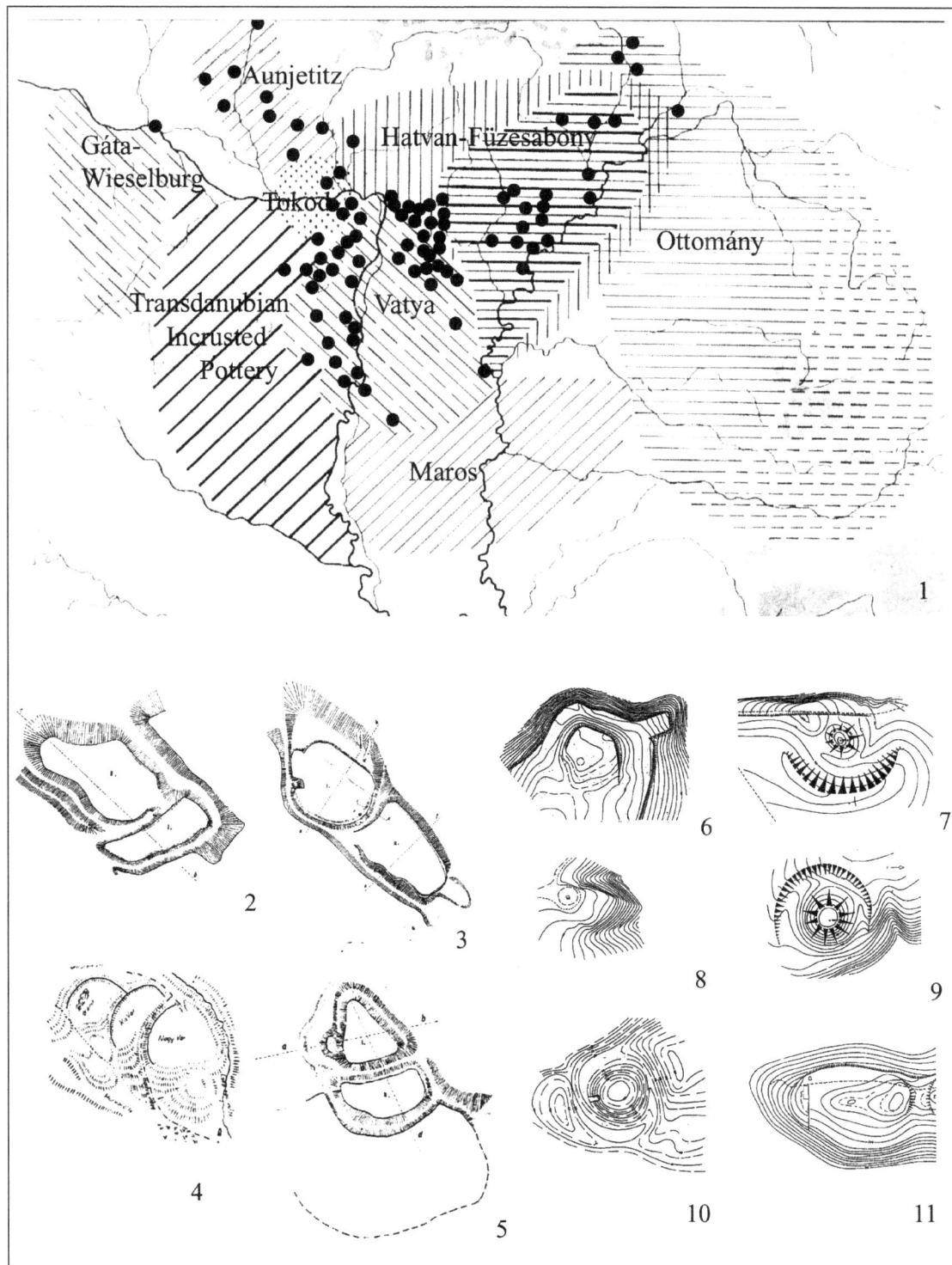

Figure 1.2 Middle Bronze Age Cultures in the Carpathian Basin with the fortified Settlements.
After Schubert 1973, Karte 2; Kalicz 1984, Taf. LIX.; Shennan 1986, Fig. 3; Bóna 1992 pp. 16-17;
Kovács 1995a, Abb. 6; Endrődi - Gyulai 1999, Fig.1; Kissne 1999; Koós 2002; Kiss 2000, Taf. 7. 2-5:
Fortified Settlements of Vatya Culture 2: Alcsút: Nováki 1952, Abb. 2; 3: Vál: Nováki 1952, Abb. 3; 4:
Pákozd: Nováki 1952, Abb. 4; 5: Sárbogárd: Nováki 1952, Abb. 5 Not to scale.

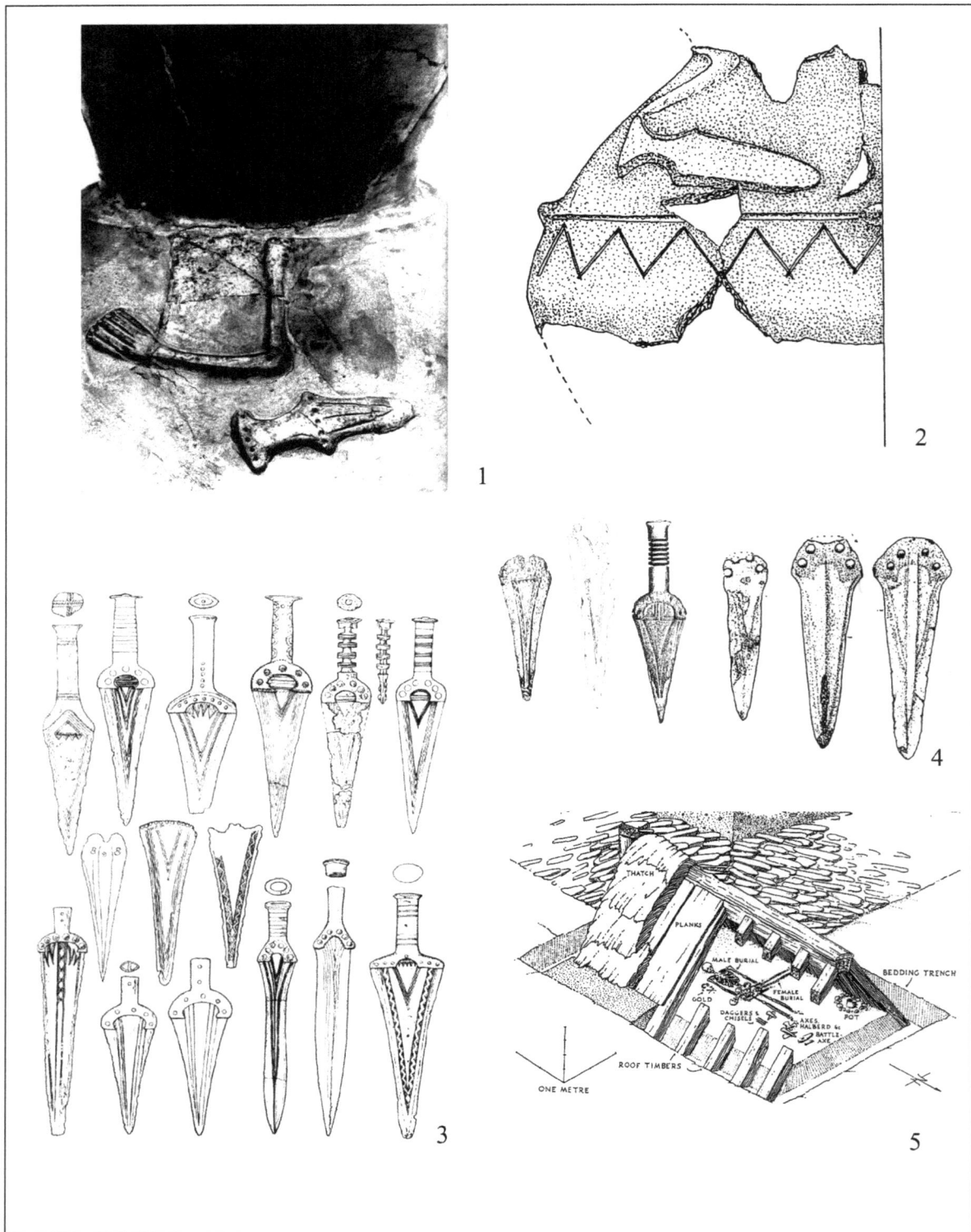

Figure 1.3. 1-4: Daggers of East-Alpine Metallurgy, 1: Pot with dagger representation from Mende, Vatya Culture (Kovács 1973, 1977, Abb. 47). 2: Pot with dagger representation from Százhalombatta,Vatya Culture (Poroszlai 2000, Platte XII). 3: Daggers of Aunjetitz Culture (Divac–Sedláček 1999, Abb. 3). 4: Daggers of Transdanubian Incrusted Pottery (Kiss 1998-1999, 2.1-3, Kiss 2000, Taf. 4.8-10). 5: Wooden mortuary house under barrow, male burial with gold jewellery, female burial with weapons from Leubingen, Aunjetiz Culture (Piggott 1965, Fig. 67). Not to scale.

Beside the weapons different masculan symbols are found in the graves in the Carpathian Basin. Drinking vessels and riding/driving in horse harness/wheeled vehicles, which I would mention as an important role in the riding in Indo-European mythology. The Heros and the ancestors became more and more important, because the social status became heritable. The occurrence of tumulus graves (in the *Tumulus* culture) and stone heaps above the graves (in the *Vatya* culture) indicated this process. As the importance of ancestors and origins increased, the gendered warrior elit was born. The covered period is not only the time of the stregthen cheifdoms but the rising of the gendered warrior elit as well (see Treherne 1995: 106 ff).

The end of the Golden Age

The final period of the Middle Bronze Age in the Carpathian basin was named *Koszider* period after the three bronze treasures found at Dunaújváros (Dunapentele)-Kosziderpadlás. The reason for this label is that the numerous bronze treasures found in this period were allocated to the same chronological unit. When researchers first tried to explain the historical background of the appearance of this "treasure unit", they came to the conclusion that these bronze treasures were buried because of a great, devastating wave of migration that destroyed the existing cultural units. This migration was attributed to the south-eastern movement of the *Tumulus* culture (Mozsolics 1957; Bóna 1958, 1992; Kovács 1975a, 1984c, 1995a:22 f).

More recent research has however changed this gloomy picture concerning the events of the *Koszider* period. The new results first of all disproved the former assumption that the wave of the *Tumulus* culture caused an overarching, total devastation. It is not completely assured today that the *Gáta-Wieselburg* culture disappeared (Neugebauer 1994:61). It is much more certain that the culture of the *Incrusted Pottery* did not disappear during the *Koszider* period (Kiss 1997, 2000; Vékony 2000). At the same time, we can also question the decline of the *Perjámos* culture (Fischl 1997:101; Szábo 1999:62).

Even though it is evident that the groups of the *Tumulus* culture and of the late *Magyarád* culture reached the Transdanubia (Simon & Horvath 1999; Vekony 2000) and the southern part of the Great Hungarian Plain (Szabó 1999) during the *Koszider* period, these groups of people did not rearrange the basic structure of the Middle Bronze Age in the Carpathian basin. The formerly created economic and social relations remained unchanged.

Thus according to the data at our disposal, the *Koszider* period cannot be described as the era of destruction, wars and sweeping migrations. On the contrary, the data implies that metallurgy was doing better than ever, both quantitatively and qualitatively. This was possible because getting hold of ore became relatively easy, and

this indicates the high standard of trade relations. The extended trade relations can also be recognised in the standardisation of metal objects, and the diffusion of these good quality items outside the Carpathian basin. The amber beads that piled up in the treasures of the *Koszider* period (Kovács 1984a:223) are very good evidence of the long-distance trade in prestige objects. The intermixing, and to a certain degree standardisation, of ceramic types, show the peaceful and intensive system of relations between the different cultures. Based on these facts, the *Koszider* period represents an integral part, or even more, the peak in the development of the Middle Bronze Age. The explanation for the appearance of the *Tumulus* culture features at this period is that (besides the permeation of some *Tumulus* groups into the area) a great, extended system of relations existed: the *Tell* cultures did not only form very intensive contacts with one another, but also with groups of the *Tumulus* culture.

Based on the above presented arguments, the hiding of the *Koszider* treasures cannot be explained by the attack of the *Tumulus* culture against the *Tells*, either. Even the earlier historical explanations were only able to prove it in the case of the *Toldanémed-type* and the *Koszider* treasures. A historical reconstruction about the conquer of the *Tumulus* culture could not explain for example why the bronze treasures of *Hajdúsámson-Apa*, and the gold treasures from the same age were hidden (Kovács 1995b:43).

What could explain then the decline of the prosperous *Koszider* period? Though it is hard to find a definite answer, the reasons must be connected to the collapse of the social-economic system of the Middle Bronze Age chiefdoms. The demographic expansion must have continued in the *Koszider* period because new settlements were established at that time. However, as the natural resources were limited, there was no possibility to expand the economy any further. The exhaustion of resources (land and ore quarries) itself could have caused the economic collapse of the chiefdoms and the weakening of the chieftains' power. In addition, a new climatic change, a less advantageous one, started around 1500-1400 BC, according to environmental research (Birks 1981; McGhee 1981; Gyulai 2001:89). The climate in the Carpathian basin became cooler and wetter, thus the groundwater level rose. The deterioration of climate must have changed the ecological conditions for agriculture.

The end of the *Koszider* period also indicates the disappearance of the Tell cultures: the earlier densely inhabited Tells became deserted. The Koszider layer always contains the topmost layer of *Tells* from the Bronze Age. The inhabitants of *Tells* left their former homes and moved into smaller, one-layered settlements probably because they had to change their living style as resources became scarce and/or the climate cooled down. At the same time the fortified settlements, centres of the chiefdoms, became deserted as well.

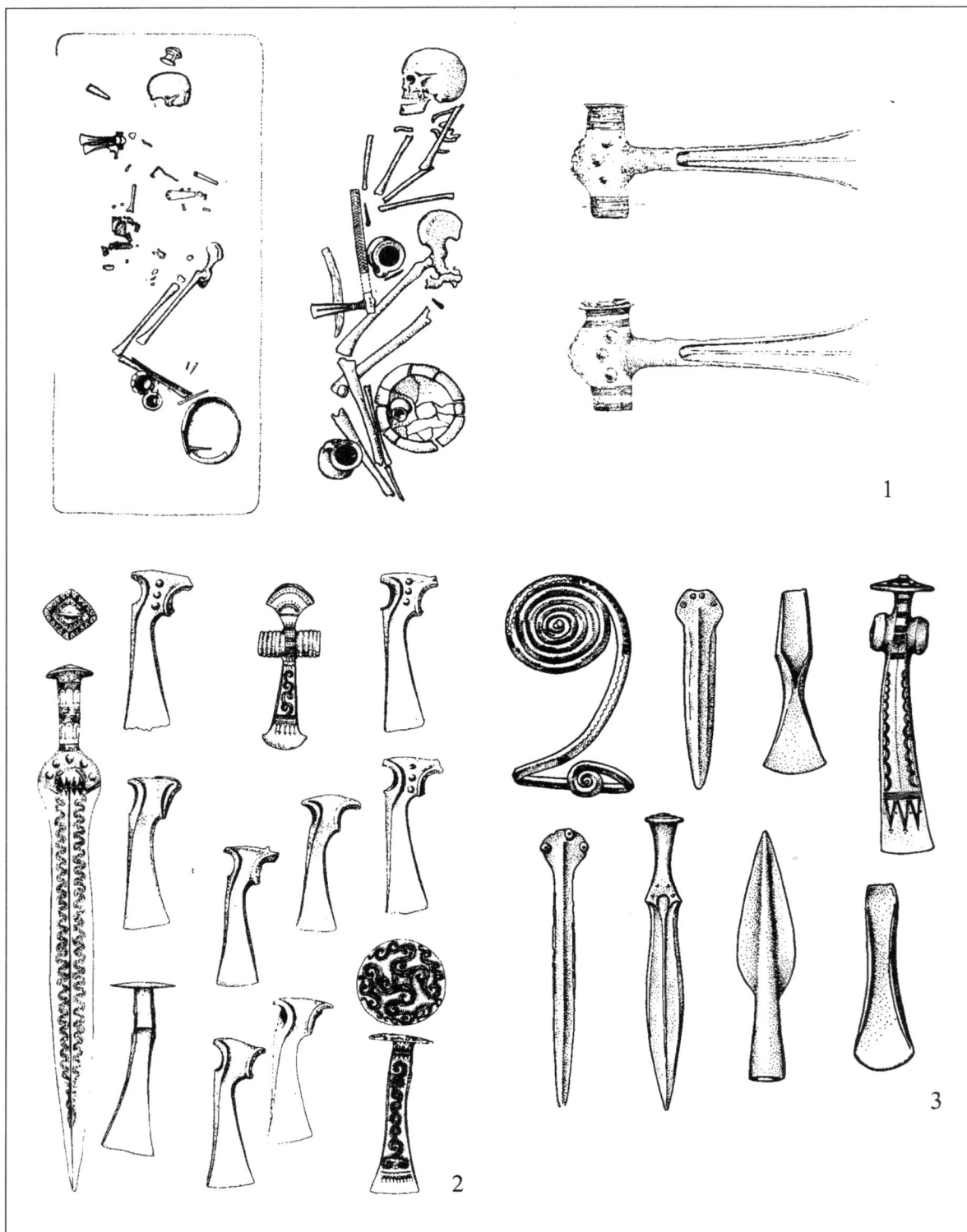

Figure 1.4 Warrior burials and weapons of eastern Carpathian metal workshops.
1: Female burials with axes from Tiszafüred (North Hungarian Plan) Füzesabony (Ottomány) Culture
(Burials: Kovács 1977, Fig. 25; Axes: Kovács 1996, Fig. 7. 2).
2. The treasure from Hajdúsámson (Mozsolics 1967, Abb. 9-11; Kovács 1995b, Abb. 21).
3. Weapons of the Koszider Period (Kovács 1984c, Taf. XCVII). Not to scale.

In the meanwhile, groups of the *Tumulus* culture continued to move in. Their infiltration since the *Koszider* period must have been facilitated by the weakening of the chiefdoms and the disappearance of borders that were presumably more rigid before. It is possible that the settlement was not completely without conflict; however it is more and more likely that it was not a devastating *Tumulus* movement that put an end to the flourishing civilisation of the Middle Bronze Age. On the contrary, the weakened economic and social base of the "golden age" opened up the opportunities for the *Tumulus* culture to move in. The inhabitants of the Tells who moved to horizontal settlements, and the *Tumulus* newcomers created the new cultural units together, the regional groups of the *Tumulus* culture. This is clearly evident in the new bi-ritual cemeteries (e.g. Kovács 1975b; Csányi 1980:154 f), and in the new cultures that were characterised by mixed elements of the earlier cultures and the *Tumulus* material culture. The groups of the *Tumulus* culture did not settle in waves, as it was pointed out by V. Szabó Gábor in connection with the southern part of the Great Hungarian Plain (Szabó 1999:64). The process was rather a slow and continuous infiltration of smaller communities of *Tumulus* and *Late-Magyarád* cultures. The process could not have been drastic either because the systems of relations in the Middle Bronze Age could be still detected until the end of the Late Bronze Age (Szabó 1999:62), thus the regional trade channels still functioned. As opposed to this, the long-distance trade that dealt with prestige objects connected to the chiefdom centres and the chieftains' power avoided the Carpathian basin. The amber-route connecting the Baltic and Northern-sea coasts with the Aegean region still existed, but it avoided the Carpathian basin and went towards southern Italy after the *Koszider* period (Sheratt 1993, *Figure 1.9*; Sheratt 1998, *Figure 1.6*). Due to the dissolution of chiefdom centres, there was no central place anymore where the chiefs could have traded with prestige objects among themselves, as explained earlier.

Conclusions

In this paper I have studied the economic and social background of the golden age in Early and Middle Bronze Age in the Carpathian basin. The economic basis of the golden age in the Early Bronze Age was created by the changes in the farming processes. Parallel to the demographical growth the farming methods were intensified. The cultivation with the plough became widespread, as a new step of the secondary exploitation of animals the horse came into general use, and besides high level metallurgy got spread. As a result of the changes the economy could produce overflow, which led to an increasingly differentiated society. The elite's position and power expanded with time. They looked after the growing resources – like strategical evident of metallurgy, and distant exchange system – by the redistributive system. The elite created visible fortified settlements in favor of defence of the territory of

chiefdom and preserve of own power. They buried with rich grave-goods, and hid rich bronze and gold treasures. The growth of population size needed a re-organisation of power based on territory. The power of the elite and defence of the community was protected by the new warrior aristocracy found in graves with weapons. The Bronze Age growth culminated in the *Koszider* period. The cultures of the Carpathian basin organized most-extended exchange system in this period. After the *Koszider* period due to various reasons the instabil system of the Middle Bronze Age chiefdoms crashed. This crisis resulted in demographical drop, so the infiltration of the *Tumulus* culture became rapid. At the beginning of the Late Bronze Age mixed groups of the *Tumulus* culture and the earlier population lived in the Carpathian basin.

References

Bándi, G. & Petres, É. 1969. Ásatás Lovasberény-Mihályváron – Excavations at Lovasberény-Mihályvár. *ArchÉrt 96*, pp. 170-177.

Birks, H. J. B. 1981. Pollen analysis and climate reconstruction. In: Wigley, T. M. L., Ingram, M., J. & Farmer, G. (eds.): *Climate and history.* Cambridge, pp. 111-138.

Bóna, I.1958. Chronologie der Hortfunde vom Koszider-Typus. *Acta Archaeologica Academiae Scientiarum Hungaricae* (Budapest) 9, pp. 211-243.

Bóna, I.1992. Bronzezeitliche Tell-Kulturen in Ungarn. In: Meier-Arendt W. (Hrsg.):*Bronzezeit in Ungarn. Forschungen in Tell Siedlungen an Donau und Theiss.* Frankfurt am Main, pp. 9-39.

Csányi, R. M.1980. Árokkal körülvett sírok a halomsíros kultúra jánoshidai temetőjében – Graves surrounded by Ditches in the Jánoshida Cemetery of the Tumulus Grave Culture. *ArchÉrt 107*, pp. 153-165.

Divac, G. – Sedláček, Z. 1999. *Hortfunde der Altbronzezeitlichen Dolche von Praha 6-Suchdol.* Fontes Archaeologici Pragenses – Supplementum 1 Prague.

Endrődi, A.–Gyulai, F. 1999: Soroksár-Várhegy. A Fortified Bronze Age Settlement in the Outskirts of Budapest.Plant Cultivation of Middle Bronze Age Fortified Settlements. *CommArchHung 1999*, pp. 5–34.

Fischl, P. K. 1997. Klárafalva-Hajdova I. Bronzkori tell település. In: Havassy, P. (ed.). *Látták Trója kaput. Bronzkori leletek a Közép-Tisza vidékéről. Gyulai katalógusok 3.* pp. 85-122. Gyula.

Fried, M.1967. *The evolution of Political Society.* New York.

Gyulai, F. 2001. *Archaeobotanika. A kultúrnövények története a Kárpát-medencében a régészeti-növénytani vizsgálatok alapján.* Budapest.

Harding, A. F. 2000. *European Societies in the Bronze Age.* Cambridge.

Honti, Sz. & Kiss, V. 2000. Neuere Angaben zur Bewertung der Hortfunde vom Typ Tolnanémedi. *Acta Archaeologica Academiae Scientiarum Hungaricae* (Budapest) *51*, pp. 71-96.

Kalicz, N. 1984: Die Hatvan-Kultur. In: Tasić, N. (Hrsg.): *Kulturen der Frühbronzezeit des Karpatenbeckens und Nordbalkans.* Beograd 1984, pp. 191–214.

Kemenczei, T. 1984. *Die Späthbronzezeit Nordostungarns.* Budapest.

Kiss, V. 1997. A mészbetétes edények népe késői fázisának sírlelete Veszprémből – Die Grabfunde der Kultur Inkrustierten Keramik von Veszprém. *Communicationes Archaeologicae Hungariae* (Budapest) 1997, pp. 39-49.

Kiss, V. 1998-1999 Neuere Funde zur der mittelbronzezezitlichen Metalkunst in Transdanubia. *Savaria – pars archaeologica 24/3*, pp. 153-164.

Kiss, V. 2000 A mészbetétes kerámia kultúrája kapcsolatai a Kárpát-medence nyugati területeivel és a közép-európai kultúrákkal a középső bronzkorban – Die Beziehungen der inkrustierten Keramik in den westlichen Gebieten des Karpatenbeckens und zur mitteleuropäischen Kultur in der mittleren Bronzezeit. *Komárom Megyei Múzeumok Közleményei*, 7, pp. 15-55.

Kissné Cseh, J. 1999 A mészbetétes edények kultúrája lelőhelyei Komárom-Esztergom megyében. – Die Fundorte der inkrustierten Keramik im Komitat Komárom-Esztergom. *Komárom Megyei Múzeumok Közleményei*, 6 (1999), pp. 23-88.

Kovács, T. 1966. A Halomsíros-kultúra leletei az Észak-Alföldön – Die Funde der Hügelgräberkultur. *ArchÉrt 93*, pp. 159-202.

Kovács, T. 1973. Representations of Weapons on Bronze Age Pottery. Folia Archaeologica 24, pp. 7-31.

Kovács, T. 1975a. Historische und chronologische Fragen des Überganges von Mittleren- zur Spätbronzezeit in Ungarn. *Acta Archaeologica Academiae Scientiarum Hungaricae* (Budapest) 27, p. 299-317.

Kovács, T. 1975b. Tumulus culture cemeteries of Tiszafüred. *Régészeti Füzetek* (Budapest) Serial II. No. 17.

Kovács, T. 1977. *A bronzkor Magyarországon. = The Bronze Age in Hungary.* Budapest.

Kovács, T. 1984a. Die Vatya-Kultur. In: Tasić, N (ed.): *Kulturen der Frühbronzezeit des Karpatenbeckens und Nordbalkans.* Beograd, pp. 191-218.

Kovács, T. 1984b. Die Füzesabony-Kultur. In: Tasić, N (Ed.): *Kulturen der Frühbronzezeit des Karpatenbeckens und Nordbalkans.* Beograd, pp. 235-256.

Kovács, T. 1984c. Die Koszider Metallkunst. In: Tasić, N (Ed.): *Kulturen der Frühbronzezeit des Karpatenbeckens und Nordbalkans.* Beograd, pp. 377-388.

Kovács, T. 1995a. A középső bronzkor: a virágkor. In: Maráz, B. (ed.): *A bronzkor kincseiMagyarországon.* Pécs, pp. 18-24.

Kovács, T. 1995b. Bronzművesek, harcosok, kincsleletek. In: Maráz B. (Ed.): A bronzkor kincsei Magyarországon. Pécs 1995, pp. 37-44.

McGhee, R. 1981. Archaeological evidence for climatic change during the last 5000 years. In: Wigley, Ingram & Farmer (eds.): *Climate and history*, pp.162-179.

Mozsolics, A. 1957. Archaologische Beitrage zur Geschichte der Grossen Wanderung. *Acta Archaeologica Academiae Scientiarum Hungaricae* (Budapest) 8, pp. 119-156.

Mozsolics, A. 1967 Bronzefunde des Karpatenbeckens. Budapest 1973.

Neugebauer, J-W.1994. Die Bronzezeit in Ostösterreich. Wien.

Nováki, Gy.1952 Fejér megye őskori földvárai. *ArchÉrt* 79 (1952), pp. 3-19.

Novotna, M.1980. *Die Nadeln in der Slowakei.* Prähistorische Bronzefunde XIII/6. München.

Novotna, M. 1983 Metalurgia opevnenych osád – Die Metallurgie in befestigten Siedlungen. *Archeologické rozhledy* (Praha) 35, pp. 63–71.

Piggott, S. 1965 *Ancient Europe.* Edinburgh 1965.

Poroszlai, I. 2000. Excavation campaigns at the Bronze Age tell site at Százhalombatta-Földvár. In: *Százhalombatta Archaeological Expedition* Annual Report 1. Százhalombatta (Hungary), pp. 13-73.

Reményi, L. 2002. A Vatya-kultúra Budatétény – Növény utcai temetője. – Das Gräberfeld der Vatya Kultur in Budatétény – Növény Strasse. *Budapest Régiségei* 35, pp. 77-101.

Schubert, E. 1973. Studien zur frühen Bronzezeit an der mittleren Donau. *Bericht der Römisch-Germanischen Kommission 54*, pp. 1-105.

Shennan, S. J. 1986. Central Europe in the Third Millennium B.C.: An Evolutionary Trajectory for Begining of the European Bronze Age. *Journal of Anthropological Archaeology* 5, pp. 115-146.

Shennan, S. J. 1993a. Settlement and Social Change in Central Europe, 3500-1500 BC. *Journal of World Prehistory Vol. 7, No. 2*, pp. 121-161.

Shennan, S. J. 1993b. Commodities, Transactions, and Growth in the Central-European Early Bronze Age. *Journal of European Archaeology 1.2*, pp. 59-72.

Shennan, S. J. 1999. Cost, benefit and value in the organization of early European copper production. *Antiquity 73*, pp. 352-363.

Sheratt, A. 1983. The secondary exploitation of animals in the Old World. *World Archaeology 15,* pp. 90-104.

Sheratt, A. 1993. What would a Bronze-Age world system look like? Relations between temperate Europe and the Mediterranean in later prehistory. *Journal of European Archaeology 1.2,* pp. 1-57.

Sheratt, A. 1997. *Economy and Society in Prehistoric Europe.* Edinburgh.

Sheratt, A. 1998. The Human Geography of Europe: A Prehistoric Perspective. In: Butlin, R. A.& Dodgshon, R. A. (ed.): *An Historical Geography of Europe.* Oxford, pp. 1-25.

Simon, H. K. & Horváth, L. A. 1999. Középsőbronzkori leletek Gellénháza-Budai szer II. lelőhelyen (Zala megye) – Mittelbronzezeitliche Funde in Gellénháza-Budai szer II. (Komitat Zala). *Savaria – pars archaeologica 24/3*, pp. 193-214.

Szabó, V. G.1999. *A bronzkor Csongrád megyében (Történeti vázlat a készülő régészeti állandó kiállítás kapcsán). – Die Bronzezeit im Komitat Csongrád. Eine historische Skizze anlässlich der künftigen ständingen Ausstellung – The bronze age in county Csongrád. A historical outline made on the occasion of the arrangement of the permanent archaeological exhibition.* Múzeumi Füzetek – Csongrád 2, pp. 51-118.Szathmári, I.1999. Adatok a kora bronzkori makói kultúra kérdéséhez. Beiträge zur Frage der frühbronzezeitlichen Makó-kultur. *Savaria – pars archaeologica 24/3*, pp. 141-152.

Treherne, P.1995. The warrior's beauty: the masculine body and self-identity in Bronze-Age Europe. *Journal of European Archaeology 3.1*, pp. 105-144.

Vékony, G. 2000. A koszideri korszak a Dunántúlon. – Die Koszider-Periode in Transdanubien. *Komárom Megyei Múzeumok Közleményei* 7, pp. 173-186.

Female interaction during the early and middle Bronze Age Europe, with special focus on bronze tubes

Sophie Bergerbrant

University of Stockholm, Sweden

Abstract

The article deals with a rather insignificant artefact category, the bronze tube. Bronze tubes have a wide geographic distribution and a close study of them can give us important social information. Here bronze tubes from the Carpathian Basin, Lower Austria, Lower Saxony and southern Scandinavia are discussed. The paper tries to show that a contextual study of the object in question in the different areas can both give information about how the object was used and information about contact routs in the European Bronze Age. Comparing their commonness between the different regions can also give us indication about their social use, and if the idea of the artefact was transmitted with the object or if it was locally defined or redefined. Another purpose of the article is to show that artefact categories that often are overlooked can give a lot of information.

Introduction

In this paper I will discuss a fairly common but often overlooked European bronze object; the bronze tubes. It is not an object with an elaborate form; one could rather say that they are fairly similar between the different areas of use. What is noteworthy, however, is the ways they are used. This seems to differ between different regions. It is this variation I intend to focus my study on. I will focus my article on the Scandinavian and the Lower Saxony examples but bring in material from both the Carpathian basin and Lower Austria.

The metal tubes have a long history of use, as cold-hammered copper tubes are known from the site of Çatal Hüyük, Turky (dating between the 7th to 6th millennium BC). These have been interpreted by Mellaart to have been used on the string end of a corded skirt (Barber 1991:255).

Bronze tubes are mainly used on the female dress even though there are a few examples on male costumes (see below). One can find the artefact category in graves from the Carpathian Basin, Lower Austria, Lower Saxony, and in southern Scandinavia to name a few (Behrens 1920:119, Schumacher-Matthäus 1985, Neugebauer & Neugebauer 1997, Bertemse 1989, Bergmann 1970, Laux 1971, Aner & Kersten 1973 and Oldeberg 1974). It is bronze tubes from these areas that this article will discuss, with a focus on the Scandinavian and Lower Saxony cases.

Style has long been used in archaeology for a variety of purposes. Martin Wobst (1977) claims that style can be used as an information exchange between an emitter and a receiver. He has divided the receivers into different groups, where the target group is socially distant from the emitter. When the group is further than that (i.e. very distant) it is not, according to Wobst, economical to send

stylistic messages. The emitter sends out only a few stylistic messages to the immediate household, close friends, and relatives according to this scheme, since stylistic messages are not viewed as necessary within close groups. Wobst presents a modern case study of clothing in (former) Yugoslavia, where he sees the male headpiece as a signal of belonging to a particular group. Polly Wiessner is another archaeologist who has used style to see whether we can find group belonging in the archaeological record. In her ethnographical study of the Kalahari San, she sees two different kinds of ways of signalling identity. Emblemic style is what is found on an artefact that has a distinct referent and sends a clear message to a defined target group; this is a conscious use of material to show group affiliation. Her second style category is the assertive style, where an artefact carries personal identity information. She found that the projectile points showed group belonging and as the different language groups could separate them (the different projectile points) this would be an example of emblemic style. Assertive style, on the other hand is shown in the headbands used by women; they show more personal information and can de used to see rates of interaction between groups (Wiessner 1983 & 1984). I do not find Wobst's use of style to be very relevant, since Wobst's cost – benefit label on style is a very big limitation upon the use of style. Wiessner's study shows that messages transmitted through style are sent to closer associates as well (For a deeper theoretical discussion about style and appearance see Bergerbrant 1999 and forthcoming).

Bronze tubes seem only to have been viewed as decoration on female costume and this might be the reason why it is an overlooked category. In excavation reports and catalogues they are often presented as a number of bronze tubes. This is probably partly due to the fact that it is a fragile material and many tubes are only partly preserved, but this cannot fully explain the superficial treatment the object often is given. As the tubes can vary in number from just a few, one to five, or to about 125 in one grave I find this lack of detail astonishing. How many are 'a number of', five, ten or 100? I can only see this lack of precision as a lack of interest. The tubes are seen as only unimportant pieces of clothing decoration. I will in this article try to show that even simple objects such as bronze tubes can give us important information about the prehistoric society. Authors tend to put importance on masculine objects such as swords and razors for analysis of social structure. Object belonging to female costume tend only to be used in analysis of regionality seen through costume, or as a way to find prehistoric marriage alliances between different groups. Female costume is seldom studied in its own right in order to find social structure or ways to female power and interregional contact.

Contacts between areas are often discussed on basis of male artefacts or specific 'cult' objects. During the Nordic period IB it is the distribution of, for example, the Hajdúsámson-Apa swords (for example see Vandkilde 1996:224ff) or the Hungarian influences of the Sögel and Wohlde sword/dagger blades (Sprockhoff 1927, Hachmann 1957). For period IV it is shown in the two almost identical objects from Barkåkra and Hasfalva (Knape & Nordström 1994). Or the late Bronze Age moulds of northern European artefact types found in southeastern Europe (Wanzek 1997). These objects tend to be discussed in terms of exchange or gifts, the objects changed area without being strictly tied to one person. Jewellery, however, is often seen as personal objects, as only moving on a person (Jockenhövel 1991, Kristiansen 2002:72). The bronze tubes are most often a part of female costume, worn as decoration of a particularly piece of clothing and should therefore with the above view be seen as only moving on a person. The different use of the artefact category should, however, indicate that at least some of the early bronze tubes moved without being placed on a person, i.e. fitted to her costume. Or in any case that the idea of bronze tubes moved even if the use changed along the line. Jan Apel (2001:340f) sees for the Scandinavian Late Neolithic the possibility of two different interactions spheres. He sees in the late Neolithic a male sphere where flint daggers are a part of the exchange elite goods and the possibility of a female exchange network where other goods are bartered. From this view point the so-called foreign women can be interpret in a different light. One could see them as an important factor in the movement of goods through the female networks, instead of as the supreme gift within a male network system. This could, for example, explain how the so-called 'Princess from Drowen' had a fibula that probably came from North Germany and a hanging bowl probably originated from North Jutland (Thrane 2001:556). The woman who had been in possession of these goods had probably got them through the exchange of artefacts through networks of her own rather than that they were part of bridal wealth.

I have chosen to have a chronological and geographical presentation of the data, starting with the early Bronze Age examples of the Carpathian Basin and Lower Austria to later focus on the middle Bronze Age case studies in Lower Saxony and Scandinavia.

Carpathian Basin

In the Carpathian basin the objects are found in cremation graves as well as in inhumation graves (Schumacher-Matthäus 1985), and it is therefore difficult to pin down the place of use in some areas. Attempts has, however, been made by, for example, Gisela Schumacher-Matthäus (1985). She uses grave material and clay figurines to interpret hoard finds in the region. The author argues that the hoards mirror different people's equipment. In the Maros group, Kistapostage-Vatya and the Encrusted Pottery Cultures the bronze tubes are mainly used as head-and back (rear) jewellery. The objects seem mainly to belong to the Early Bronze Age in this region.

Some of the bronze tubes are found in graves with heart-shaped pendants (Schumacher-Matthäus 1985), and one example of this is grave number three from Dunapentele, Kom Fejér, Hungary which contains exceeding the bronze tubes; pins, bronze spirals, and heart-shaped pendants among other things (Behrens 1920:119ff). This can be compared with the grave from Fallingbostel, Lower Saxony (see below). The hearth-shaped pendants are, however, of different kinds, in Dunapentele it is of Hänsel type one and in Fallingbostel it is of Hänsel type three (Hänsel 1968). Hearth-shaped pendants are only known from female graves in this region (Schumacher-Matthäuser 1985:165). The pendant is an important part of the female inhumation burials during the time. It has been suggested that they symbolise motherhood (Blischke 2000:34ff).

Lower Austria

One can find bronze tubes in many early Bronze Age cemeteries from Lower Austria. Here I have chosen to bring in two cemeteries as examples, as these are well published and come from the same region.

In the cemetery Gameinlebarn the majority of the bronze tubes are placed in the shoulder-neck region, even though there are a few placed in the vicinity of the head. There also exists tubes made out of dentalium, these have the same placement on the dress as the bronze examples. In Gemeinlebarn the bronze tubes have a date from late Reinecke A1 and early A2 (Bertemse 1989).

Below I will focus on one big cemetery that has been excavated in more recent times, Franzhausen I[1]. The early Bronze Age part of the cemetery was used for c. 700

---

years. The individuals buried there probably lived in the near by settlement and it is calculated that there lived c. 30 people per generation (Neugebauer 1994:80ff). It can therefore be presumed that the cemetery represents the remains from a fairly homogeneous group Franzhhausen I is situated in the Traisen valley close to the river Danube. It contains 716 graves and of these over 80 graves contains bronze tubes of different kinds. The burials with bronze tubes in Franzhausen I belongs to Unterwölblingen (c. Re A_{1b}- A_{2a}) and Böheimkirchner (c. Re A_{2b}-A_{2c}/B) culture groups of the early European Bronze Age (Neugebauer & Neugebauer 1997). The use of copper tubes in the region, however, goes back to the Corded Ware Culture as seen in the cemetery in Inzersdorf (Neugebauer-Maresch 1994:32). Bronze tubes can be found in children's', youth's, women's and males' graves, however, children and youth dominate in the material. Of all the graves containing bronze tubes 56% are children and youth, 33% are adult/mature/senior female, 7% are adult men, and 4% are of unknown sex. The skeletal material from the children's graves has generally not been osteologically determined to either sex. As the placement of the dead generally is related to the sex of the deceased (Neugebauer 1994) one could probably find out the children's sex by such a study (see for example Sofaer Derevenski 1997 & 2000) this is, however, a too big project for this study. A large percent of the graves have been disturbed in prehistoric times, out of the studied material 65% lacks information about the position of the artefact category on the body. Only 35% of the graves can be used to show how the bronze tubes had been worn. Out of these 86% were placed in the region of the neck/upper torso, and only 10% on the head. In a grave of a young female aged between 16 and 18 the tubes were placed on the side of the body. In the burial of one mature female (50-70 yeas old) bronze tubes was placed both on the head and on the hip.

As we can see, the majority of the people in this region had worn their bronze tubes as either part of a necklace or as a decoration on the top of the clothing worn on the upper torso. There are, however, some minor variations on this team. All variation, except one, is of adult or senior women. The child grave, which has the bronze tubes placed in the head area, contains a child between 3 and 4 years old. The child has a fairly complex headgear including amber beads, glass beads, spiral tubes, Noppenrings as well as tubes made out of denatlium. These graves, which differ from the norm, might represent people who originate in another region and therefore wore the dress used in their area of origin. As most of them are grown up women, it is possible that they indicate exogamic marriages. To verify such a hypothesis one would need to make a analysis of a larger area to study the placements of the tubes and the other artefacts found in the grave in order to see if local dress customs can b defined. This again is a too large study to do for this article.

On the local level bronze tubes are a commonly used object; more than one individual would probably had worn them at any time of the settlements/cemeteries history. If we assume that the graves containing bronze tubes were evenly spread out over the cemeteries 700 years then c. three people out every generation wore bronze tubes. In Franzhausen I the tubes seems to have been worn by a few people in every generation. Many children graves contained bronze tubes one reason for this could be that the bronze tubes were connected to a role, which one was born into rather than an acquired role. If this were the case then the death of a childe wearing bronze tubs would create the need to transform this role to another child or a new born. It is c. 1.3 adult per generation who wore the bronze tubes, using the above assumption, this could be the result of that some of them survived to an age older than the average age (for example the three graves containing Maturus-Senilis women) and therefore the community had two grown ups holding the same position a one time. It seems to be mainly a female role but the cases of males with bronze tubes might be explained with the lack of a suitable female child to take over the role.

Lüneburger Group

In the Lünerburger area the bronze tubes and spirals are placed in the graves in a position that indicates that they were worn as part of the headdress (Piesker 1958 & Laux 1971). In the beginning, however, the researchers based on the Scandinavian material believed that bronze tubes were placed somewhere around the hip in Lower Saxony as in southern Scandinavia. Sprockhoff (1930:199ff) in interpretation of one grave in mound B, Vorwohlde, discovered that the bronze tubes had been placed on a headgear, as they were placed round the remains of a skull. The tubes and some other smaller bronze objects were laid in neat order around the skull remains. Below the head had some amber beads and bronze spiral tubes been placed, creating a probable necklace. Under the head one finger ring was found, this led to the author's interpretation, after a short discussion of other possibilities, that the head must have been beheaded and placed in the hands of the deceased woman. He then goes into one discussion about vampires. However, it is more likely that authors' first suggestion, that the hands were placed under the head, is the correct interpretation. Studying the drawing from the grave and the situation of the objects, all indicate that the hands were placed under the head. Sprockhoff himself points out that the remains of the forearms were angled, which indicate that the most likely position of the arms was angled to be placed under the head.

There are bronze tubes in 45 graves, one hoard, and one stray find from the region, all graves, except one, are probable female graves[2] (Bergmann 1970, Laux 1971 &

---

[2]   Gender is assumed from artefact assembles in the graves in most cases, as many of the graves lack skeletal material or osteological

1984). Out of these we know the placements of 30, 28 are a part of a headpiece and two probably decoration of the cape[3] (Laux 1984). The hoard in Schmalenbeck (Bergmann 1970 list A 16,3) can easily be descried as a hoard containing one woman's equipment. In the region we have two different kind of headdresses rich on bronzes, the first one a kind of winged headpiece some times with an addition hanging down the back (see *Figure 2.1*) and one containing a thin bronze metal sheet placed around the forehead (see *Figure 2.2*), graves with the latter sometimes contains bronze tubes as a decoration on the cape. During later middle Bronze Age periods there exists a headpiece involving a fibula placed on the back of the head (Laux 1984). In his study Wobst (1977) example of style is a headdress used to indicate group belonging. In this case one cannot say that the main use of the headpiece is to signal group in the sense of people belonging to one area. Laux (1984:60f) has shown that even though the winged headpiece has a limited distribution there is only one per generation on the bigger largely excavated mound cemeteries, such as the Hengstberger group in Wardböhmen or Wittenberger group in Bleckmar that wears the headdress. Neither does it seems to be used in one mound group in more than three generations. Wobst cost – effect label on style seems wrong here, it seems rather to be used as a symbol for the local community, including family and friends, even though it probably also signals to people within the region that here walks a woman of some specific kind.

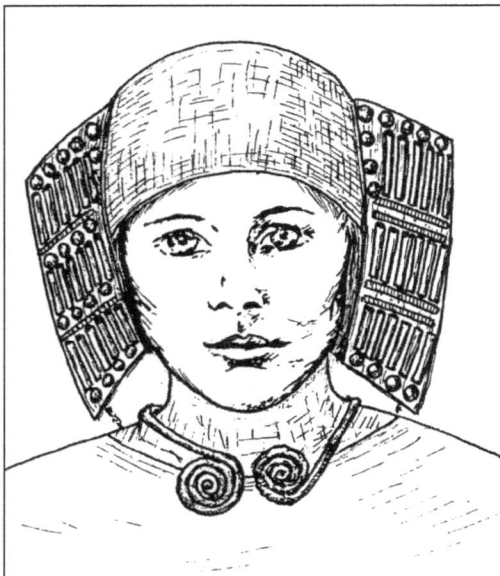

*Figure 2.1 Winged headpiece
(from Laux 1984 part of Fig. 10).*

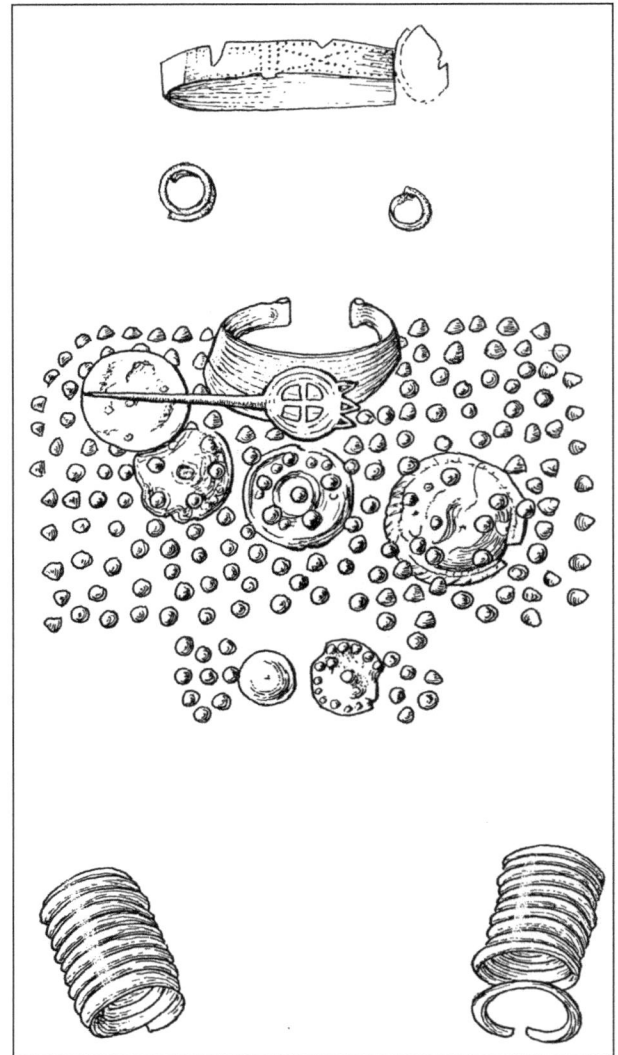

*Figure 2.2 Headpiece containing metal sheet
(from Laux 1984 Fig. 13).*

One grave, which in the question of contact and transformation appears to be of special interest, is a female grave from Fallingbostel, Lower Saxony. The grave contains; 32-conical shaped small stud, 50 larger or smaller bronze tubes, four Lockenspirals, 13 amber beads, seven hearth shaped pendants, eight neck rings with Ösenende, one wheel headed-pin and two spiral arm rings and fingerings. Laux has on the basis of the small stud and the pendants dated the grave to the Sögel-Wohlde time, i.e. period IB (Laux 1972:43ff, 1976 Nr 81 & 1985:81ff). The heart-shaped pendants are of Hänsel type three and are dated to the Middle Danubian Bronze Age II, which is more or less equal to Reinecke B1, which is more or less contemporary to the Sögel-Wohlde period (Nordic Period IB) (Hänsel 1968; Vandklide 1996). The author interprets the grave as one of a foreign woman. This is mainly based on the pendants, which he claims to have a Hungarian origin. Based on his determination of the pendants and the small stud, Laux

---

analysis of existing remains. The possible male grave has uncertain find circumstances.

[3] Grave II from mound 7 in Wardböhmen are reconstructed to be decoration on the cape by Laux (1984) but in the publication by the excavator they are written to be by the waist (Piesker 1958). Here we might have a case of tubes placed on a corded skirt in Lower Saxony.

(1971:24f) decides that the wheel headed pin is an imported piece from the Austrian-Hungarian area. The hearth-shaped pendants of type 3 had its main distribution in the Tisza region (Hänsel 1968:222f, Furmánek 1980:28f). I agree with Laux that this grave probably represents the remains of a woman who originated in the Carpathian basin. How she ended up buried in Lower Saxony, on the other hand, is harder to determine. Maybe she was a middle-aged woman who travelled by herself or with a group. There are ethnographic examples of women who after their menopause travel for family, religious, or trade reasons (Brown 1982). She might even have been a woman who arrived to the area through marriage, but to her knowledge of the exotic, gained a lot of influence in the local society. Kristiansen (2002) has argued for the importance of travel and knowledge about faraway places. Who would have more knowledge about a distance place than someone who grew up in it? There is no doubt that the woman buried in Fallingbostel had a great impact on the appearance of female dress on the Lüneburger heath, she probably also had a large effect on the social structure (see below) in the region.

Nordic Bronze Age

I will here deal with the bronze tubes from the Early Bronze Age (1700-1100 BC), this even though there also exists bronze tubes from younger Bronze Age (Thrane 1975:157). In the Nordic Bronze Age the use of bronze tubes are restricted to the north and eastern parts, i.e. northern Jutland, the Danish Isles and Scania. All bronze tubes can be found in these areas except the one find in a period III[4] hoard in Turinge, Södermanland, Sweden (Aner & Kersten 1973, Broholm 1943, Oldeberg 1975, Strömberg 1975:58ff).

Four hoards in Scandinavia are found which contain bronze tubes, and all of them except the above-mentioned hoard from Turinge, belong to period II. If one follows Kristiansen's (1974) idea that the bronze hoards containing female jewellery in one or more sets can be viewed as one woman's (or a number of women's) personal equipment, the hoard from Rye, Holbæk County (Ke 669) can easily be seen as a hoard contain the personal jewellery from three women. This as the hoard among other things includes three belt plates and three collars. The hoard from Vognserup, Hobæk County (Ke 1043I) can be categorised as two women's equipment, it has two belt plates and two neck collars[5]. It differs from the Scandinavian norm with a high number of tutulus, two of the tutulus has buckle ornamentation and one might be able to see a connection to the Lünerburger

group. In Martørv, Hjørringe County a hoard containing bronze tubes, belt plate, collar and tutuli (Thomsen 1929:192) indicates that it was one woman's personal equipment. The bronze tubes were found gathered on a string (ibid.). this would indicate that the tubes were deposited with/on a corded skirt. These three hoards are the only three in southern Scandinavia that hold bronze tubes from the Earlier Scandinavian Bronze Age. There are two hoards in southern Scandinavia containing bronze tubes from the younger Bronze Age (Broholm & Hald 1940:151f), these have a different distribution than the finds of the earlier tubes. The hoard from Turinge, Södermanland is outside the main area of use of bronze tubes and it shows a very different picture. It accommodates both women's jewellery, for example, two belt plates, unisex jewellery, tools, as well as weapons, for example, spearheads. This hoard does not fit in the pattern of a hoard containing different women's personal belongings; it is probably rather a case of long distance exchange of mixed assembly.

Larsson (1997:71 & 88) has suggested that the Trundholm chariot indicates that one during the Early Bronze Age, people believed in/worshipped a sun goddess. Maybe the belt plate as a clothing related ornamentation was chosen on purpose to increase the status of women, by emphasising their connection to the sun goddess. While 61% of the graves with bronze tubes from period II include a belt plate, during period III this relationship diminishes into only 12%. During period III the relationship between the belt plate and the tubes can only be seen in the areas were the use of the tubes are new or relatively new, i.e. Scania and Bornholm. If one adds the Danish hoards the relationship with the belt plate grows even stronger, all three hoards show this relationship. The hoards, which can be seen as hoards of more than one woman's equipment all have more than one belt plate. Maybe the introduction of the bronze tubes into Scandinavia had clear associations to women carrying a specific, maybe ritual, role in the society. This association might be further strengthened by the sacrifice of many women's equipment in to the hoards. Perhaps the tubes played a dual role, in creating sound as part of a preformed ritual and giving high status in the daily life of the women, as they would have been heard a long way when the tubes rattled.

Most of the bronze tubes found in graves where information about the placement on the body can be obtained are placed in the region of the hip, often under the belt plate. In some occasions the tubes contain remains of textile. These remains indicate that the bronze tubes have been placed on corded skirts[6]. When there are many tubes in a grave they are generally placed in two rows on what seems to be the front of the corded skirt, the

---

[4]   The hoard contains both Period II and III objects, it seems to have been deposited during the latter period (Montelius 1917 (reprint 1984):40) and is placed outside the main area of the Nordic Bronze Age.

[5]   In the Aner and Kersten volume it is described as existing 6 belt plates and 4 less tutuli, however, a study of the artefacts show that there is only 2 belt plates and that the other 4 objects are tutuli rather then belt plates.

[6]   In the Egtved grave we have a complete corded skirt, there are indication of corded skirts from most regions of the Nordic Bronze Age (Broholm & Hald 1940:149ff). The Bronze tubes, however, has only a limited distribution.

most well known example of this is the Ølby grave (Ke 299) (see *Figure 2.3*). There is, however, one exception to this, namely the grave found in Måløv (Ke 335), Smørum District, Copenhagen County, where the bronze tubes were placed in three parallel rows on the corded skirt and possibly also on seven on the fringes of the belt (Thrane, Archive Nationalmuseum, Copenhagen 648/65). Among the excavated cases there is only one grave that indicates a different placement than on a corded skirt. A stone formation in a mound in Kværkeby, Sorø County (Ke 1104G) contains different concentrations of skeletal parts, not placed in anatomically correct position, behind a skull bronze tubes were found (Petersen 1883, Archive Nationalmuseum, Copenhagen). Some authors have seen the use of corded skirt as having a wide distribution in both time and space. Neolithic examples of a corded skirt made out of plant fibres can be found in Robenhausen near Zürich, Switzerland (Hägg 1996:140ff). Other scholars want to bring the corded skirt as far back as to the Palaeolithic (Barber 1991:255ff). The corded skirt therefore seems to have been a well-established type of skirt. One question that comes to mind is why the use of bronze tubes on the skirt only has such a limited distribution?

One can see a difference in the distribution in time between the different local regions (see *Figure 2.4*). The use of bronze tubes seems to have begun on Zealand for a later spread both west and east. In Copenhagen County and Scania they seem to have come into use during late period II but the main use seems to have been during period III. On the island of Bornholm the use of the bronze tubes did not start until period III. In both Scania and Bornholm there are indications that the bronze tubes were used during later Bronze Age as well, this, as they exists as single finds and in cremation graves as the only grave goods. The occurrences of bronze tubes in graves and hoard during the Later Bronze Age have a wider distribution pattern. The distribution of bronze tubes during period II is coherent with Vandkildes zone I for period I.

Period I of the Nordic Bronze Age have been divided into two zones. Northern, central and eastern Denmark comprises zone I, and southern and western Denmark zone II. A line can be drawn between Aarhus – Lemvig in Jutland. Vandkilde has shown that there is a difference during period IB of the Nordic Bronze Age in both depositional practises of bronze objects and, mainly, in artefact groups, i.e. the Valsømagle and the Sögel-Wohlde types (Vandkilde 1996:190ff). According to Vandkilde (1996:289ff) this difference in depositional practices can be interpreted as difference in social structure. One could read this as showing that in zone I there was a marked quantitative differentiation in burial wealth. Most burials only contain one metal object but a few hold three to six objects. In zone II, although, there are more graves and a more uniform metal wealth, none contains more than three bronze artefacts. Vandklide has interpreted this as an example showing that there was a

broader and more equal based male elitehood in zone II than in zone I, and that in zone I the upcoming individual male elite group needed to be more explicit about expressing themselves as socially different from the old social order of group dominance. One can see a difference between the intensity and type of female objects during later periods between these two areas. Herner (1987:160) has pointed out that there are more belt plates in the regions that compare to the earlier period's zone I.

Figure 2.3 The Ølby grave from Boye (1896 reprint 1986) Taf XXVI.

One interpretation of the local distribution of the bronze tubes could be that women in the region equal to period I's zone II had a longer tradition of a male elitehood (see Vandklide 1996) and thus did not have the same possibility to gain and exercise power. Whereas the women in the other region had the possibility to use the new technology, i.e. bronze production, to negotiate a new status position with a higher access to personal bronze objects and to important social roles. This differing pattern occurs despite the fact that there is an overall unity of artefact types and preferred combinations in period II of the Scandinavian Bronze Age. Period III still shows a larger unity between the male associated objects (types and combination) whereas the female objects have much more localised traits (Rønne 1986 a, b). Maybe this could be seen as a result from the period IB's zone I structure indicated by Vandklide (see above). If there was an ongoing negotiation between the new uprising individual male elitehood and the older elite groups, some women may have been able to use their knowledge regarding rituals and/or clay, for example, to change their power position within the group.

Discussion

One can see a chronological difference between the different areas of use. The earliest example given here, are the ones from the Carpathian basin. They belong to the Early Bronze Age, in come cases the transition to the Middle Bronze Age, whereas the most of the examples in the north belongs to the Middle Bronze Age[7]. Here the grave from Fallinbostel might be a key in the acceptance of the bronze tubes in the Lüneburger Heath. The grave seems to be an example of a so-called foreign woman, who arrived to Lower Saxony from Hungary or an area close to Hungary. It is exceptional in many ways, most so-called foreign women only moved within a shorter distance. Jockenhövel (1991) has shown that most cases of female mobility happened within an area of 50 to 200 km. In this case the distance is much greater. This grave is also important due to the fact that this is the only identifiable female grave in Lower Saxony from the Sögel-Wohlde time that contains metal. One can see that it has a big influence on the formation of the female appearance in Lower Saxony. Traits that continue in the following time periods are the use of bronze tubes, generally placed as part of a headdress, the wheel-headed pin are transformed into local production[8], conical shaped Small stud, arm rings and neck rings. The hearth-shaped pendants are the only elements that were not taken up in the local tradition. Maybe the symbolism of motherhood in the hearth-shaped pendant was not viewed as suitable for a community with a patriarchal tradition. The road to more power and access to bronze production might rather have been through production, rites and cultural practices than through a motherhood ideology.

The appearance of foreign women, however, does not explain why the bronze tubes begun to be used in Skandinavia. The grave from Kværkeby might be one of a so-called foreign woman; it seems to have the bronze

tubes placed as part of the head gear, however, the find is not part of a regular grave of one person so it is hard to be sure about the original dispositional place. If the placement of the tubes around the head were original it would indicate an origin of the deceased from Lower Saxony or the Carpathian Basin. There is nothing, however, to indicate that this was the first example of the use of bronze tubes in Scandinavia. There is so far no find found that points to the arrival of the bronze tubes to Scandinavia would have been through a foreign woman such as the case is in Lower Saxony. How then did bronze tubes come into use in Scandinavia? Is it a local development out of earlier used decorations on corded skirts or did someone who had seen them elsewhere adopt the idea of the bronze tubes locally?

There are examples of contact between the Lower Saxony and eastern Denmark from both period I and II. In Lower Saxony there are no clear cases of Scandinavian women from these periods, however, there are example of Scandinavian males. One example of this is *Figure 2.4* from a mixed find from a mound in Ehestorf, Bremervörde, Lower Saxony were both a spearhead of Valsømagle type and a belt hook of Nordic origin are found (Laux 1971:164). Examples from later period can also be found. In eastern Denmark it seems, however, to be foreign women that are found, one example of this is the woman from Lüneburger Heath excavated in Smidstrup, Præstø County (Ke 1264A), rather than foreign men. As seen above we have evidence of contact between the different regions but no clear evidence that the idea of the bronze tubes came from Lower Saxony to eastern south Scandinavia. There are also proof of contact between southeastern Scandinavia and Hungary during period I. This can be seen in the Hajdúsámson-Apa swords were some of them seem to have been bartered goods and some seems to have been locally produced (Vandkilde 1996:224ff). One can therefore show that southeastern Scandinavia was in contact with two areas where bronze tubes were worn; two regions where the tubes were worn as part of a headdress. We know from the Lower Austrian example that the bronze tubes were a fairly commonly used object during the early Bronze Age in Central Europe. Neither in Lower Saxony nor in Scandinavia did the object become commonly used but seems to have been explicitly used by a low number of women, maybe just one woman per generation within a region. In Lower Austria there is an indication that on the local settlements they were worn by one individual per generation, whereas in Scandinavia and Lower Saxony they where worn by one individual in the local region per generation.

One puzzling questing is why bronze tubes were not used in Schleswig-Holstein and on southern Jutland. During Late Neolithic and period I of the Bronze Age there are many similarities between these regions and Lower Saxony, the use of Sögel-Wohlde bronze objects is just one of them. However, a big change occurs in the transition between periods I and II.

---

[7]   In the local Nordic Bronze Age chronology the objects belong to the Early Bronze Age, but this is mainly contemporary with the south and central European Middle Bronze Age. In order to avoid confusion I use the central European chronological scheme in this part of the article.

[8]   The wheel-headed pin from a more southern region is double sided profiled, whereas the Lüneburger examples are single sided profiled (Laux 1976:35ff).

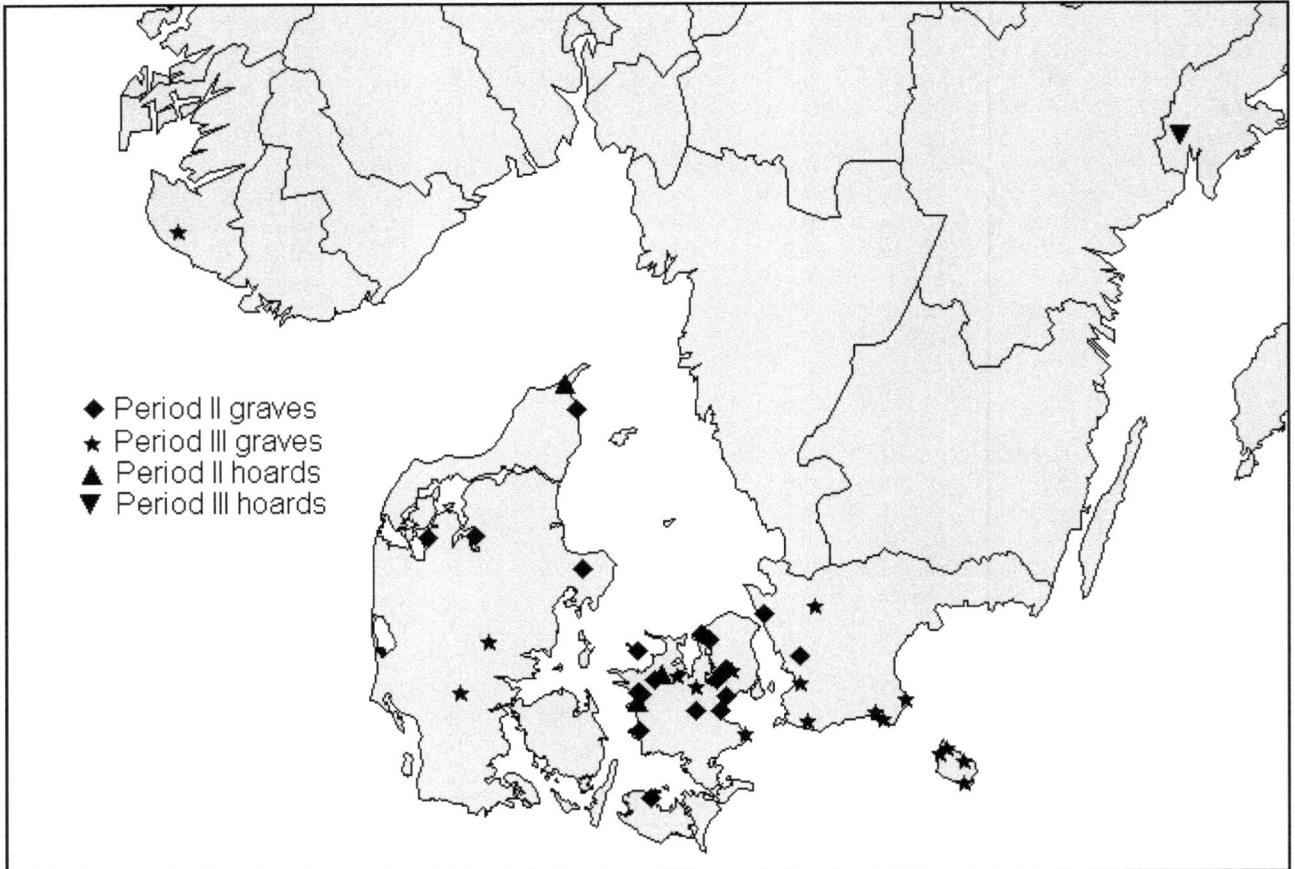

Figure 2.4 Distribution of bronze tubes in Scandinavia.

In the Lüneburger Heath swords became a very rare object while in the Nordic tradition they are common both in graves and in hoards (Bergerbrant forthcoming). Another big difference, which appears between the regions, is the wealth and number of the buried females. Female graves are sparse in Schleswig-Holstein and southern Jutland, whereas on the Lüneburger Heath there are plenty of female graves and some very richly furnished. This question is, however, too broad to be further discussed in this article, and will instead be further examined in my forthcoming dissertation. One hypothesis is that in Schleswig-Holstein and southernmost Jutland was the central region for the Sögel-Wohlde bronze production, already had a very stable male hieratical system, which was hard to renegotiate. While the Lüneburger Heath was in the outskirt of this system and not as set in their ways, one individual, the woman buried in Fallinbostel, had the opportunity to have a great say in the society. Her influence can be seen both in the social structure, distribution of wealth and the appearance of the females.

Kristiansen (2002) has argued for the importance of knowledge of foreign places and practices during the Nordic Bronze Age. The author sees these travelling individuals as male. He does not take into account the knowledge of the so-called foreign females. Even if we assume that they were mere supreme gifts (see Lévi-Strauss 1969:65) they would have had knowledge about another culture's norms and practices. Unless we believe that these women never were integrated in the society, they would have had an opportunity to use this knowledge to gain an important position in the society. These women would also have contacts within there old society, which they might hand down to their daughters and that way expand the female networks in the region. Such contacts might explain why the period V hoard in Druwden, Holland withheld artefacts from both North Germany and North Jutland. Similar networks between women in different regions might explain the appearance of bronze tubes in southeastern Denmark during period II and its spread to the surrounding regions during late period II and early III. Then again the use of bronze tubes might have been picked up by one woman who herself travelled to faraway places. One grave, which might indicate female travellers is the period III grave from Store-Loftsgård, Bornholm (Ke 1477), among other things the grave contains bronze tubes, the local fibula called Bornholms fibula as well as a typical central European fingering and European types of hooks. The possible importance of the exotic in the northern European older Bronze Age did not only give men an opportunity to create a position in the society through travel, it did also increase the women's opportunity to gain a position through their own network system, marriage alliances and travel. The variation of the placement of the bronze tubes on the dress between the different regions indicates that it in some cases, such as Lower Austria and Scandinavia the idea of the bronze tubes travelled rather than that they moved on a person. To Lower Saxony, however, they seem to have arrived through a so-called foreign woman.

One difference between the Scandinavian and the Lower Saxony examples is that in the latter there are bronze tubes with ornamentation. The lack of ornamentation on the Scandinavian bronze tubes might be connected to the placement of the tubes. The placement slightly beneath the hip and the lack of ornamentation might indicate that the objects most important function was the sound they would have created when the woman moved or the wind blew through the corded skirt. Whereas the placement of the tubes around the head in the Lower Saxony area might appeal to a view of the objects at a closer range than the Scandinavian bronze tubes. The sound would most likely also here have been an important purpose of the objects. The present or absences of ornamentation might be an important clue for us to trace cultural rules about how, were to and how to, look at another person.

One can say that the bronze tubes in themselves do not make an example of emblemic style but it is rather the way they are used, i.e. placed on the body/clothing, which creates an emblemic style. This as their placement on the dress can differ between different regions, and there for can indicate group belonging. However, especially in Scandinavia and Lower Saxony, they also seem to be part of an assertive style. This, as it seems to indicate a specific role the bearer holds. Following Wiessner (see above) then the bronze tubes should be a good material for studying interactions.

Conclusions

In this article I have shown that one from artefacts, which often is seen as small and often not given any importance, can be important to the study of social structures within prehistoric societies.

The bronze tubes seem to have been used by specific people in the society, the position of the wearer in Scandinavia and Lower Saxony was more exclusive than it was in Lower Austria and in the Carpathian Basin. To find out more about the role these women played, who wore the tubes, one must make a larger study than the one possible here. One suggestion that one can put forward is that to wear bronze tubes, involved ritual practises.

There are also indications that the positions of the tubes wearing women were inherited in Lower Austria whereas in Lower Saxony and Scandinavia they might have been gain by knowledge of the exotic.

Acknowledgment

I would like to thank the scholarship STINT for making it possible for me to temporarily become a foreign woman in Berlin. I am also very grateful to Herr Professor Dr Hänsel and his co-workers and students for making my visit at the Institut für Prähistorische Archäologie, Freie Universität Berlin so pleasant and fruitful.

Sources
Archive Nationalmuseum, Copenhagen, Denmark.

References

Aner, E. & Kersten, K. 1973. *Die Funde der Älteren Bronzezeit des nordischen Kreises in Dänemark, Schleswig-Holstein und Niedersachsen.* Nationalmuseum, Copenhagen.

Apel, J. 2001. *Dagger, Knowledge & Power. The Social Aspects of Flint-dagger Technology in Scandinavia 2350-1500 cal BC.* Coast to Coast-book 3, Uppsala.

Barber, E. J. W. 1994. *Prehistoric Textiles. The Development of Cloth in Neolithic and Bronze Age with special reference to the Aegean.* Princeton University press. Princeton.

Behrens, G. 1920. Frühbronzezeitliche Gräber aus Ungarn. *Prähistorische Zeitschrift* vol. 11 & 12, pp. 117-123.

Bergerbrant, S. 1999. Body, Sex and Gender – Constructing Appearance in Archaeology. In: Nordström, Patrik & Svedin, Marie (eds.), *Aktuell Arkeologi VII*, pp. 147-154. Stockholm Archaeological Reports Nr. 36.

Bergerbrant, S. Forthcoming. *Cut from a different cloth: Changing styles in the southern Scandinavia and northern Germany Period IB and II of the Bronze Age.* Preliminary title Ph.D. dissertation.

Bergmann, J. 1970. *Die ältere Bronzezeit Nordwestdeutschland. Neue Methoden zur Ethnischen und Historischen Interpretation Urgeschichtlicher Quellen.* Teil A + B. N. G. Kasseler Beiträge zur vor- und Frühgeschichte Vol 2. Elwert Verlag, Marburg.

Bertemes, F. 1989. *Das Frühbronzezeitliche Gräberfeld von Gemeinlebarn. Kulturhistorische und Paläometallurgische Studien.* Saarbrücker Beiträge zur Altertumskunde Band 45. Dr Rudolf Habelt GMBH, Bonn.

Blischke, J. 2000. Die Sprache der Toten. Grabbeigaben und ihr gesellschaftlicher Kontext. *Mitteilungen der Berliner Gesellschaft für Anthropologie, Ethnologie und Urgeschichte* vol 21, pp. 29-36.

Boye, Vilhelm. 1896 (reprint 1986). *Fund af egekister fra bronzealdern i Danmark* Wormianum, Århus

Broholm, H-C. 1943. *Danmarks Bronzealder*, Bind I. Copenhagen.

Broholm, H-C & Hald, M. 1940. *Costumes of the Bronze Age in Denmark*. Copenhagen.

Brown, J. K. 1982. Cross-cultural Perspectives on Middle-aged Women. *Current Anthropology*, vol 23, no 2, pp.143-156.

Ehlers, S. K. 1998. *Bronzezeitliche Textilen aus Schleswig-Holstein. Eine Technische Analyse und Funktionsbestimmung*. Dissertation zur Erlangung des Doktorsgrad der Philosophischen Fakultät der Christian-Albrects-Universität zu Kiel.

Furmánek, V. 1980. Die Anhänger in der Slowakei. *Prähistorische Bronzefunde XI, 3*. C.H. Beck-Verlag, München.

Hachmann, R. 1957. *Die frühe Bronzezeit im westlichen Ostseegebiet und ihre mittel- und südosteuropäischen Beziehungen*. Fleming Verlag, Hamburg.

Hägg, I. 1996. Textil und Tracht als Zeugnis von Bevölkerungsverschiebung. *Archäologischie Informationen* vol 19 nr. 1 & 2, pp.135-147.

Hänsel, B. 1968. *Beitrage zur Chronologie der Mittleren Bronzezeit im Karpatenbecken*. Part I and II. Rudolf Habelt Verlag GMBH, Bonn.

Herner, E. 1987. *Profession med tradition. Teknisk-kvalitativ analys av den äldre bronsålderns spiralornamentik, dess central- och lokalproduktion*. Acta Archaeologica Lundeinsia Series in 8° Nr.15.

Jockenhövel, A. 1991. Räumliche Mobilität von Personen in der mittleren Bronzezeit des westlichen Mitteleuropa. *Germania* 69 (1), pp. 49-62.

Knape, A. & Nordström, H-Å. 1994. Der Kultgegenstand von Balkåkra. *The Museum of National Antiquities/Stockholm Monographs 3*. Statens Historiska Museum, Stockholm.

Kristiansen, K. 1974. Glerupfundet. Et depotfund med kvindesmycker fra bronzealderens femte period. *Hikuin* I, pp. 7-35.

Kristiansen, K 2002. Langfærder og Helleristninger. *In Situ* 2000-2002, pp. 67-80.

Larsson, T. B. 1997. *Materiell kultur och religiösa symboler. Mesopotamien, Anatolien och Skandinavien under andra förkristna årtusendet*. Arkeologiska studier 4, Institutionen för arkeologi, Umeå universitet.

Laux, F. 1971. *Die Bronzezeit in der Lüneburger Heide*, August Lax Verlagsbuchhandlung, Hildesheim.

Laux, F. 1972. Ein bronzezeitliches Frauengrab aus Lüneburger Heide. *Harburger Jahrbuch* 1968/72 XIII, pp. 43-51.

Laux, F. 1976 Die Nadeln in Niedersachsen. *Prähistorische Bronzefunde XIII, 4*. C.H. Beck-Verlag, München.

Laux, F. 1984 Flügelhauben und andere Kopfbedeckungen der Bronzezeitlichen Lüneburger Gruppe. *Hammaburg* 1981-83 vol 6, pp 49-76.

Lévi-Strauss, C. 1969. *The elementary structures of Kinship*. Beacon press, Boston.

Montelius, O. 1917 (reprint 1984). *Minnen från vår forntid, Sten och Bronsåldern*. Faksimiltryck ARKEO-Förlaget, Gamleby.

Neugebauer, C. & Neugebauer, J.-W. 1997. *Franzhausen. Das Frühbronzezeitliche Gräberfeld I*. Fundberichte aus Österreich Materialheft A 5/1 & 5/2. Horst Adler, Wien.

Neugebauer, J.-W. 1994. *Bronzezeit in Ostösterreich*. Verlag Niederösterreichisches Presshaus, Wien.

Neugebauer-Maresch, C. 1994. Die Lokalgruppe der Schnurkeramik des Unteren Traisentales. In: Neugebauer, J.-W. (ed.), *Bronzezeit in Ostösterreich*, pp. 23-34. Verlag Niederösterreichisches Presshaus, Wien.

Piesker, H. 1958. *Untersuchungen zur älteren Lüneburischen Bronzezeit*. Hermannsburg.

Rønne, P. 1986a. Stilvariationer i ældre bronzealder. Undersøgelser over lokalforskelle, brug af ornamenter og oldsager i bronzealderns anden periode. *Aarbøger for nordisk Oldkyndighed og Historie*, pp. 71-124.

Rønne, P. 1986b. Overgangen fra periode II til III på de danske øer. En kronologisk analyse af den sene periode II milieu i de danske øers ældre bronzealder. *Aarbøger for nordisk Oldkyndighed og Historie*, pp. 125-146.

Schumacher-Matthäus, G. 1985. *Studien zu bronzezeitlichen Schmucktrachten im Karpatenbecken. Ein Beitrag zur Deutung der Hortfund in Karpatenbecken*. Marburger Studien zur Vor- und Frühgeschichte Band 6. Verlag Philipp von Zabern, Mainz am Rhein.

Sofaer Derevenski, J. 1997. Age and gender at the site of Tiszapolgár-Basatanya, Hungary. *Antiquity* Vol 71, pp. 875-889.

Sofaer Derevenski, J. 2000. Rings of life: the role of early metalwork in mediating the gendered life course. *World Archaeology* Vol. 31(3), pp. 389-406

Sprockhoff, E. 1927. Die ältesten Schwertformen Niedersachsens. *Prähistorische Zeitschrift*, vol 18, pp. 123-141.

Sprockhoff, E. 1930. Hügelgräber bei Vorwohlde im Kreise Sulingen. *Prähistorische Zeitschrift*, vol. 21, pp. 193-236.

Strömberg, M. 1975. *Bronsålder på Österlen. Undersökningar i Valleberga – Löderup – Ingelstorp*. Berlingska Boktryckeriet, Lund.

Thrane, H. 2001. Why did the rainbow end at Drouwen – if it did? In: Metz, W. H., Beck, von B. L. & Steegstra (eds.), *Patina*, pp. 551-560.

Vandkilde, H. 1996. *From Stone to Bronze. The Metalwork of Late Neolithic and Earliest Bronze Age in Denmark*. Jysk Arkæologisk Selskabs Skrifter XXXII. Aarhus.

Wanzek, B. 1997. Nordica im bronzezeitlichen Südosteuropa. In. Becker, C. et al (eds.), Χρόνος Beiträge zur Prähistorischen Archäologie zwischen Nord- und Südosteuropa. Festschrift für Bernhard Hänsel, pp. 527-541. Verlag Marie Leidorf GmbH, Espelkamp.

Wiessner, P. 1983. Style and social information in Kalahari San projectile points. *American Antiquity*, vol. 48, pp. 253-276.

Wiessner, P. 1984. Reconsidering the behavioral basis for style. *Journal of Anthropological Archaeology*, volume 3, pp. 190-234.

Wobst, M. H. 1977. Stylistic behavior and information exchange. *University of Michigan Museum of Anthropology, Anthropological Paper 61*, pp. 317-342.

Engendering cultural communication networks:
Gender related exchange systems of North Caucasian Iron Age societies between high mountains, piedmonts and the steppe

Sabine Reinhold

Institute of Archaeology RAS, Moscow, Russia

Abstract

This paper surveys gender relations in piedmont and mountain societies of the Late Bronze and Early Iron Age in the Caucasus. Here the so called Koban culture took shape amid the larger cultural networks of Eurasia and the Near East. The base of this study is made up of about 340 inhumation burials of the pre-Scythian period, i.e. from the 10th to the end of the 8th century BC. The main endeavour of this paper is to present a review of the social organisation of these societies with a focus on gender related communication networks. Mainly two different gender groups are defined, a male and a female one, but each of them with an internal ranking system. Three cultural networks can however be defined by artefact distribution and similarities in costume, armour, fighting techniques and other criteria. Two of them involve the male sphere – armour and prestige goods exchange, and one of them shows female aspects like costumes and costume elements. The female network, geographically link the two male circles, which otherwise stand rather against each other. Alternative explanations to the differences in male and female networks are tried, but the two gendered network systems were not impermeable of interaction with each other.

Introduction

Gender is a concept that deals with the roles and relationships between men and women related to social, political, and economic contexts in a community and is not determined by biology. It regulates the activities ascribed to men and women and relates to the ways in which a culture or society defines rights, responsibilities, and identities of both sexes in relation to one another (ICIMOD Newsletter No. 29). These general statements refer to recent pre-modern traditional societies but should be postulated for prehistoric societies as well. In doing so gender archaeology has developed as an individual field of social studies in prehistory during the last decade (Conkey & Spector 1984; Sofaer Derevenski 1997; Sørensen 2000). In 1992 Marie Louise Stig Sørensen outlined an agenda for an archaeology that predominantly takes the awareness of gender and its link to material culture as a principal organising criterion of society. With the human individual reappearing in archaeology since the post-processual critique of functionalist approaches of both processual and traditional archaeology, and through emergence of gender related studies in the humanities (Völger 1985; MacCormac & Strathern 1987; Völger & von Welck 1990; Di Leonardo 1991), it was only consequential to draw attention to the relationship between males and females in prehistoric societies, and to the role gender relations had in the creation of the material culture we deal with.

This paper surveys gender relations in piedmont and mountain societies of the Late Bronze and Early Iron Age in the Caucasus. With reference to European prehistory this area seems to be rather peripheral. But considering the geographical position at the boundary of the Near Eastern and the Eurasian cultural *koïnes*, this area is an interesting case study.

In mountain societies, gender is a crucial element not only in regulating the division of labour but also the radius of a persons mobility and communication networks. Like in many mountain societies the traditional migration between villages and summer or winter pastures in the Caucasus associated males and females with different activities and mobility patterns (Wixman 1980:58-60; Stadelbauer 1984). During summer women customarily remained in the villages, dealing with agriculture, haymaking and micro-scale pasture while men went on large scale pasture migrations or even lived as mountain nomads. In consequence of these male communication networks during the pre-Soviet period span over much of the mountain territories, while women's role in exterior relations was that of demonstrating the local identity and preserving local traditions (Chenciner 1997; Shami 1999).

Gender relations in prehistoric societies of the Caucasus therefore can be seen against various backgrounds. There are on the one side e.g. the topics of a social gender archaeology outlined by Sørensen (2000). Is gender a relevant criterion of social classification in the studies society at all? How can gender be related to material culture? What kind of gender relations can we reconstruct from the archaeological record? Another side is that of the ethnographical analogy. Do prehistoric gender relations reflect a similar pattern like those in the pre-modern societies? Thus, is geographical diversity indeed responsible for the diversity of cultures, subsistence strategies and traditions, the cultural patchwork which is found still today in this area?

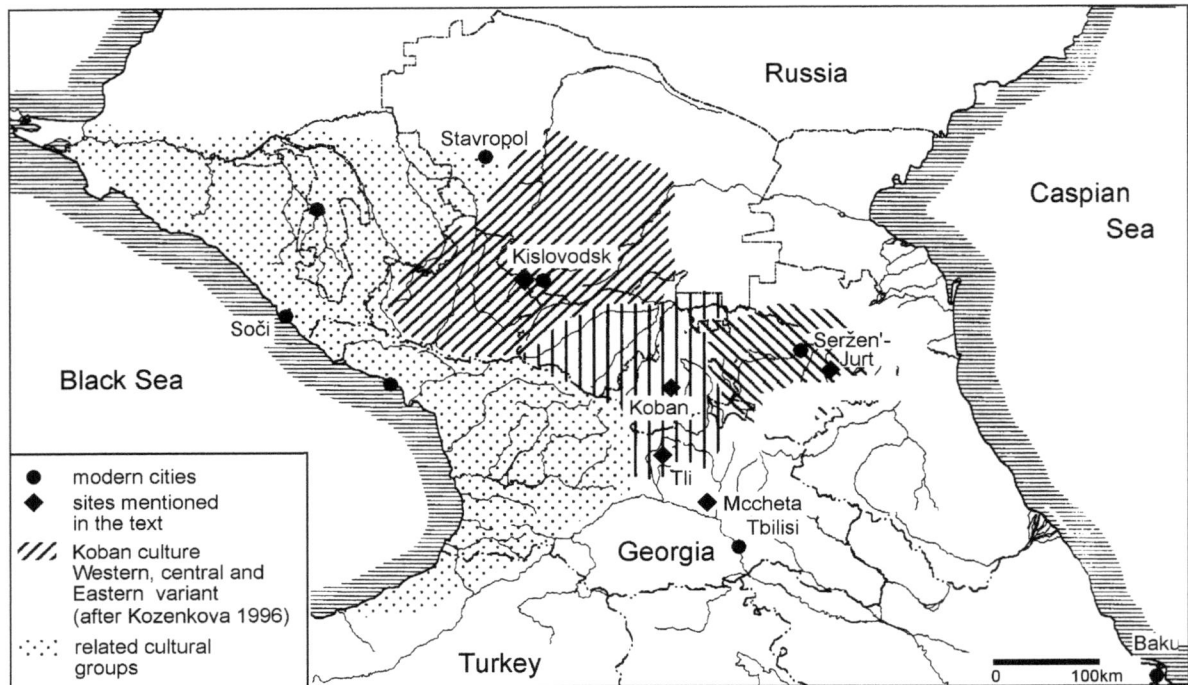

Figure 3.1 The Northern and Western Caucasus

Cultural Networks of the Koban Area

During the Late Bronze and Early Iron Age in the West and North Caucasus a powerful and autonomous cultural area traditionally known as 'Koban' (or 'Koban/Kolchis') culture took shape amid the larger cultural networks of Eurasia and the Near East (*Figure 3.1*). Located in a high mountain and piedmont environment, the archaeological evidence indicates a densely settled landscape with small farmsteads including cemeteries in the lower valleys of the piedmont zones (Afanas'ev, Korobov & Savenko 2004). The high mountains are less densely settled, but several large sites like the famous Koban are found there as well, pointing on high mountain communities which controlled the high mountain passes, pastures and mining areas (Kozenkova 1996). Based on mainly objects from burials, the Koban/Kolchis culture is divided into four major chronological phases: the formation phase, Koban A (14th-12th century BC), an early stage, Koban B (11th-9th century BC), the classical phase, Koban C (9th/8th century BC) and the late or Scythian phase, Koban D/E (7th-5th century BC) (Kozenkova 1990; Reinhold 2002).

The rich and complex grave good assemblages make it possible to define male and female representations relatively easy through the correlation of burial assemblages with anthropological data (Belinskij, Dudarev & Härke 2001). The distribution of different aspects of material culture – metal and ceramic types, costumes and armament, raw materials – enable us as well to outline different local groups which perhaps can be related to tribes or even ethnic groups (Kozenkova 1996: 62ff, Fig. 26; Reinhold 2002; 2003, 18f, Fig. 7).

Despite this excellent basis for studies of gender relations or cultural communication networks, social relations have not received much attention in Caucasian archaeology so far. The principal topics of previous studies have been the definition of cultural groups and a chronology based mainly on warrior graves. Social aspects were chiefly discussed with regard to the influence of alien mounted warriors ('Reiterkrieger') from Eurasia, the Cimmerians, who presumably passed the Caucasus during the 8th century BC on their raid to the Near East (Šarafutdinova 1993; Leskov & Erlich 1999: 32f).

The main endeavour of this paper, therefore, is to present a review of the social organisation of these societies with especial inquiry of gender related communication networks. This means not only to include female aspects into the study but also to discuss the comparative topics of gender archaeology. The paper will focus on one of the several regional groups in the Northcaucasian piedmont zone, the basin of Kislovodsk, and on the pre-Scythian period. Here the archaeological situation is ideal for a case study of gender relations since not only gender related material culture is found but also the cultural orientations of females and males seem to differ substantially. The bases of this study are about 340 inhumation burials of the pre-Scythian period, i.e. from the 10th to the end of the 8th century BC.

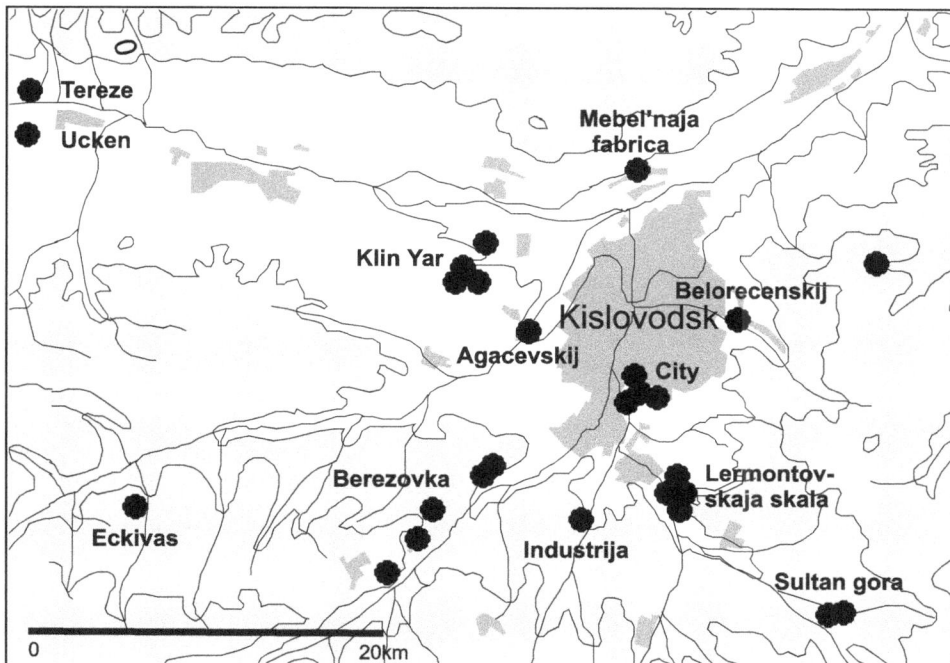

Figure 3.2. The Kislovodsk basin with the main sites

During this period a stable settlement pattern indicates the presence of at least eight communities in the valleys surrounding the present city of Kislovodsk (*Figure. 3.2*).

Asking for cultural and social identities in these prehistoric communities, however, we are confined to burial evidence, as settlement excavations are rare and poorly published. The cemeteries, however, provide a good source of indicators which are associated with social factors such as rank, age, gender and participation in broader cultural networks. Anthropological studies are limited because of early excavations and poor preservation of bones, but some sites have been studied well enough to outline a relation between socially constructed facts like graves with weapons or with ornaments with male or female individuals (Belinskij & Härke 2000). From this point we may use the present gender division in burial assemblages as a guideline to look for the presence of male and female in the graveyards, the artefacts and ritual standards associated with them, the artefact diversity, quantity and quality of male and female burials and the ranking pattern of the two genders. This will lead us to the investigation of regional variance within the cultural network of the Kislovodsk men and women and the relationship that both genders had with members of other groups.

Gender related artefacts and ritual standards

Gender related artefacts in the Kislovodsk burials are easy to identify, if we follow the line of gender specific grave assemblages. This allows us to relate arms and tools like whetstones, awls and 'lighters' to males,

ornaments and jewellery to women. There are only a few graves which include arms and jewellery. In these cases, however, like in grave 34 of Mebel'naja fabrica, the ornaments were placed in a separate deposit beside the armed individual. This practice is rarely observed in the Kislovodsk area (Dudarev 1999: Fig. 138; 144; Berezin & Dudarev 1999: Fig. 11-12; Kozenkova 1989: Pl. XXXIX-XL), but frequently at another Koban site, Seržen'-Jurt in Chechnya (Kozenkova 1992). In this area it is an interesting fact that female costumes seem to have been a special burial gift for armed men.

It is proven by small figurines from the Northern Caucasus that the burial equipment is a correlate of gender related identities (Markovin 1986). This also relates to belt-plates from Transcaucasia decorated with figures (*Figure 3.6*) (Esayan 1984; Chidaseli 1986). Physically identifiable men in these representations are associated with arms, depicted particularly in warfare and hunting scenes. Women on the contrary, are depicted wearing jewellery and carrying vessels, offering food, children or sitting on horses. Even if we allow these objects to be from a highly ideological and/or religious context, different spheres of activities and objects associated with them are obvious.

But not only are the combinations of objects related to females or males, but the objects themselves seemed to be gender related as well. The ceramic in the graves, for instance, vary greatly in form and decoration between burials with arms and ornaments (*Figure 3.3 A-B*). Especially during the earlier periods in the 10th and 9th century BC females were associated with slim high pots with fingernail imprints, while in male graves open bowls with geometric decoration are found. Only in the later phase, during the 8th century BC bowls appeared in female graves. The small number of pottery published from settlements (Kozenkova 1989:Ppl. XIII-XVI; Kozenkova 1998: pl. XXX-XXXIII), however, indicates that among others both these forms were present and thus the selection of specific vessel types for burial equipment was indeed an intentional act. Unfortunately no settlement material is published to such a degree that for instance female or male spheres in houses could be postulated. However, the studies presented open up for the question of gender representation in the production of pottery. Generally females are associated with pottery production and decoration (Knopf 1999: 182ff). How about pottery for male burials?

Gender specific burial customs are evident as well in the placement of the bodies. While most of the armed individuals are placed in a right position, those with ornaments are predominantly found lying on the left side. The cemetery of Mebel'naja fabrica 1 is a good example for this custom (*Figure 3.4*). It shows after all that there is not such a strict gender related burial position as for instant during the Late Neolithic and Early Bronze Age Europe since a considerable percentage of individuals do not fit this rule.

Other aspects of the burial ritual seem not to be gender related. The orientation of the dead was very heterogeneous and shows only preferences within the different cemeteries, not between the genders. Likewise, the size and types of graves – pit-graves or stone-cists – vary only between the sites, not between the genders. Similar, gender related burial places or special areas in the cemeteries for men and women respectively, are not observable, either.

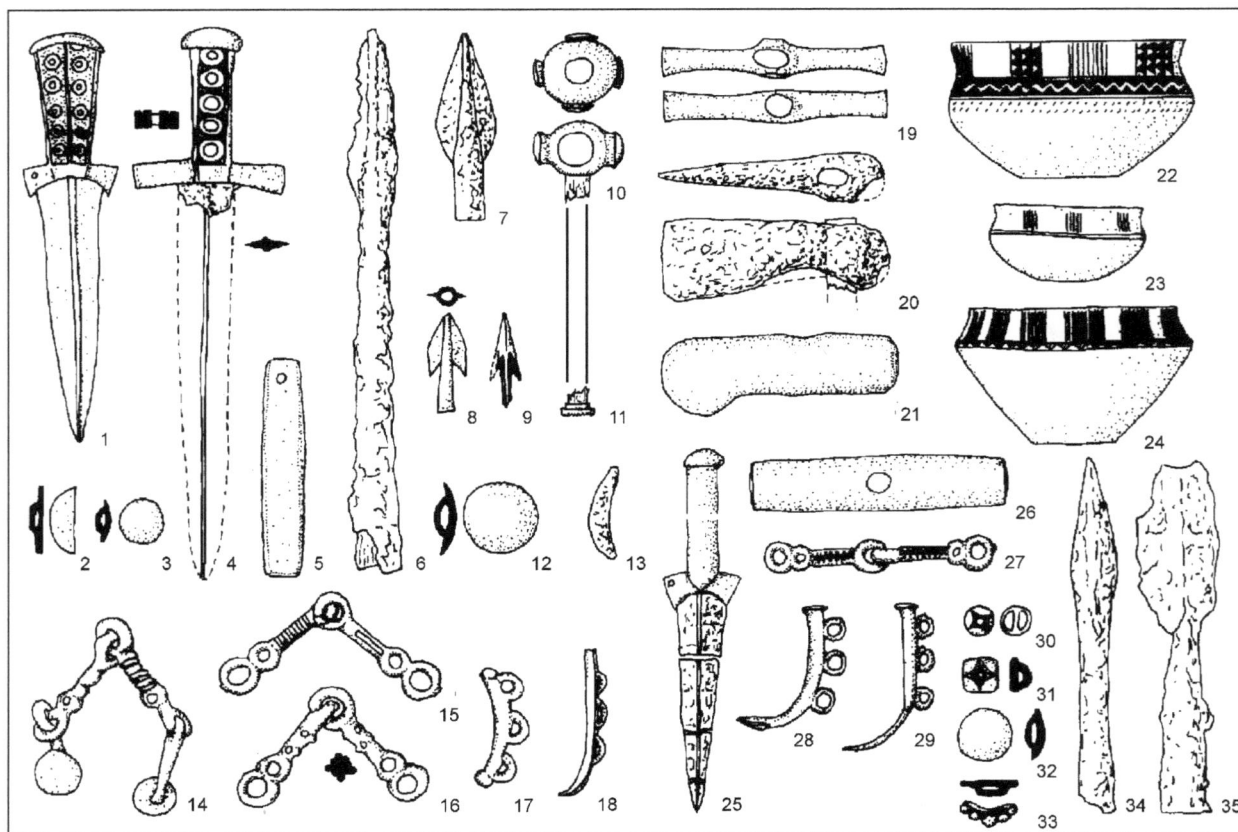

Figure 3.3A. The typological spectrum of warrior/male graves.
Mebel'naja fabrica 1: grave 4: 15; grave 5: 24; 26; grave 6: 4; grave 11: 7;
grave 14: 25; grave 15: 10-11; grave 26: 2, 22; grave 34: 2-3; 5; 8; 12; 14; 18; 20; grave 36: 13; 32-
33; Klin Yar 3: grave 26F: 29-30; grave 135F: 9; grave 18B: 35; grave 20B: 28; grave 23B: 16; grave
186Bel: 27; 31; 35; destroyed graves 1987: 6; Ostjoinik, grave 3: 17
(all after Dudarev 1999. Without scale)

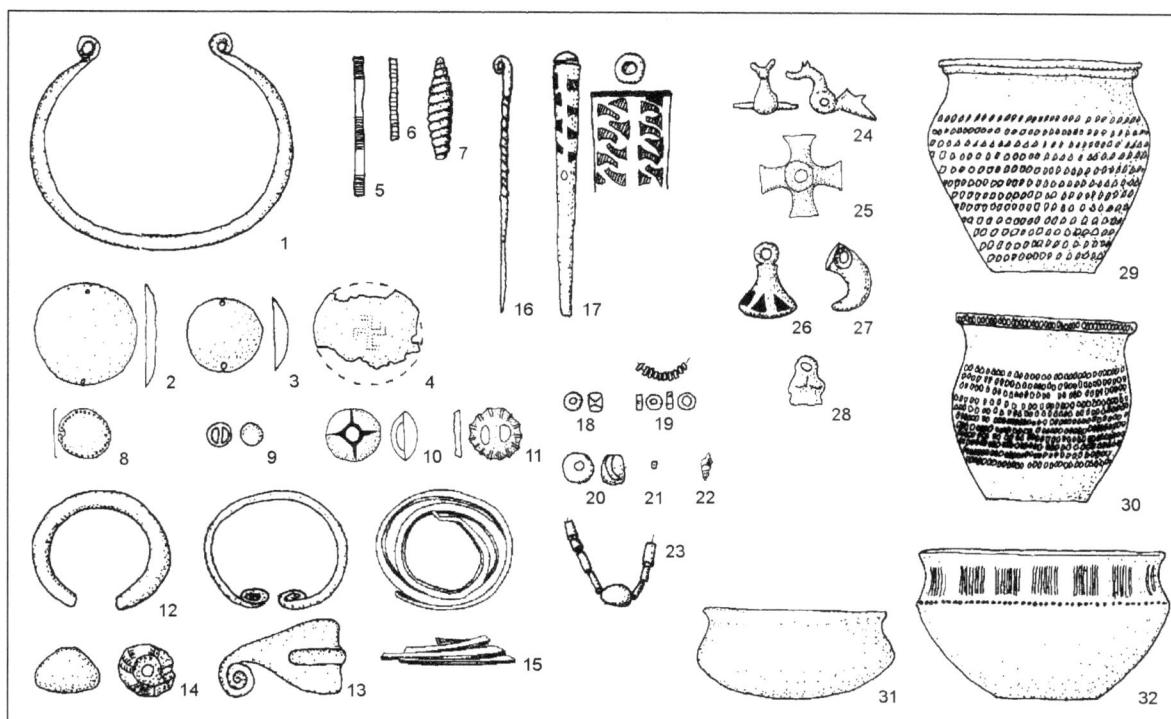

Figure 3.3B. The typological spectrum of female graves.
Mebel'naja fabrica 1: grave 25:1; 6-7; 10-13; 16-17; 32; Industrija 1, grave 9:
2-3; 14; 19-21; 23; grave 15:9; 18; 24-29; 31; Klin Yar 3, 1987/2B: 8;
Ostjoinik, grave 1: 4-5; 22; 30 (1, 6-7; 9; 10-13; 16-18; 24-29; 31-32 after Kozenkova 1989,
pl. XLI V and pl. XLII A; 2-3; 14; 19-21 after Afanas'ev and Kozenkova 1981, fig. 2
(there grave 1/1971); 4-5; 8; 22, 30 after Dudarev 1999, fig, 11 and 137, 1-5. Without scale)

Gender was consequently important to the Kislovodsk social identities at different levels. Material culture, its style and potential as part of costumes or armament was definitely significant. For the burial ritual gender apparently was less important. This makes it reasonable to suppose that the corporate gender identities displayed in the burial equipment were important to be preserved even after death as a representation of the social order of these communities, while the ritual used to preserve these representations remained less important.

**Social ranking according to burial equipment –
inequality of genders?**

In many recent societies the relation between the genders is one of inequality. Female status is defined in regard to the status of their fathers or spouses, their outside activities are often restricted. Although mountain societies usually have less restrictions on women, which is basically due to the importance of their working labour in the extreme terrain, gender equality is rarely reported (ICIMOD Newsletter 29). In a prehistoric society where gender related identities are apparent, the question of equality or inequality between men and women is a significant detail for the reconstruction of social relations.

To verify levels of inequality in the burial assemblages of Kislovodsk a comparative analysis of combinations of functional artefacts classes such as weapon combinations or ornament arrangements was carried out for both genders. Costumes and/or armour – the factors which lead to such specific artefact combinations – are well known symbols of social representation and thus likely to be used to reconstruct the social organisation of a community (Sørensen 1997; Reinhold 2003). The result was then compared to an analysis of the burial's 'wealth', including artefact quantity and quality, as well as the labour involved in the construction of the grave, using a method first applied by Mechtild Freudenberg to grave inventories of the Danish Bronze Age (Freudenberg 1989: 56ff; Jørgensen 1990).

For the male population the excavators of the largest excavated site Klin Yar have proposed a sophisticated ranking system, in which the presence or absence of arms, horse gear or tools classify the buried individuals in six social groups (Belinskij, Dudarev & Härke 2001). The first group includes horse gear, 1-3 weapons, 1-3 tools, a ceramic vessel and sometimes gold-decorated objects, parts of an armour of Western Asian (Assyrian or Urartean) and Transcaucasian origin; the second represents a group with 2 kinds of weapons, a ceramic vessel and 1-4 tools; the third group includes warriors armed, chiefly with spears, and a vessel; the fourth group incorporates unarmed men with a vessel and tools; the fifth group has only one vessel, and the sixth group includes individuals without grave goods. Yet, the result of their analysis was, that besides in the uppermost class, the graves do not show too sharp differences in burial wealth or size, and thus a rather equal social position among the warriors is postulated.

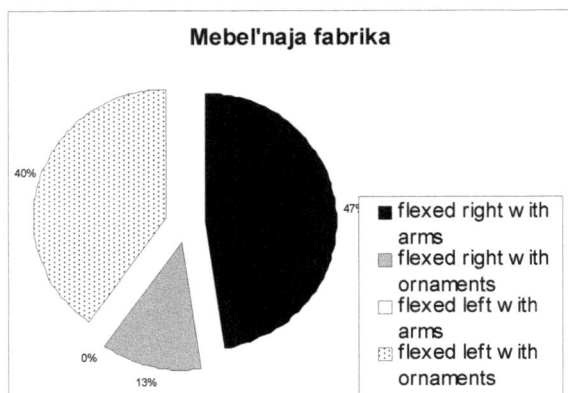

Figure 3.4. Burial customs Mebl'naja fabrica 1

The main classification criterion in this system is the presence or absence of horse gear, i.e. the status of mounted or non-mounted warriors. This definition, nevertheless, is chiefly a reflection of the traditional view, which relates the 'mounted warrior' graves, i.e. those with horse gear, to nomadic Cimmerians (see Metzner-Nebelsick 2000 for the paradigm and its critique). This nomadic population which emerges during the late 8th century BC in the Near Eastern sources, are supposed to have come from the Eurasian steppe as horse breading nomads with a specific mounted warrior class, adopted by the local Caucasian groups. The definition, yet, is ambiguous since the graves with horse gear are rather heterogeneous in their other equipments, as are those without horse gear. As I could show elsewhere (Reinhold 2005) the differentiation of warrior equipment according to the combination of weapon classes is much more promising, since it leads to homogeneous units with strictly regulated armour. It as well places the 'mounted warriors' at the top of a system of warrior ranks corresponding to well known ancient fighting techniques.

If we therefore exclude the horse gear as defining criteria we find that the basic weapon in Kislovodsk was the spear and the most frequent tool the whetstone (Tab. 1). About 44% of the armed individuals are equipped with a spear, 65% have whetstones, predominantly in combination with spears. Combined with spears and whetstones we find daggers in 13 inventories and axes in 11 inventories (warrior level 2). Very seldom these three items were combined in a triple set (level 1), for

instance in Ėčkivaš, grave 4, or Mebel'naja fabrica, grave 15 and 26 (Dudarev 1999: fig. 104, 11-22 (Ėčkivaš, grave 4), fig. 141: 1-11 (Mebel'naja fabrica, grave 15); fig. 142: 8-13 (ditto, grave 26)) (*Figure 3.5, E*). The first two of the last mentioned inventories are among the wealthiest graves in Kislovodsk and both have nearly identical mace-heads made of silver.

At the other end of the spear-whetstone combination we find the most numerous group, which is that of the warriors with a single spear (level 4A). And besides the spear-carriers there is a noteworthy group without spears. They carry daggers and axes or battle-hammers (level 3), or a single weapon of these categories (level 4B/C). Combinations, however, are rare and graves like Mebel'naja fabrica 14 and 36 (Dudarev 1999: fig. 140 (grave 14), fig. 147, 1-12 (grave 36)), range among the extraordinarily rich burials. The lowest level includes burials with tools and/or whetstones (level 5) and males without arms (level 6).

As for the 'mounted warriors' which constitute the upper social rank in Dudarev, Belinskij and Härkes system, there is indeed an obvious relationship between rich burials and horse gear, and hence to the combination of spear and battle-axes/hammers/maces or spears and daggers. In ten out of the twenty-two warrior graves with horse gear, a combination of arms was found. But four of the horsemen were equipped with only a spear and no further arms; another five only with battle-axes/hammers/maces, and two of the Klin Yar warriors with horse gear, had only a whetstone and an arrowhead (Reinhold 2005). This fact allows the association of horses with the upper class of warriors, but does not allow the reconstruction of a mounted elite warrior class. Horses rather can be regarded as a symbol of social prestige, which is added to the other symbols of a warrior of a higher rank, or perhaps of a higher age. It is also very likely that some of the Caucasian warriors were mounted warriors and took possibly part in a raid to the Near East, as for instance the man in grave 186 from Klin Yar (Belinskij 1990) (*Figure 3.5, G*), who has an Assyrian style helmet. Yet, another very wealthy warrior from the site Industrija, grave 4 (Dudarev 1999: fig. 148, 1-12) (*Figure 3.5, F*), with a combination of a spear, two central Caucasian axes, a flat-axe and an Urartean scale armour was not mounted. These examples show that the principal structure of the Kislovodsk warriors is most obviously represented in the standard weapon combinations to which additional and exceptional burial goods – like horse gear – could have been added. In consequence, excluding the concept of a particular mounted warrior class, the ranked but not extremely hierarchical society proposed by Dudarev, Belinskij & Härke (2001), is an adequate basis for further studies. It allows the hypothesis of the attendance of outstanding warriors, like the 'big men' of Marshal Salins (*Figure 3.6*), but relate otherwise to a rather vertically ranked society.

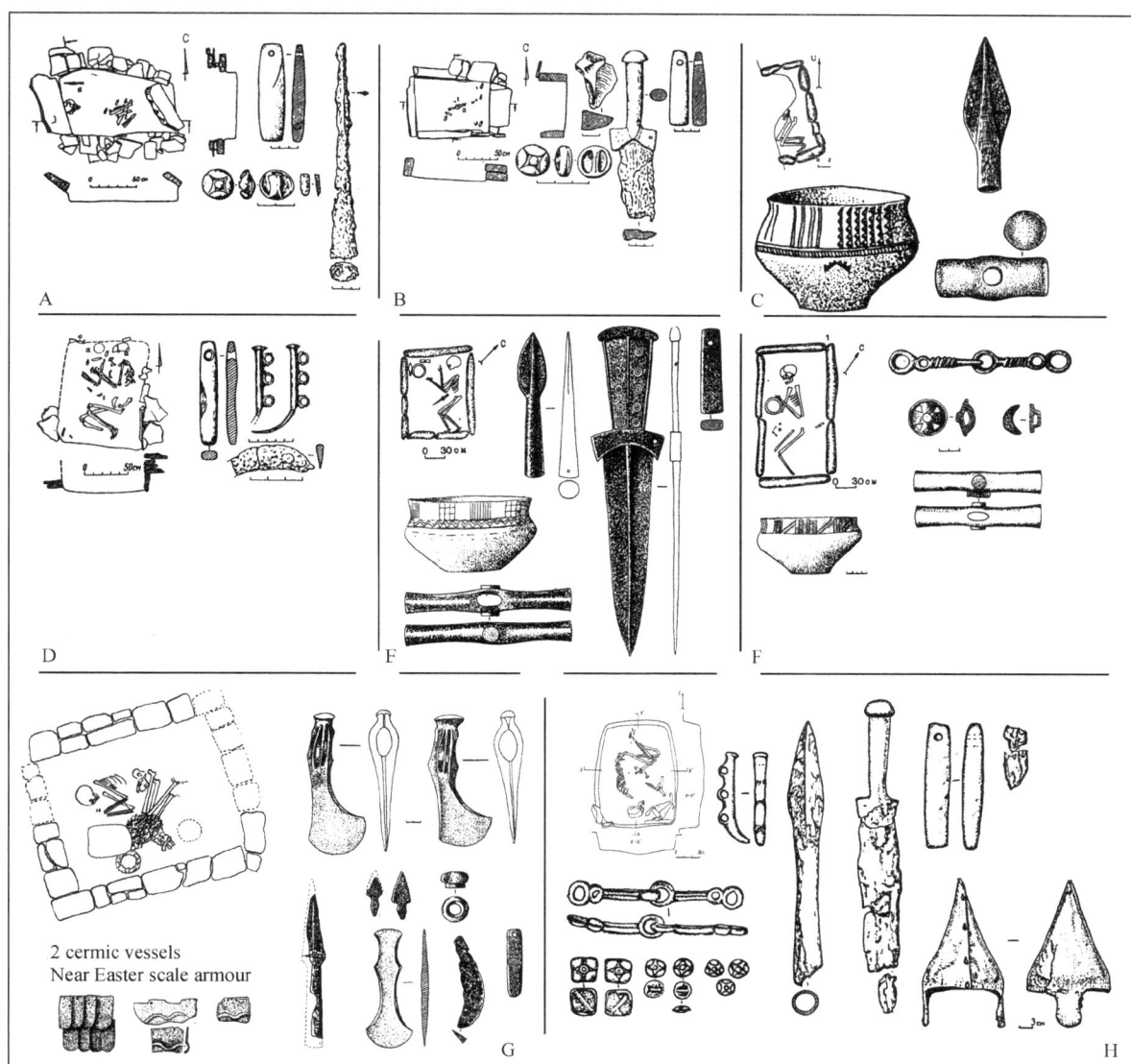

Figure 3.5. Warrior graves from Kislovodsk.
A=Klin Yar 3, grave 87F; B=Klin Yar 3, grave 121F; C= Mebl'naja fabrica 1, grave 11; D= Klin Yar 3, grave 26F; E= Mebl'naja fabrica 1, grave 26; F= Mebl'naja fabrica 1, grave 17; G=Industrija 1, grave 4; H=Klin Yar 3, grave 186Bel (A,B,C,E,F,G,H after Dudarev 1999, fig. 113, 1-5; 114; 1-5; 115, 1-5; fig. 139, 5-8; fig. 142, 8-13; fig. 142, 1-5; fig. 148, 1-12; fig. 117. Scale 1:6)

The female manner of dress reveals a similar classification among women (Tab. 2). The structures, however, are less clear than in the male sphere, because the number of costume elements is larger all the way through. The costumes include head and plait gear, neck rings and necklaces, pins and arm spirals in various, but regular combinations. Their combinations are to some degree site specific. For instance in Mebel'naja fabrica, Ėčkivaš, Berezovka and in the sites of the city centre, the costumes can be divided into three levels by their attributes; a very elaborated costume level with head gear, arm spirals, neck ring or necklaces and pins; a second costume level with head gear, necklaces and pin(s), and a third one, with head gear. In Klin Yar,

Belorečenskij or Industria, on the contrary, the most elaborate female costume level includes a specific plait gear, neck rings and pins (*Figure 3.7, A, B*), or rich sets of bracelets and neck rings; the second level only a pair of bracelets and the neck ring (*Figure 3.7, C, D*), and the third one, only small head ornaments and necklaces (*Figure 3.7, E, F*).

Altogether the costumes are more individualistic than are the male equipment, but in general there are three major levels; rich costumes with a lot of bronze objects and beads, a middle level with less bronze but similar amounts of beads, and a lower level with only small numbers of beads and very few bronzes.

31

Figure 3.6. Warfare, feasting and hunting scenes on decorated belts from Transcaucasia.
1=belt from Stepanavan after Esayan 1984, fig. 38; 2=belt from Tli, grave 74 after Techov 1977, fig. 100,
3=belt from Tli, grave 350 after Techov 2002, fig. 296.

When we compare the two genders on this level, we find both of them ranked in a hierarchical system respectively that, however, has no extreme poles. The ranking is rather categorical, and in all categories the number of individuals is equal enough to exclude a ranking in rich and poor families. There are some extraordinary warrior graves, which indicate a kind of social elite. But they are neither limited to one site, as for instance around the princely sites ('Fürstensitze') in the Western Hallstatt culture, nor are they outstanding in a principal ritual (Kossack 1974). These warriors appropriate to their outstanding grave goods, were part of one or another of the standard warrior group. Similarly, rich female graves are represented, but they do as well keep to the principal representation of their respective costume group. Tradition thus had been strong enough to prevent any social fissure and forbid outstanding persons like the warriors from Klin Yar or Industria, to establish themselves as princely elite (Reinhold 2005). Both genders show a similar structure in social ranking, which basically involve a descending number of artefact combinations. In addition, a detailed study of artefact numbers, the metal involved in the

burial goods or other criteria, which are related to the resources disposed of in a grave show, that both genders were treated quite equally (*Figure 3.8A; 3.8B*). The expenditure rises similar with the levels of either armour or costume. Thus, while gender was clearly defined through the material culture involved in the burial, the resources to furnish were not related to gender, but to the social position of the deceased.

Unfortunately the anthropological data of the Kislovodsk burials are not substantial enough to make sure to what extent age and age classes are in charge for this social classification. Until today in Caucasia age is the crucial criterion for both genders in certifying their position in society (Shami 2000). Along this line run the abilities of social intercourse and political decision making, and the e.g. young warriors are at the disposal of the old men (Plaetschke 1929). In the same way women's status within the female sphere do not depend too much on their husband's status but rather on their age and martial status. If these criteria, yet, was equally the background of the prehistoric societies' structure remains open.

Grave	spear	dagger	axe/hammer	arrows	knife	whetstone	lighter	awl	horse gear	scale armour	ceramic vessel	anthropology	armament
MF1/26	1	1	1			1					1	♂	1
MF1/15	1	1	1						1			♂ 20-25	1
MF1/6	1	2				1					2	♂ ~70	2
MF1/43	2	1			1	1	1	1	1		1		2
MF1/11	1		1			1					1		2
MF1/4	1		1		1	1			1			♂	2
MF1/27	1				1	1						♂	4 A
MF1/49	1				1	1	1				1		4 A
MF1/2	1					1					1		4 A
MF1/12	1										1	♂ 45-50	4 A
MF1/31	1				1	1					1		4 A
MF1/19	1				1	1					1		4 A
MF1/24	1					1			1				4 A
MF1/38	1				1	1							4 A
MF1/14		1	1	2		1							3
MF1/36		1	1		1	1			1				3
MF1/28		1			1			1					4 B
MF1/34			1	3			1		1		1		4 C
MF1/5a			1			2			1		1		4 C
MF1/17			1			1			1		1		4 C
MF1/44					1		1				1		5
KY3/362Bel	1		1			1					1	♂ adult	2
KY3/14B	1		1	4		1			1		1		2
KY3/23B	1		1			3	1		1		1		2
KY3/186Bel	1	1			1	1			1	1			2
KY3/128F	1	1											2
KY3/20B	1	1				1	1		1		1		2
KY3/18B	1				1	1			1		1		4 A
KY3/358Bel	1				1	1					1	♂	4 A
KY3/143F	1						1	1			1		4 A
KY3/16B	1									1	1		4 A
KY3/126F	1												4 A

	1	2	3	4	5	6	7	8	9	10	11		
KY3/87F	1				1								4 A
KY3/121F		1			1	1							4 B
KY3/316Bel			1	4	1	1	2	2			1		4 C
KY3/135F			1	1	1								4 C
KY3/184Bel			1	1	1	1					1		4 C
KY3/138F				1	1						1		5
KY3/164Bel				1	1						1		5
KY3/196Bel				2	1	2					1		5
KY3/297Bel				4		1			**1**		1		5
KY3/309Bel				1	1								5
KY3/325Bel				3		1		1			1		5
KY3/82F					1								5
KY3/95F					1								5
KY3/26F				1	1				**1**		1		5
KY3/13B				1									5
KY3/127F				1									5
KY3/376Bel				1	1						1	♂	5
KY3/74F				1									5
KY3/12F					1						1		5
KY3/377Bel											1	♂	6
IN1/4	1		3	2	2	1	2	1		1			1
IN1/3	1				1								4 A
IN1/17	1												4 A
IN1/10				2		1							5
IN1/14					1	1					1		5

Table. 3.1 Warrior equipment of selected sites (Mebel'naja fabrica 1, Klin Yar 3 and Industrija 1), disturbed and younger graves are excluded (after Dudarev 1999; Berezin and Dudarev 1999; Belinskij and Härke 2000; Belinskij and Dudarev 2002; Afanas'ev and Kozenkova 1981; for Klin Yar the excavators are labelled F = V.S. Flërov, B = Ja.B. Berezin and Bel = A.B. Belinskij)

Artefact distribution and exchange systems

Both of the genders present in the archaeological material from the Kislovodsk burial grounds, have been part of wide-ranging exchange networks, since a considerable quantity of male and female burials clearly include imported objects. Such objects are rare or singular in Kislovodsk, but they are on the contrary, frequent in neighbouring areas like the Kuban region, or in the high mountains of the Central Caucasus range. Similarly, objects of a presumably Kislovodsk origin are distributed over a vast area. However, artefacts usually related to the female sphere, are found in fairly different areas than are those related to warrior burials. These circumstances lead to another aspect of gender related social structures in this area.

During the pre-Scythian period a large quantity of Northcaucasian arms and horse gear is found throughout Eastern Europe (*Figure 3.9*). Traditionally it is related to the already mentioned nomadic Cimmerian tribes, which appear as invaders first in the late 8th century BC in Near Eastern sources, and later are believed to have inhabited the Eurasian steppe in the early 7th century BC, previous to the Scythians (Chochorowski 1993).

With a considerable change in the absolute chronology of the Caucasian (Kossack 1983; Kossack 1994; Reinhold 2002), Northernpontic, and Eastern European Early Iron Age (Metzner-Nebelsick 1994), that is from the late 8th-6th to the 10th-8th century BC, this paradigm has to face fundamental critique. Not only is the underlying historical and ethnic connotation of the objects highly questionable (Metzner-Nebelsick 2000). The entire paradigm of nomadic horse breeding tribes inhabiting the Eurasian and Northernpontic steppe, which conquered the Northcaucasian piedmonts on their way to the Near East, is called into question. A new synthesis of the Northpontic Early Iron Age has shown, that the tribes were much more territorially restricted and settled, than previously thought (Dubovskaja 1997). Likewise, the 'Cimmerian' objects are by means of quantity and quality, now regarded as to be of Northcaucasian or Middle-Wolga origin, and the Kislovodsk area is seen as one of the main sources for these objects (Berezin and Dudarev 1999: 195).

Nevertheless, Northcaucasian objects are present far outside their homeland; and if we do not accept the 'Cimmerian' paradigm, i.e. their widespread distribution by 'Cimmerians' and as an indicator for 'Cimmerian raids' across Eurasia anymore, it becomes necessary to establish another model to explain their passage across the steppe.

Carola Metzner-Nebelsick has suggested such an alternative through her model of a complex system of seasonal pasture migration, prestige good exchange, shift

of an elite warrior ideology, and 'warrior societies' to account for the presence of Eastern types in the Carpatian basin (Metzner-Nebelsick 1998: 400-411, fig. 31). A similar model is applied by Olga Dubovskaja for the Northenpontic Early Iron Age Černogorovka culture, too (Dubovskaja 1997). Both authors see an intense and permanent Caucasian influence in all parts of the Eastern European steppe and its fringes, which primarily is indicated by the mentioned Caucasian weapons. This allows us to reconstruct a long standing and complex communication network among the warriors over a vast area. The exchange of arms and military techniques, like fighting on horseback and from war chariots with the necessary horse gear, associate this network with an elite concept of warfare (Reinhold 2005). It reminds us of the world of political and military alliances, established via exchange of prestige goods and elite marriages, as Homer describes in the prelude of the Trojan War.

Grave	head gear	snail head gear	plait gear	neckring	necklace	pins	spiral bracelets	bracelets	pendants	cowrie	spindel whorle	ceramic vessel	anthropology	costume levels
MF1/25	1		1	1	m	1	6	2	m			1		1 A
MF1/1	1					1	6					1		1 A
MF1/18					m	1	4	2	m	3		1		1 A
MF1/48	1	1			m	1		2						1 B
MF1/13					m	2		2			1			1 B
MF1/5b	1				x	2					1	1		2
MF1/7	1				x	2					2		♀	2
MF1/32	1	1			x	1						1		3
MF1/29	1	1			x	1					1	1		3
MF1/30	1				x	1						1		3
MF1/8	1				x	1					1	1		3
MF1/3	1					1					1	1		3
MF1/47	1				x	1					1			3
MF1/33					x	1				18	1	1		3
MF1/10	1	1										1		4
MF1/39	1	1										1		4
MF1/16	1											2		4
MF1/35	1										1	1		4
MF1/37					x							1		5
MF1/46					x									5
KY3/366Bel	1			1	m		4					1	♀?	1 A
KY3/350Bel	1			1	m		2						♀ subadult	1 A
KY3/11B							2		1			1		1 A

KY3/25B	1			1	m	1		2		1	1		1 B
KY3/10B					x			2			1		1 B
KY3/9B				1	m			2		7	1		1 B
KY3/2/1987 B	1	1			x	1					1		3
IN1/9	1		1		m			2		1	2		1 B
IN1/6	1		1		m			2	1				1 B
IN1/5			1		m						1		2
IN1/15	1			1	m				4		2		2
IN1/2					m			2			2		2
IN1/16				1	x			1			2		3
IN1/13				1							1		3
IN1/1	1				x						2		5
IN1/12	1										2		5

Table 3.2 . Female costumes of selected sites (Mebel'naja fabrica 1, Klin Yar 3 and Industrija 1), disturbed and younger graves are excluded (after Dudarev 1999; Berezin and Dudarev 1999; Belinskij and Härke 2000; Belinskij and Dudarev 2002; Afanas'ev and Kozenkova 1981; for Klin Yar the excavators are labelled B = Ja.B. Berezin and Bel = A.B. Belinskij)

Yet, this communication and exchange network was a purely male affair. Caucasian objects of female association are nearly never found in the Eastern European steppe and vice versa. One or two bracelets in a hoard near Tripolje in Ukraine (Val'čak 1997a), some Kislovodsk head gear elements in a second hoard from Zalevki (Terenožkin 1976: 74, fig. 40, 4-5), a Caucasian pin from Chmel'na (Terenožkin 1976: 97, fig. 60, 1) and a golden templering of Northwest Caucasian origin in a hoard from Šarengrad in Croatia (Metzner-Nebelsick 1994) are the sole examples of Caucasian female artefact types in Eastern Europe. And from all North Caucasian female graves only one from the site Kislovodsk-Industrija included a typical Northernpontic, i.e. Černogorovka type, earring (Kozenkova 1998, pl. IX, 21).

The Eastern European-Caucasus communication network apparently did not include women, not even the women of the higher social level. Perhaps the female aspect of this network is hidden behind similarities in ceramic decoration linking some of the North Caucasian and Northernpontic groups. But obviously Caucasian women were not married – and buried! – outside their homeland, and no 'alien' women according to burial costumes are found in the Northern Caucasus.

The communication network of the Kislovodsk women on the contrary, looks like an apparent contrast to their male contemporaries. Neither qualitative analysis, nor the distribution pattern of female artefact types, lead into the steppe but, on the contrary, into the opposite direction; it links the Kislovodsk area with the Central Caucasus and Western Transcaucasia.

The most abundant objects in Kislovodsk female graves are beads and small pendants. Two thirds of the beads are made from yellow, white or light blue glass paste, and were very likely produced locally. But the last third of the beads includes carnelian beads of different types common in the high mountain areas and in Transcaucasia. Moreover, carnelian deposits are localised only in the central Caucasian range. Especially the riffled beads from several sites in Kislovodsk which always appear singular within the colliers have clear links to the site Tli in the high mountains. Equally other precious stones among the beads of the Kislovodsk women, e.g., garnet beads in Mebel'naja fabrica, grave 5b or an agate bead from the site Belorečnskij have parallels only in Tli or the Transcaucasian site Mccheta-Samtavro (Lemmlejn 1950). This site has also the only parallels to deer teeth ('Hirschgrandeln'), of which some have been found in a female grave in the Kislovodsk city centre (Zamjatin 1933: 222). Further, about 1500 antimony beads and pendants are found in the Kislovodsk female graves. They make up an amount of at least 3kg of this material that also must have come from the high mountains. Antimony deposits and ancient mines are well known in the central range of the Caucasus, especially in Rača and Svanetia (Čartolani 2001; Maisuradze & Gobedišvili 2001) but not in the Kislovodsk area. It is obvious that an extensive exchange or trade in raw material and/or jewels existed throughout the whole Central and Western part of Caucasia and the Kislovodsk females took part in it.

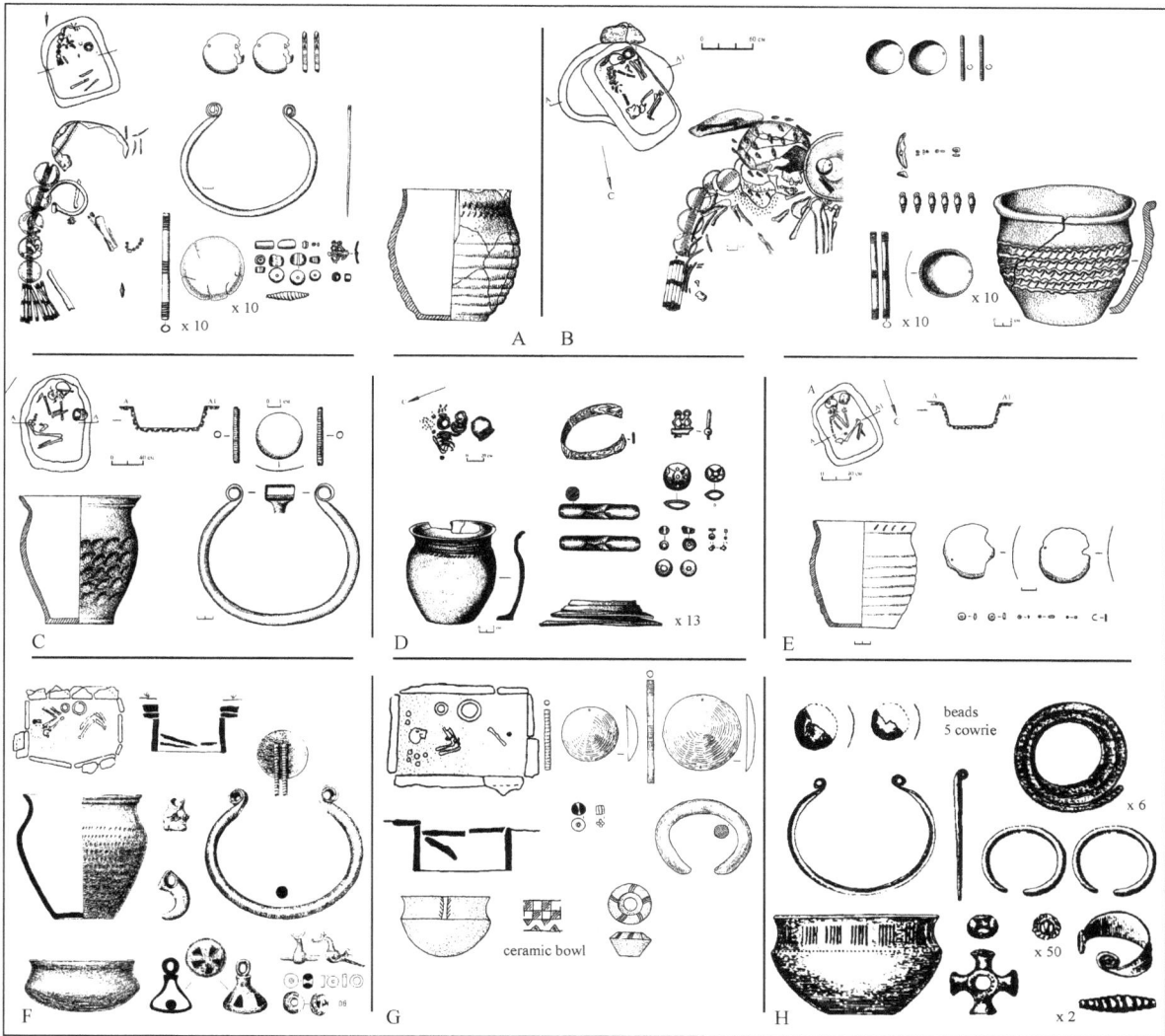

Figure 3.7. Female graves with costumes from Kislovodsk.
A=Belorečenskij, grave 26; B=Belorečenskij, grave 18; C=Belorečenskij, grave 31; D=Belorečenskij,
grave 15; E=Belorečenskij, grave 22; F=Industrija 1, grave 15; G=. Industrija 1, grave 9;
G=Mebl'naja fabrica, grave 25 (A,B,C,D,E after Dudarev 2004, fig. 20-21; fig. 13-1; fig. 25, 1-6; fig.
17, 1-10; F,G after Afanasev/Kozenkova 1981, fig. 2; fig. 5; H after Kozenkova 1989, pl. XLII A)

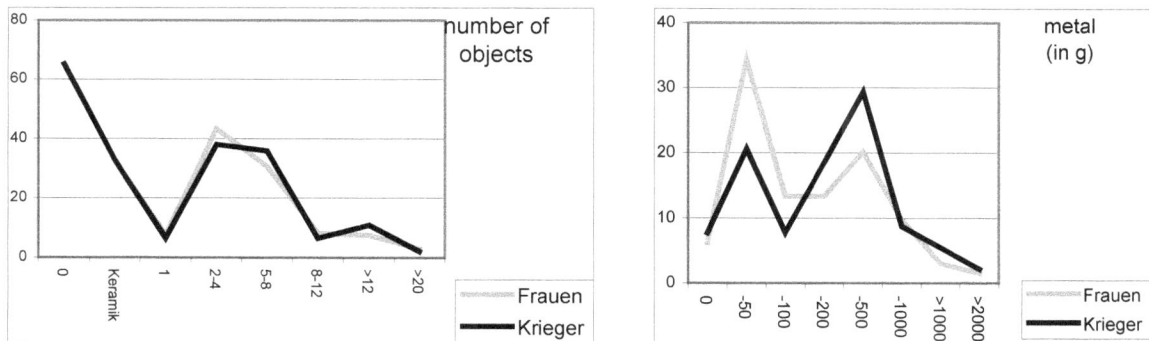

Figure 3.8A. Metal weight of male and female grave goods.
Figure 3.8B. Number of items in male and female graves.

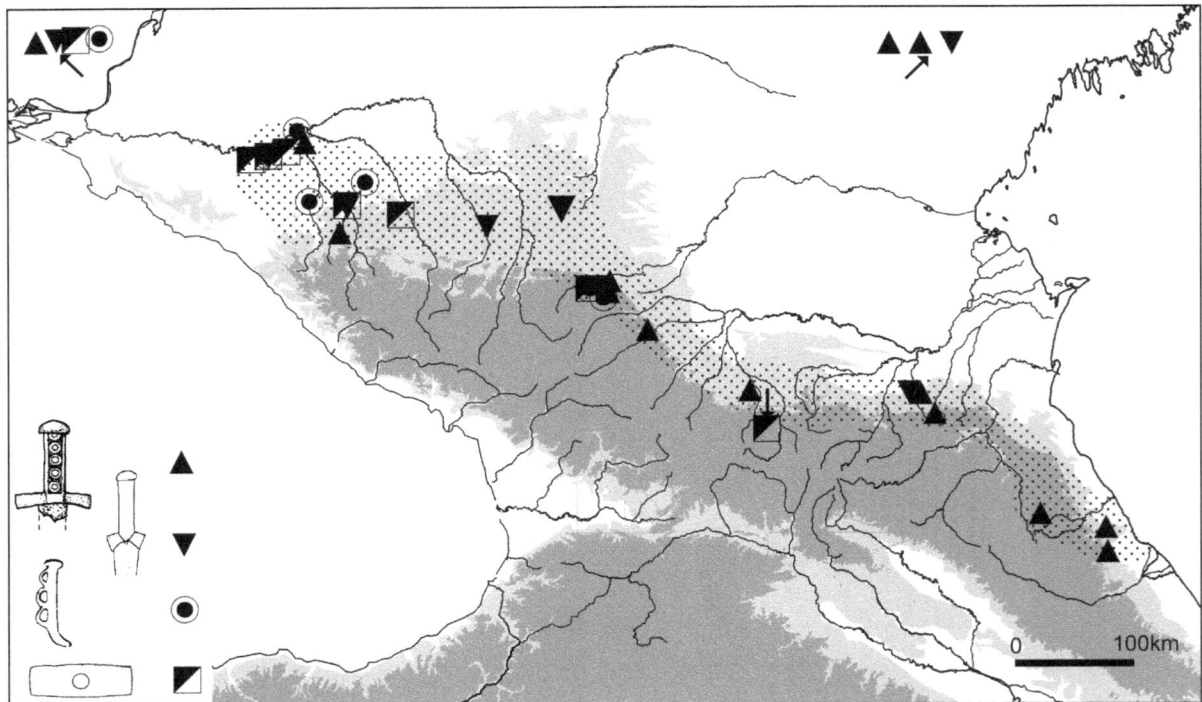

Figure 3.9. Typical elements of the North Caucasian armour and the distribution across the Eurasian steppe.Dagger A=KoB (10/9th century BC); horse gear=KoC1 (9/8th century BC); dagger B (Type "Golovjatino" and relations)=KoC2 (end of 8th century BC), battle hammer=KoC

It is, however, not only the interchange of beads which illuminates the exchange system of the female sphere linking the Kislovodsk women with those of the high mountains. Unlike the male armament which is rather local, some of the ornament types used in Kislovodsk, are distributed across the entire Western and Central Caucasus. Massive bracelets (*Figure 3.3B, 12*), bracelets with spiral ends (Fig. 3B, 13), neckrings ('Ösenhalsringe') (*Figure 3.3B*, 1), pins with rolled head ('Rollenkopfnadeln', *Figure 3.3B*, 16) and the typical elements of head gear, buckles and tubes (*Figure 3.3B*, 2-3), have a distribution ranging from the Kuban region and Abkhazia in the West across the Kislovodsk basin and the Kabardinian piedmonts up to the high mountains at both sides of the central Caucasian range (*Figure 3.10*). Their frequency in the different regional groups of this vast area is similar, thus it is not possible to determine a single production centre. Within the regional groups these ornaments were part of different costumes (Reinhold 2002: fig. 221; Reinhold 2003: fig. 7), and combined with local types – in Kislovodsk e.g. spiral bracelets and some of the pins. This links the women of several regional groups either to one commonly used centre of production, i.e. imply an intensive trade of ornaments, or to a general and trans-regional style which was shared by all this local communities.

Central Caucasian imports are as well frequently part of the more elaborated costumes in Kislovodsk. In grave 15 from Industrija (Afanas'ev & Kozenkova 1981: fig. 165-167, fig. 5) a wealthy woman was buried with a costume including a neck ring, a carnelian bead collier and a typical Kislovodsk head gear. On the necklace she wore several pendants of obviously Central Caucasian origin: a birdlike pendant, a symbolised tooth, an animal head and a rattle pendant (Fig. 7, D 29-32). Analogies for these pendants are found only in the high mountain sites of Koban and Tli (Chantre 1886: pl XVII, 1-2; XVIII, 1; Kozenkova 1998, pl. XVI, 2).

While the imports are generally part of the upper level costumes, the presence of at least one or two ubiquitous types, is the rule also in the midlevel female costumes. And even the poorest and least elaborate dresses had at least a few carnelian beads. This suggests that the female exchange system included a bigger part of the community's women and was not regulated by the hierarchical, internal structure of the Kislovodsk communities.

The distribution pattern of the female artefact types in fact resembles, to some degree, an area of a second male network in the Central and Western Caucasus mountains, marked by the occurrence of Central Caucasian battle-axes (*Figure 3.*11), specific types of daggers, and a common tradition of figural ornamentation on arms and other artefacts (Skakov 1997). The warfare techniques of these high mountain warriors did not include fighting on horseback. This is indicated by the absence of horse gear and of the importance of arms for hand-to-hand combat. Their network had very little contact with the former male network of the piedmonts and steppe.

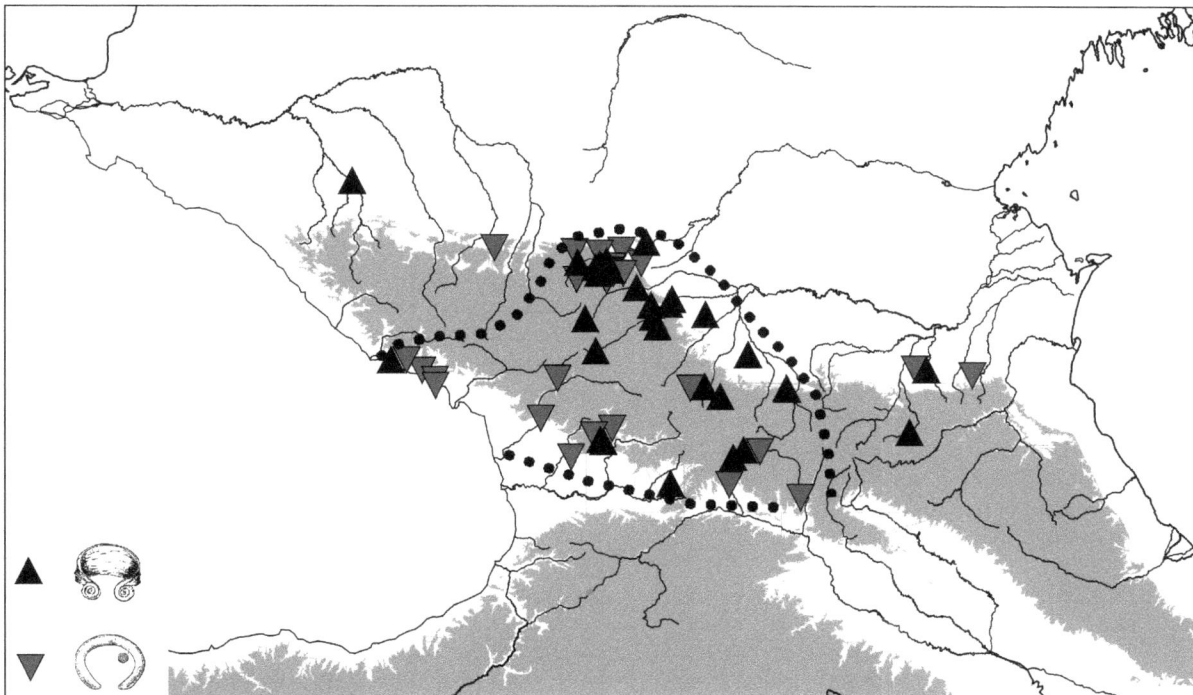

Figure 3.10. Common types of female costumes in the western part of Caucasia

Only a limited number of artefacts were exported from the mountains to the piedmonts. In Kislovodsk only one battle-axe from Klin Yar (Härke & Belinskij 2000: 196f) and a dagger blade from Berezovka, grave 29 (Dudarev 1999: fig. 147, 13-20), can be dated in the earlier stage of the pre-Scythian period (10th/9th century BC). The number increases towards the end of the 8th century BC when in four of the richest graves, Industria, grave 4 (*Figure 3*.5, G 17-18), Tereze, grave 3, Sultan gora 1, grave 1 and the burial mound of Učkeken central Caucasian battle-axes and bronze vessels appear. Conversely, the situation is similar. Only in the Northcaucasian site of Koban a number of piedmont horse gear is present (Chantre 1886: pl. XXX-XXXbis; Val'čak 1997b). In the roughly 450 graves of the site Tli at the southern slope of the central range, not a single typical piedmont male object was found during the whole pre-Scythian period.

Communication networks and gender

The analysis of the grave finds from Kislovodsk has in this sense exposed the occurrence of a very divergent distribution pattern of gender-related artefact types. The male warriors of these communities have been part of a broad cultural network that included warrior elites across the Eurasian steppe. Their female counterparts on the contrary, were linked to the opposite geographical area, and besides, another male network operated within the high mountains and Western Transcaucasia. The artefact distribution and the quantity of imported or exported objects within each network are so regular, that co-

ordinate communication structures and a regular exchange of goods, ideas and persons must be presumed.

In order to understand the relationship between these communication networks it is important to recapitulate once more their gender specific foundation. Piedmont, here Kislovodsk, and high mountain men used the quantity, diversity and quality of weapons to classify their members. Warfare and hunting were recognised as the preferred male activities. This is depicted on the decorated belts (*Figure.3.6*) and axes, and this warrior identity is what men wanted to be preserved in the life hereafter. The warrior concept itself can be compared with similar phenomena all over prehistoric Europe (Treherne 1995; cf. Reményi this volume). Therefore it is possible to complete it with cultural mechanisms related to warrior networks in general: social and judicial ranking according to an age related(?) right to carry weapons (Härke 1992), the control of prestige goods as a basis of social power (Müller & Bernbeck 1996; Eggert 1991; Burmeister 2000), the importance of heroic ancestors, membership in brotherhoods or warrior societies (Völger & von Welck 1990) and participation in forays into the lands of enemies. Unlike in the European Iron Age, however, the segmented tradition in Caucasia did not allow the elite to monopolise this concept and transform itself into a princely caste (Dudarev, Belinskij & Härke 2001; Reinhold 2003: 22-27). But the presence of closely related areas, prestige goods exchange, and common warrior identities are obvious. The frontier between the piedmont and the mountain male network which is represented in the distribution of the archaeological material, may represent a border between two such 'politically' corporate areas with less – or at least not very peaceful – intercourse.

Female networks in contrast, are much more difficult to decipher, which is basically due to a lack of useful concepts. Far less ethnographic studies deal with female networks, and analogies are not easily found. Female identities usually are not linked with warfare, and emphasise more a local origin or kinship (Baker 1997; Lindisfarne-Tapper 1997). Age and matrimony are significant criteria of female ranking and marriage is also a mean of female mobility, especially in patrilocal societies (Völger 1985). Female agency and moral authority result from social knowledge and their importance lies in the preservation of traditions and the cultural identities of their communities (Watkins 1996, 14-15; Shami 2000). But none of these aspects leads directly to an answer of the question of why women can have their own exchange networks.

However, in societies with gender equivalence, where balanced gender relations do not restrict women's mobility and ownership, large scale trade networks include women as well as men (Watkins 1996). Pasture mobility or religious pilgrimage is another aspect of female mobility in mountain landscapes and known from the Caucasus. The organisation of marriage by women and the marrying out of females into neighbouring groups, which is documented e.g. in Caucasus for the strictly exogamic Ingush (Anc'abaje

2001), is perhaps the most likely analogy for the described links among the Early Iron Age females. But why do the communication networks of men and women differ so considerably?

Turning back to the archaeological case study, it is quite difficult to bring these concepts together. Societies with a strong military component including competition in prestige and social power are usually associated with male dominance and patriarchal structures. Thus the notion of Dudarev, Belinskij & Härke of a 'military democracy' is at first sight a convincing concept for the Kislovodsk community. However, the female perspective contradicts a strong male dominance. An inequality between men and women as categories cannot be distinguished neither in the structure of the corporate identities nor in wealth, or access to prestige and imported goods (*Figure 3.8*). If we do not presume the Kislovodsk women as a sheer passive reflection of their husbands' status, we have to acknowledge their ability to operate in their own ways. A positive argument for this is the almost absent exchange of arms between the two male networks, while artefacts of the female sphere pass to and fro. If women's possession were only a reflection of male communication structures, one would expect a much more equal exchange of male goods, especially when these goods – such as North Caucasian armour - are well known to have been exported to other areas as prestige goods to affirm social relationship.

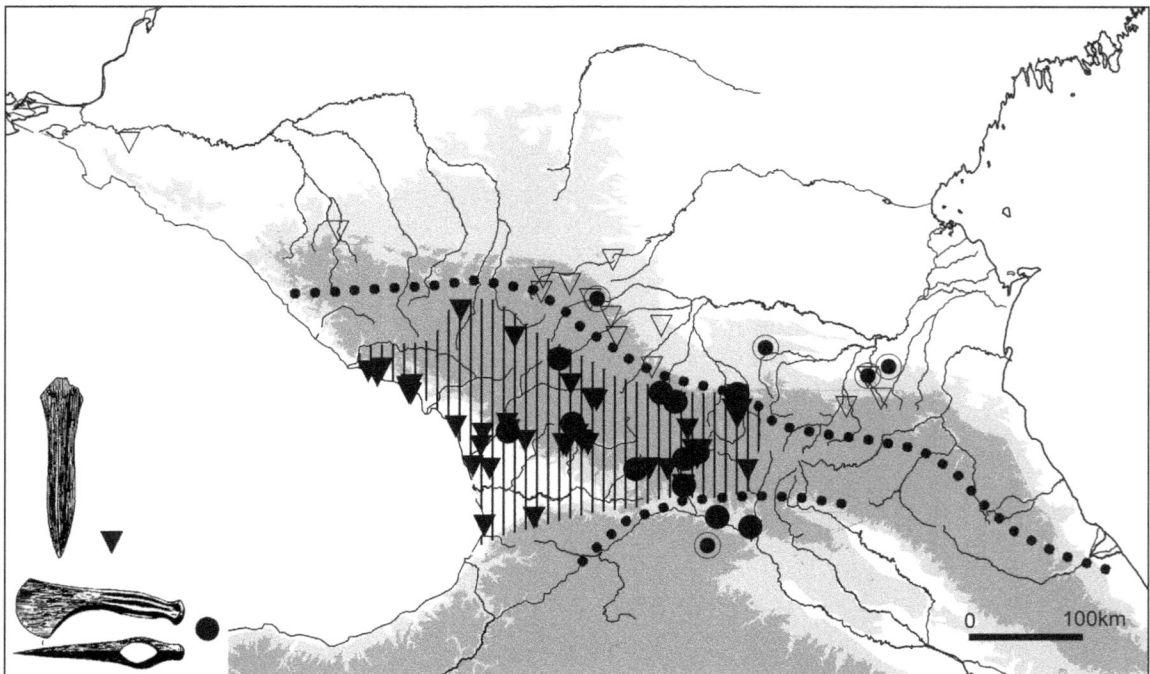

Figure 3.11 Typical elements of the Central Caucasian armour and its distribution. Dagger A=KoB, Koban Axe Type I=KoC, open signs imports from the core area of distribution

There are several possible scenarios in which the described archaeological configurations could be placed. The distribution of female costume elements across a wide territory might be explained by a marriage system delocalising women and placing them within a new environment. Sooner or later this would cause an intermixture of artefact types from their origin and the new residences, or even the formation of a common style. It would back the network with a strong kinship component and explain the lines along which goods and raw material were exchanged. Why the piedmont males are not visible in such a system, however, remains unclear.

Another possible scenario is that of mobile bronze workers and tradesmen. Ulrike Wels-Weyrauch (1989) argues in this way to explain the similarities of ornaments, in of else totally different costumes from the South German Middle Bronze Age. The control over raw materials, bronze working and metal trade must have been a crucial basis especially for the high mountain communities in the Caucasus. Places like Koban or Tli are situated at the fringe of the present-day arable land. During the first half of the first millennium BC the agricultural situation must have been much more complicated, as climate conditions had been harsher than today (Kvavadze & Efremov 1996). These places, yet, control the access to the major mining areas in the central range in Rača and Digorja, and the community which buried their dead in these large cemeteries must have been greatly involved in bronze working (Reinhold 2002). They could have produced all the objects found in the lower parts of the mountains. But on the other hand, artefact trade or mobile bronze workers again do not explain the limitation of the contacts to the female sphere alone.

Pasture migration and linked artefact exchange is the next possible plot. Such seasonal migrations are well known from all over the Caucasus in the pre-modern era until today (Wixman 1980: 54ff; Stadelbauer 1984). In the ethnographically documented period it was often limited to males, but under different gender relations it could easily include women as well. The modern migration patterns in the Central and Western part of the Caucasus cover exactly the territory described for the female communication network. Again the question arises, why the men are not visible through the artefacts when women could exchange objects and carry them back to their homesteads.

Conclusion

Since none of these scenarios are satisfactorily, a comprehensive analysis of the possible background for the situation in Early Iron Age Kislovodsk must allow the possibility of engendered communication networks for which we cannot find a proper analogy today. While the female sphere controlled relations with the high mountain communities and consequently secured the supply of

metal, precious stones or other products from the mountains, and most likely regulated pasture rights as well; the male sphere in the piedmonts associated itself with the steppe communities. This possibly secured pasture rights in the steppe zone, prevented raids and allowed the exchange of local products for those of steppe environments, especially horses and livestock.

An engendered agenda of external relations, however, does not imply that men and women had totally different cultural orientations. Nor does it imply the absolute impossibility of both genders to take part in the network of the other. Rather, it highlights the presence of ideology in a society, in this case that of gender ideologies related to different geographical and cultural areas. For a community at the fringe between different ecological zones such as the Kislovodsk basin a system like this could secure stability into both major geographical directions. That the system was indeed not as impermeable as the artefact distribution, i.e. the ideologically determined one, can be seen in some structural resemblance among the females in the steppe and adjacent areas. Similarities in ceramic decoration already have been mentioned. But there are convergences in female costumes as well. Among the most precious objects in female graves in Kislovodsk and in the high mountains area, are amber beads and cowries. They are part of a general distribution pattern that resembles the Eurasian male network. The major military techniques of horse riding and chariot fighting highlighted by the Kislovodsk men, were in fact developed south of the mountains in an area stretching from Eastern Anatolia across Transcaucasia to Western Iran during the early second millennium BC. Likewise, the beginning of iron production in Transcaucasia and Western Iran starts slightly earlier in this area than in the Northern Caucasus (Chachutajšvili 1987; Piggott 1989). Technical inventions, military technologies and other cultural aspects therefore indeed passed along the female communication network into the North Caucasian-Eurasian male sphere even if the material culture does not directly reflect these contacts.

The different scenarios for such contacts lead to the consequence that during the Early Iron Age a social system existed in which gender relations were characterised by relations of equivalence rather than by inequality and dominance of males. Both genders had they own sphere, but both spheres together secured best the stability of the whole society. This conclusion contradicts the critique of the use of analogies in gender archaeological reasoning as highly contaminated by contemporary notions of gender inequalities (Conkey & Spector 1984; Conkey & Gero 1991; di Leonardo 1991). Analogies indeed allow us to compare different models of gender relations with the archaeological case-study. Rather than to abolish analogical reasoning, gender studies should extend the knowledge about female classification and communication networks in ethnography as well as in archaeology (Bernbeck 2001).

The Kislovodsk example illustrates the fact that female communication systems can operated differently from male networks, but likewise include similar basic concepts – the exchange of prestigious goods, raw materials and cultural values. Since such arguments are habitually used to describe the relations within and between archaeological cultures, the notion that male and female spheres could seriously differ is another important result of this case-study.

Summary

Gender related material culture is a well known occurrence both from archaeology and modern ethnography. This article expands the archaeological analysis of such gender related archaeological material to the level of cultural communication networks. The bases of this study are rich grave finds from the North Caucasian Early Iron Age which form an excellent case study for such a reconstruction. They show an internal differentiation along criteria as gender, social status and presumably age, as well as a transregional aspect which allows the reconstruction of cultural communication networks. Three cultural networks can be made out by artefact distribution together with similarities in costume, armour, fighting techniques and other criteria. Two of them involve the male sphere – armour and prestige goods exchange – one female aspects like costumes and costume elements. The female network, geographically link the two male circles, which otherwise stand rather against each other. The deeply gender divided communication networks of the Early Iron Age in the Northern Caucasus, nevertheless, reflect the complementary character of gender relationships in general and the possibility to detect such even in the fragmented archaeological record.

Zusammenfassung

Geschlechtsspezifische materielle Kultur ist ein oft beobachteter Sachverhalt sowohl in archäologischen wie in ethnographischen Studien. Mit diesem Aufsatz möchte ich versuchen, die üblichen Untersuchungen zu geschlechtsspezifischer Kultur auf die Ebene allgemeiner kultureller Kommunikationsnetzwerke auszudehnen. Als Basis dienen reich ausgestattete Gräber aus der frühern Eisenzeit im Nordkaukasus. Sie erlauben nicht nur eine interne Gliederung der Bestattungen entsprechend sozialen Kriterien wie Geschlecht, Status und wahrscheinlich Alter. Sie beinhalten darüber hinaus einen überregionalen Aspekt, der es erlaubt kulturelle Kommunikationsnetzwerke zu rekonstruieren. Drei solche Netzwerke lassen sich anhand Übereinstimmungen in Tracht, Bewaffnung, Kampftechniken und anderen Kriterien festmachen. Zwei Zirkel betreffen die männliche Sphäre gekennzeichnet durch Austausch von Waffen und ‚männlichen' Prestigegütern (z.B. Reit- oder Streitwagenpferde), ein Netzwerk fasst verschiedene Trachtgruppen aus der weiblichen Sphäre zusammen. Dieses Netzwerk verbindet die beiden, männlichen'

Netzwerke, die ansonsten wenig Gemeinsamkeiten aufweisen. Die geschlechtsspezifischen Kommunikationsnetzwerke der frühen Eisenzeit im Nordkaukasus spiegeln insofern ein sehr komplexes Geschlechterverhältnis wieder, zeigen aber gleichzeitig die Komplementarität beider Geschlechter.

References

Afanas'ev, G. E. & Kozenkova, V. I. 1981. O neizvestnych pogrebal'bych kompleksach predskifskogo perioda iz okresnostej Kislovodska. *Sovjetskaja Archaeologija (2)*, pp. 161-177.

Afanas'ev, G. E., Korobov, D. S. & Savenko, S. N. 2004. *Drevnosti Kislovodskoj kotloviny.* Moscow. Naučnij Mir. Anc'abaje, G. 2001. *The Vainachs (the Chechen and Ingush).* Tbilisi, Caucasian House.

Baker, P. L. 1997. Politics of Dress: the Dress Reform Laws of 1920-1930s Iran. In: Lindisfarne-Tapper, N. & Ingham, B. (eds). *Languages of Dress in the Middle East.* Richmond, Curzon Press, pp. 178-192.

Belinskij A. B., Dudarev S. L. & Härke, H. 2001 Ob opyte social'nogo ranžirovanija pogrebenij predskifskoj epochi mogil'nika Klin Jar III. *Donskaja Archeologija 2001 (3/4)*, pp. 47-59.

Belinskij, A. B. 1990. K voprosu o vremeni pojavlenija šlemov assirijskogo tipa na Severnom Kavkaze. *Sovjetskaja Archeologija 1990 (4)*, pp. 190-195.

Belinskij, A. B. & Dudarev, S. L. 2002. *On The Problem of Social and Property Differentiation among the Early Koban Culture: The Klin-Yar III Tomb Finds, Kislovodsk, Northern Caucasus.* http://www.bilkent.edu.tr/~arkeo/blacksea/session 7b.htm

Belinskij, A. B. & Härke, H. 2000. *The Iron Age to early medieval cemetery of Klin Yar (North Caucasus): excavations 1994-96* (Summary of fieldwork and ongoing post-excavation analysis). http://www.rdg.ac.uk/archaeology/Research/Russi a/klinyar.htm

Berezin, J. B. & Dudarev, S. L. 1999. Neue präskythische Funde aus der Umgebung von Pjatigorsk, Nordkaukasien. *Eurasia Antiqua 5*, pp. 177-209.

Bernbeck, R. 2001. Towards a Gendered Past – The heuristic value of analogies. In: Gramsch, A. (ed.), *Vergleichen als archäologische Methode. Analogien in den Archäologien.* Oxford, BAR, pp. 143-150.

Burmeister, S. 2000. *Geschlecht, Alter und Herrschaft in der Späthallstattzeit Württembergs.* Münster, New York, München, Berlin Waxmann.

Burström, M. 1996. Reconstructing the Spatial Extension of Ancient societies. A Scandinavian Viking Age Example. *Archaeolgia Polona 34*, pp. 165-182.

Čartolani, S. 2001. Alter Bergbau in Svanetien. *In: Georgien. Schätze aus dem Land des Goldenen Vlies.* Bochum, Deutsches Bergbaumuseum, pp. 120-129.

Chachutajšvili, D. 1987. *Proizvodstvo železa v drevnej Kolchide*. Tbilisi, Mecniereba.

Chantre, E. 1886. *Recherches anthropologiques dans le Caucase 2. Periode protohistorique*. Paris, Reinwald.

Chenciner, R. 1997. Felt Capes and Masks of the Caucasus. In: Lindisfarne-Tapper, N. & Ingham, B. (eds), *Languages of Dress in the Middle East*. Richmond, Curzon Press, pp. 80-92.

Chidaseli, M. 1986. Die Gürtelbleche der älteren Eisenzeit in Georgien. *Beiträge Allgemeine und Vergleichende Archäologie 8*, pp. 7-72.

Chochorovskij, J. 1993. *Ekspania kimeryjska na tereny Europy Srodkowej. Cracow*, Universitet Jagiello'nski.

Conkey, M. W. & Gero, J. M. 1991. *Engendering Archaeology. Women and Prehistory*. Cambridge, Blackwell.

Conkey, M. W. and Spector, J. 1984. Archaeology and the Study of Gender. In: Schiffer, M. B. (ed)., *Advances in Archaeological Method and Theory 7*, pp. 1-38.

Di Leonardo, M. 1991. Introduction. Gender, Culture and Political Economy: Feminist Anthropology in Historical Perspective. In: Di Leonardo, M. (ed.). *Gender at the Crossroad of Knowledge: Feminist Anthropology in the Postmodern Era*. Berkley, University of California Press, pp. 1-48.

Dudarev, S. L. 1999. *Vzaimootnošenija plemen Severnogo Kavkaza s kočevnikami Jugo-Vostočnoj Evropy v predskifskuju epochy (IX – pervaja polovina VII v. do h.e.)*. Armavir, Mešdunarodnaja Akademija Informacii.

Dudarev, S. L. 2004. Belorečenskij 2 mogil'nil – Pamjatnik epochi rannego železa Kavkazskich Mineral'nych Vod. Armavir, Centre ASPU.

Eggert, M. K. H. 1991. Prestigegüter und Sozialstruktur in der Späthallstattzeit: Eine kulturanthropologische Perspektive. *Saeculum 42 (1)*, pp. 1-28.

Esayan, S. A. 1984. Gürtelbleche der älteren Eisenzeit in Armenien. *Beiträge Allgemeine und Vergleichende Archäologie 6*, pp. 97-198.

Freudenberg, M. 1989. *Studien zur vertikalen sozialen Struktur: eine Analyse der Grabfunde der jüngeren Bronzezeit in Dänemark*. Oxford, BAR.

Härke, H. 1992. *Angelsächsische Waffengräber des 5. bis 7. Jahrhunderts*. Köln, Reinlandverlag.

Härke, H. & Belinskij, A.B. 2000. Nouvelles Fouilles de 1994-1996 dans la necrople de Klin-Yar. In: Kazanski, M. & Soupault, V. (eds.). *Colloquia Pontica. Les sites archeologiques en Crimea et au Caucasus durant l'Antiquite tardiv et le Haut Moyen-Age*. Leiden, Boston, Köln, Brill, pp. 194-210.*ICIMOD Newsletter No. 29*. Gender and Mountain Development http://www.icimod.org/publications/newsletter/News29/news29.htm

Ivančik, A. I. 1997. Das Problem der ethnischen Zugehörigkeit der Kimmerier und die kimmerische archäologische Kultur. *Prähistorische Zeitschrift 72*, 12-53.

Jørgensen, J. 1990. *Bækkegård and Glasergård. Two cemeteries from the Late Iron Age on Bornholm*. København, Akademisk Forlag.

Knopf, Th. 2002. *Kontinuität und Diskontinuität in der Archäologie: quellenkritisch vergleichende Studien*. Münster, New York, München, Berlin, Waxmann.

Korobov, D.S. 2000. *Geografo-informacionnaja sistema "Archeologičeskie pamjatniki Kislovodskoj kotloviny"*. http://www.archaeology.ru/ONLINE/Korobov/index.html

Kossack, G. 1974. Prunkgräber. Bemerkungen zu Eigenschaften und Aussagewert. In: Kossack, G. & Ulbert, G. (eds.), *Studien zur Vor- und Frühgeschichtlichen Archäologie*. München, Beck, pp. 3-33.

Kossack, G. 1983. Tli Grab 85. Bemerkungen zum Beginn des skythenzeitlichen Formenkreises im Kaukasus. *Beiträge Allgemeine und Vergleichende Archäologie 5*, pp. 89-177.

Kossack, G. 1994. *Neufunde aus dem Novočerkassker Formenkreis und ihre Bedeutung für die Geschichte steppenbezogener Reitervölker der späten Bronzezeit. Il Mare Nero 1*, pp. 19-54.

Kozenkova, V.I. 1989. Kobanskaja kul'tura. Zapadnij variant. Archeologija SSSR. SVOD Archeologičeskich istočnikov, V2-5. Moscow, Nauka.

Kozenkova, V.I. 1990. Chronologija kobanskoj kul'tury: dostiženija, opyt utochenija, nerešennye problemy. *Sovetskaja Archeologija 1990 (4)*, pp. 64-92.

Kozenkova, V.I. 1992. *Seržen Jurt. Ein Friedhof der späten Bronze- und frühen Eisenzeit im Nordostkaukasus*. Mainz, Philipp von Zabern.

Kozenkova, V.I. 1996. *Kul'turno-istoričeskie processy na Severnom Kavkaze v èpochu pozdnej bronzy i v rannem železnom veke (Uzlovye problemy proischoždenija i razvitnaja kobanskoj kul'tury)*. Moscow, Nauka.

Kvavadze, E. & Efremov, Ju. B.1996. Palynological Studies of Lake and Lake-Swamp Sediments of the Holocene in the High Mountains of Arkhyz (Western Caucasus). *Acta Paleobotanika 36 (1)*, pp. 107-119.

Lemmlejn, G. G. 1950. Opyt klassifikacii form kamennych bus. *Kratkie soobščenija Instituta istorii material'noj Kul'tury 32*.

Leskov, A. M. and Érlich, V. B. 1999. *Mogil'nik Fars/Klady. Pamjatnik perechoda ot èpochi pozdnej bronzy k rannemu železnomu veku na Severo-Zapadnom Kavkaze*. Moscow, Naučnoe Izdatelstvo.

Lindisfarne-Tapper, N. 1997. The dress of Shasevan Tribespeople of Iranian Azerbaijan In: Lindisfarne-Tapper, N. and Ingham, B. (eds), *Languages of Dress in the Middle East*. Richmond, Curzon Press, pp. 67-79

MacCormac, C. P. and Strathern, M. 1987 *Nature, Culture and Gender*. Cambridge, Cambridge University Press.

Maisuradze, B. and Gobedišvili, G. 2001 *Alter Bergbau in Ratscha. In: Georgien. Schätze aus dem Land des Goldenen Vlies*. Bochum 2001, Deutsches Bergbaumuseum, pp. 130-135.

Markovin 1986. Kul'tovaja plastika Kavkaza. In: Markovin, V. I. (ed.), *Novoe v archeologii Severnogo Kavkaza*. Moscow, Nauka, 74-124.

Metzner-Nebelsick, C. 1994. Die früheiesenzeitliche Trensenentwicklung zwischen Kaukasus und Mitteleuropa. In: Schauer, P. (ed.), *Archäologische Untersuchungen zum Übergang von der Bronze- zur Eisenzeit zwischen Nordsee und Kaukasus [Kolloquium Regensburg 1992]*. Regensburger Beiträge zur Prähistorischen Archäologie 1. Regensburg, Universitätsverlag, pp. 383-447.

Schauer, P. 1998. Abschied von den „Thrako-Kimmeriern"? – Neue Aspekte der Interaktion zwischen karpatenländischen Kulturgruppen der späten Bronze- und frühen Eisenzeit mit der osteuropäischen Steppenkoine. In: Hänsel, B. & Machnik, J. (eds.), *Das Karpatenbecken und die osteuropäische Steppe. Nomadenbewegungen und Kulturwandel in den vorchristlichen Metallzeiten (4000-500 v.Chr.)*. Rahden, Leidorf, pp. 361-422.

Schauer, P. 2000. Kimmerier. *Reallexikon der Germanischen Altertumskunde 16*. Berlin, New York, Walter de Gruyter, pp. 504-523.

Müller, J. and Bernbeck, R. 1996. *Prestige - Prestigegüter - Sozialstrukturen. Beispiele aus dem europäischen und vorderasiatischen Neolithikum*. Archäologische Berichte 6, Bonn, Habelt.

Piggott, S. 1989. The Emergence of Iron Use at Hasanlu, In: Dyson, R. &. Voigt, M. M. (eds.), *East of Assyria: The Highland Settlement of Hasanlu. Expedition 31 (2-3)*, pp. 67-79.

Plaetschke, B. 1929. *Die Tschetschenen*. Hamburg, Friederischsen, de Gruyter & Co.

Reinhold, S. 2002. *Untersuchungen zur späten Bronze und frühen Eisenzeit im Kaukasus. Materielle Kultur, Chronologie, Fernkontakte*. Unpublished PhD thesis, Berlin.

Reinhold, S. 2003. Traditions in transition: some thoughts on late Bronze Age and early Iron Age burial costumes from the northern Caucasus. *European Journal of Archaeology 6 (1)*, pp. 4-36

Reinhold, S. 2005. *Warriors of the Caucasian Late Bronze and Early Iron Ages*. Moscow.

Šarafutdinova, È. S. 1993. O social'noj granicii v protomerotskom pogrebal'nom obrjade *Kratkie Soobšenija Institut Archeologii (Moscow) 203*, pp. 54-62.

Shami, S. 1999. Engendering Social Memory: Domestic Rituals, Resistance and Identity in the North Caucasus. In: Acar, F. & Günes-Ayata, A. A. (eds.), *Gender and Identity Construction. Women*

of Central Asia, the Caucasus and Turkey. Leiden, Boston, Köln, Brill, pp. 306-331.

Skakov, A. Ju. 1997. K voprosu ob èvolucii dekora kobano-kolchisdkich bronzovych toporov. In: Demidenko, S. V. &. Žuravlëv, D. V (eds.), *Drevnosti Evrazii*. Moscow, Naučnoe Izdatelstvo, pp. 70-87.

Sofaer Derevenski, J. 1997. Linking age and gender as social variables. *Ethnologisch-Archäologische Zeitschrift 38*, pp. 485-493.

Sørensen, M. L. S. 1992. Gender Archaeology and Scandinavian Bronze Age Studies. *Norwegian Archaeological Review 25* (1), pp. 31-49.

Sørensen, M. L. S. 1997. Reading dress: the construction of social categories and identities in Bronze Age Europe. *Journal of European Archaeology 5* (1), pp. 93-114.

Sørensen, M. L. S. 2000. *Gender Archaeology*. Malden Mass., Polity Press.

Stadelbauer, J. 1984. Bergnomaden und Yaylabauern in Kaukasien. Zur demographischen Entwicklung und zum sozioökonomischen Wandel bei ethnischen Gruppen mit nicht-stationärer Tierhaltung. *Paideuma 30*, pp. 201-225.

Terenožkin, A. I. 1976 *Kimmerici*. Kiew, Naukova Dumka.

Treherne, P. 1995. The warrior's beauty: the masculine body and self identity in Bronze Age Europe. *Journal of European Archaeology 3* (1), pp. 105-144.

Val'čak, S. B. 1997a. Predmeti èpochi pozdnej bronzy-rannego železa iz kollecij vostočnoj Ukrainy i ich analogii. *Istoričeskij-Archeologičeskij Almanach 3*, pp. 19-21.

Val'čak, S. B. 1997b. Predskifskaja uzda Vostočnoj Èvropy: uzdečnye komplekcy s trechpetel'čatymi psalijami (klassifikacija i chronologija). In: Demidenko, S.V.and Žuravlëv, D.V. (eds.), *Drevnosti Evrazii*. Moscow, Naučnoe Izdatelstvo, pp. 88-119.

Völger, G. 1985. *Die Braut: geliebt, verkauft, getauscht, geraubt; zur Rolle der Frau im Kulturvergleich*. Ausstellung Josef-Haubrich-Kunsthalle Köln, 26. Juli bis 13. Oktober 1985. Köln, Rautenstrauch-Joest-Museums für Völkerkunde.

Völger, G. & von Welck, K. 1990 (eds.). *Männerbünde - Männerbande: zur Rolle des Mannes im Kulturvergleich*. Ausstellung Josef-Haubrich-Kunsthalle Köln, 23. März bis 17. Juni 1990, Köln, Rautenstrauch-Joest-Museums für Völkerkunde.

Voronov, Ju. N. 1969 *Archeologičeskij karta Abchazii*. Suchumi, Istatelstvo Alasara.

Watkins, J. 1996 *Spirited Women: Gender, Religion and Cultural Identity in the Nepal Himalaya*. New York, Columbia University Press.

Wels-Weyrauch, U. 1989. Mittelbronzezeitliche Frauentrachten in Süddeutschland (Beziehungen zur Hagenauer Gruppierung). In : *Dynamique du Bronze Moyen en Europe Occidentale. Actes du 113e congrès national des sociétes savantes,*

Strasbourg 1988. Strasbourg, Comité des Travaux Historiques et Scientifique, pp. 117-134.

Wixman, R.1980 *Language Aspects of Ethnic Patterns and Processes in The Northern Caucasus.* Chicago, University of Chicago, Department of Geography.

Zamjatin, S. N. 1933, Raboty na stroitel'stae sanatorija KSU v Kislovodske. Archeologičeskie raboty Akademii na novostrojkach v 1931-1933 g. Izv. *GAIMK 109*, 1, 218-226.

The Significance of Children, animals, and teeth in life and death Kin- and gender negotiations at Styrmansberget, Gotland, Sweden, 100-550 AD

Marie Svedin

Gothenburg University

Abstract

In the henged hill of Styrmansberget several graves containing children, adults, animals and human teeth were placed in and outside the henge as well as inside the stone foundation of a house. The choice of burial place and the burial practice in the graves at Styrmansberget were unexpected for the period. The different burial practices among the children are not only determinated by their different age. The preferences of places and contexts in which they are buried have been important as well. Children of the same osteological age appear in different burial contexts at different places. In this article I state that it probably means that children in prehistory also were categorized on the basis of other ideas than on the idea of age categories and life courses. This notion should also have implications on the significances of children in the society. I further claim that even if a burial place seems to bee particular it could have been filled with symbolic meaning and played an important part in the discussion, construction and negotiations of gender relations, status, kin, generations, transformations, life and death in society.

Introduction

During the last decade research has paid attention to children and their upbringing as an important part of how gender relations are constructed, maintained and changed (Lillehammer 1986; 1989; 2000; 2002; Johansson & Welinder 1995; Welinder 1998; Sofaer Derevenski 1997:a; 1997b; 2000; Scott 1999; Meskell 2000). Sex, gender and material culture are intertwined aspects in the cultural construction of society. By the act of loading the artefacts, rites and places with gender symbolism, nuances such as sex, gender and status can be expressed (Sofaer Derevenski 1997b:876). In the transformation stages, from newborn to "adult", a socialization of the individuals takes place according to the norms of society. In this transformation the gender identity of the individual is created as well as it is an understanding of society. The socialization takes place through playing, expectations, self-apprehension, inhibitions, upbringing and changes of both social and biological kind, and becomes important for the person's whole life cycle (Sofaer Derevenski 1997a; Gilchrist 2000).

I find the concept of *life cycle* to be problematic, because in the concept is embedded the idea of reincarnation. The concept also favours an idea of prescribed stages in life and death for all members of society, repeated according to a decided pattern. By the use of this model, many persons are excluded. These are e.g. persons who do not get children or persons who do not live together as a couple at adult stages (Hauptman-Wahlgren 2002:129). Today many researchers use the concept of *life course* because it stresses the idea of the biological life as a contextual and cultural process that could be marked in different ways to different persons (Gilchrist 2000:326; Sofaer Derevenski 2000; Hauptman-Wahlgren

2002:129f). It is though important in discussions about different genders and children's position in prehistory to use the concept of life course. It is fundamental in order to understand how children and their development during their individual life course were apprehended during prehistory. The concept of life course takes into consideration the distinctions in a gender group that are related to age (cultural, social and biological) transformations, but it is not the only aspect to consider in discussions about differences in a gender group. Other dimensions as status, kin, group or ethnic belonging, are also important to consider.

Archaeologists often attend children in burial context by their different initiation rites to become adults (Joyce 2000), and seldom for their own importance as children in prehistoric society. In archaeological literature about children, children are often discussed as an isolated theme and the signification of children are rarely discussed in relation to adults and society. This could be a result of the fact that this is a relatively new topic area in archaeology, but maybe this separation between children and adults also is a product of our modern Western thoughts and life style. Many children in the Western world live today in specially created pedagogically reservations and they are in many ways excluded from the rest of society. We tend to separate children from the life of the adults. In prehistory the mode of apprehending children probably were totally different.

The social and cultural significances and definitions of childhood differ between societies and cultures (for discussion about the concept of "childhood", see for instance Ariès 1960). The concept of child is not only different in different societies. In a cultural context the concept of child probably was a heterogeneous category with differences based on age, gender, status, kind and individual character. It is possible to compare this discussion with the discussion of the concept of women that have been criticized because it favourites one type of women and do not recognize the huge amount of variations of age, status, ethnical group, education, kind etc. for the women in a society. It is important in the discussion about children to make distinctions between biological/ostelological, social and chronological age (Gilchirst 1999 chap. 5). Generally children are osteologically divided in the group foetus, Infants (0-1 year), Infants I (0-7 year), Infants II (5–14 year), Juveniles (10–24 year). In my material the ostelological data are not so specified, instead the designations given are foetus/newborn, young child and child. In the material from Gotland, Sweden in the Baltic Sea (*Figure 4.1*), it seems like children between 0-7 have been categorized in different ways in different burial contexts. The different burial practices among the children are not only determined by their different biological age. Children of the same age appear in different burial contexts at different places. I state that it probably means that children in prehistory also were categorized on the basis of other ideas than the idea of age categories and life courses. This notion should also have implications on the significances of children in society.

In this article I will discuss the relation between children, adults and gender constructions in society by focusing the significance of 13 child burials from different places in Gotland. The mode of burying the children varies, as 4 of the children are placed at 3 different common burial fields, and 2 children are laid in a grave in the middle of a settlement. Seven children are buried together with adults in 15 graves in a "hill fort" named *Styrmansberget,* and situated in Fröjel parish near the coast of Gotland (*Figure 4.2*).

The child-adult burials at Styrmansberget show various signs of complex ritual practices, with the possibility of secondary openings and manipulation of the graves in prehistoric time, as known from other burial context from the Roman Iron Age period and the Migration period from other areas in Sweden (Petré 1999:205). These practices partly separate them from the ordinary burial pattern of Gotland from the same period. The graves contain a huge amount of bones from eight different animal species and from 17 different species of birds. Most remarkably are the findings of several teeth and jaws, from adults, which could not be related to any of the skeletons in the graves.

Generally, the interpretations of burials which do not fit into the general grave pattern, have been interpreted as containing burials of individuals who were different in some way, and hence were not permitted to be buried at the communal burial ground (Strassburg 2000). This interpretation is particularly common concerning newborn and young children, who have been buried in other places than the communal burial ground (Scott 1999:107; Finlay 2000). This assumption might possibly not be transmitted to Styrmansberget, as both children and adult, of different sex and age, were buried together in the same grave.

Figure 4.1. Map of the Baltic Sea with the Island Gotland and the place Styrmansberget marked (Partly after CSA1998:205. The figure is part off, edited and redrawn by author).

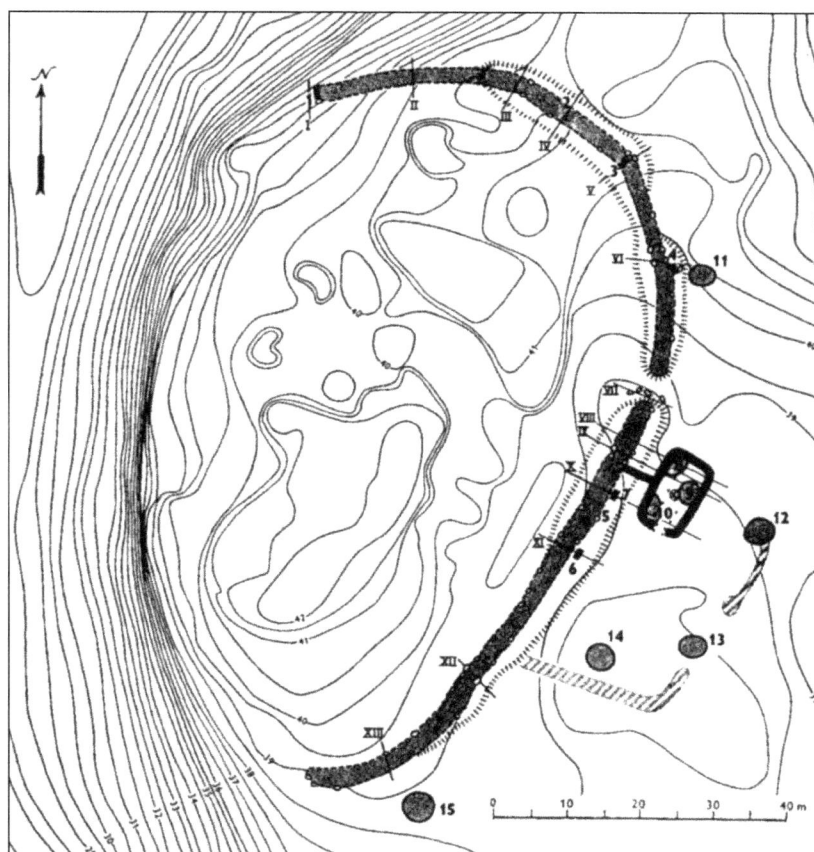

Figure 4.2. The henged mountain of Styrmansberget with the stone foundation of the house, graves, enclosures, terraces and finds marked out at the plan (Partly after Stenberger 1955:611. The figure is partly drawn and edited by the author).

I want to stress Styrmansberget as a place with human made constructions where different practices occurred, as a method to achieve a special place where it was possible to express and create different meanings about various important relations. By placing the child-adult graves at Styrmansberget an individual's position in the kin, relations between different genders, ages and relations between adult and children in life and death could be negotiated. Attention is given to the relationship between different animals, especially between birds, humans and children. Furthermore, the significance of teeth, life course and kin is drawn attention to. The graves from Styrmansberget are compared to 6 other child burials from Gotland. A discussion about the relation between a special and the general is important for the concluding discussion. In the discussion arguments from a microarcheological perspective are used. The paper is closed by a preliminary interpretation of some general aspects of gender relations in Gotland during the Roman Iron Age and the Migration period.

Styrmansberget - a significant and special place

Styrmansberget is what usually is called a "hill fort". Contemporary research has questioned the concept of

"hill forts", mainly due to the fact the connection to defence and war is far too strongly embedded in the concept (Olausson 1995:9ff; Cassel 1998:145ff; Wall 2002, 2003). In a study from Uppland parish, east central Sweden, Michael Olausson has demonstrated that hill forts were constructed during many different periods and for many different purposes (Olausson 1995). The concept *henged mountain* has been proposed as an alternative to hill fort (Wall 2002), because it takes more caution of the variations of the different categories of henged mountains (hill-forts, grave and ceremonial walls or enclosures) (Olausson 1995; Johansen & Pettersson 1993).

I therefore use the concept of henged mountain because, in my opinion, it is obvious that the henges at Styrmansberget have not primarily been built for fortificatiory purposes. Per Lundström, who led the excavation of the site, discusses the possibility of an interpretation as defence of the henges. In his opinion the henges were not constructed for the purpose of achieving a high defence. The height of the henges is only 0, 5 meter and there are no traces of stone constructions that could have made up a foot for a wooden palisade on top of the henges (Lundström, P. 1955:613).

Styrmansberget is thus, an unusual place for a burial ground in comparison to other known burial grounds from the Roman Iron Age and the Migration Period in Gotland. The concept of *"place"* has been discussed in contemporary archaeology, and the nature interpretations have been questioned (Tilley 1994, Bradley 1991, 2000). Instead, the social meanings of places, and the landscape, have been paid attention to. In prehistory special places with significant nature formations were selected, where it was possible to communicate with the spirits, it is suggested. These places were often situated in close connection to water (Helskog 1995:253). The henged mountains could be described as borderlands (Wall 2002:106) or liminal places. In these places it was possible for the living to get in contact with the dead, and the deceased could transform from one world to another or to be in-between two different worlds (Johansen 1997:145).

The henged mountains have been interpreted as places for meetings (Hegardt 1991b:62; Cassel 1998:146). I find this assumption to be a good point of departure: I would like to interpret Styrmansberget as a liminal place or border and a place for meetings, negotiations and communication between the living and the dead and possibly with animals. The burials in Gotland from the period in question show a great variation in size, chronological composition and structure. My suggestion is that the high degree of variation between the different burial grounds is related to the diversity of use among different groups of people in Gotland. These groups probably had different ritual- and burial practises used to enhance their own identity. I advocate that these burial ground "belonged" to different groups or kin, who used them for assembling and for performance of different rituals and ceremonies. In the same way I want to suggest that Styrmansberget was a place which belonged to a special group or a kin.

The house, the enclosure and the terrace constructions

The henged mountain Styrmansberget was excavated as a part of the large international Vallhagar project in 1946-50. Vallhagar consists of a settlement with 24 stone foundation houses from the Roman Iron Age and the Migration Period besides three burial grounds with graves from the Pre-Roman Iron Age (500-0 BC) to the Vendel Period (550–850 AD) (Stenberger & Klindt-Jensen 1955). As a part of this project Styrmansberget, situated 2,5 km west of the Vallhagar settlement, was partly excavated by Per Lundström (Lundström, P. 1955:610ff.). Styrmansberget has a construction of a semicircular stone wall, about 150 meters in length, ending at the western border of the cliff. Outside the henges, a hearth and three pits with fire cracked stone were found. Next to the henges there was a rectangular house foundation, stone made, with three burials inside the structure. Between the house foundation and the henges, there is a stone enclosure that can be followed westwards up from the house foundation to the henges,

and a "terrace" marked with stones.

The house foundation that was severely damaged probably occurred in connection with the construction of the graves, in the house foundation (Fig.3). One hearth was situated in the middle of the building. It consisted of a large and a smaller pit, both of them filled with fire cracked stone and charcoal. There were few objects in the building (50 potsherds, few animal bones, a few lumps of iron slag and a grinding stone) (Lundström, P. 1955:618, 620). About 70 house foundations are excavated or partly excavated (Carlsson, D. 1979:34) in Gotland, and around 40 of them have given dates from the younger Roman Iron Age to the Migration period (200–550 AD) (Cassel 1998:214ff). There is only one more henged mountain with building foundation in Gotland, namely *Herrgårdsklint*, Gammelgarn parish. However, the buildings at Herrgårdsklint are smaller, with thin walls of a thoroughly different construction. The constructions have been interpreted as folds or wind shelters for animals (Biörnstad 1955: 916ff).

Michel Olausson has suggested that Styrmansberget is a grave henge and a place for different fire rituals connected with death and burial (Olausson 1995:205). I agree with the author in his reading of the graves and the fire rituals, even though I differ from his opinion on the house as a "cult house" (Olausson 1995:205). Generally, cult houses are interpreted as houses without artefacts like the "Broby houses" from the Bronze Age (Victor 2002), or houses with artefacts which could be related to ritual or cultic activities (Scott 1999:86). The house foundation at Styrmansberget has all the characteristics in common with the other 2000 stone house foundation of the same type elsewhere on Gotland, generally situated near arable land (Carlsson, D. 1979:34f). However, this house is situated in an unusual and significant place.

The burials show many signs of complex ritual practices

In Gotland there are 32 hedged mountains, 32 circular hedges on low land, and 10 circular hedges in moors (Cassel 1998:132). It is generally assumed that hedged mountains are constructed in the early Roman Iron Age and the Migration Period, or in the Viking Age (800-1050 AD) to the Middle Age period (1050–1400 AD) (Engström 1984; Cassel 1998:141ff). In the investigation of Styrmansberget the hedges were trenched in thirteen places. In six of these sections, burials were found. In all, 15 graves were found in the surroundings of the hedges (Lundström, P. 1955:612). The graves have been dated to the Roman Iron Age Period IV: 2 – V: 1 (0-200 AD) by the excavator Per Lundström, but he stresses the fact that none of the objects in the graves allow an absolute date of the graves (Lundström, P. 1955:640). Lately there have been discussions about the date of the graves (Carlsson, A. 1983:24; Cassel 1998:93). Some of the equipment, like rectangular belt mountings are found both in the

Roman Iron Age and the Migration period. Circular Iron buckles also persist into the Migration period, and make it impossible to date the graves with any more accuracy than within the time span of the Roman Iron Age and the Migration period (Cassel 1998:93). At Styrmansberget there are no other leading artefacts, and there also is a chronological complexity of the burial artefacts which makes it impossible to determine the exact date of the graves without further excavations, C-14 analyses, investigations of the skeletons or detailed chronological studies of the artefacts. We cannot know if the graves were placed at Styrmansberget during a short period of time or if they were placed there throughout the whole period. For this article I will leave this problem unsolved and assume that the graves are dated within the span of the Roman Iron Age and the Migration Period.

The 15 graves at Styrmansberget demonstrate some unusual characteristics and constructions in comparison to graves from the rest of Gotland and mainland

Sweden. In Gotland, graves from the Roman Iron Age and the Migration Period generally consist of a circular stone construction above the surface, and often with an inner limestone cist in which the dead person was buried (Almgren, O. & Nerman, B. 1923; Nerman 1935). The burial grounds are generally placed in the low land. There are examples from different periods, and from other areas in Sweden of graves in hedged mountains (Olausson 1995:220ff). In Gotland some of the hedged mountains have graves inside the enclosure or in close connection to the enclosure (Andre Raä 6, Eke Raä 49, Fröjel Raä 8, Gamelgarn Raä 38, Hangvar Raä 2, Linde Raä 6, Lärbro Raä 17, Otem/Slite Raä 76). None of them have been excavated but by the grave forms they are supposed to date to the Vendel and Viking Ages. At Gudinge slott, Eke parish in Gotland, ten graves occur in the close surroundings of the hedge, three graves were excavated and dated to the late Viking Age (940-1050 AD), by their typical leading Viking age grave artefacts (Hegardt 1991a:46).

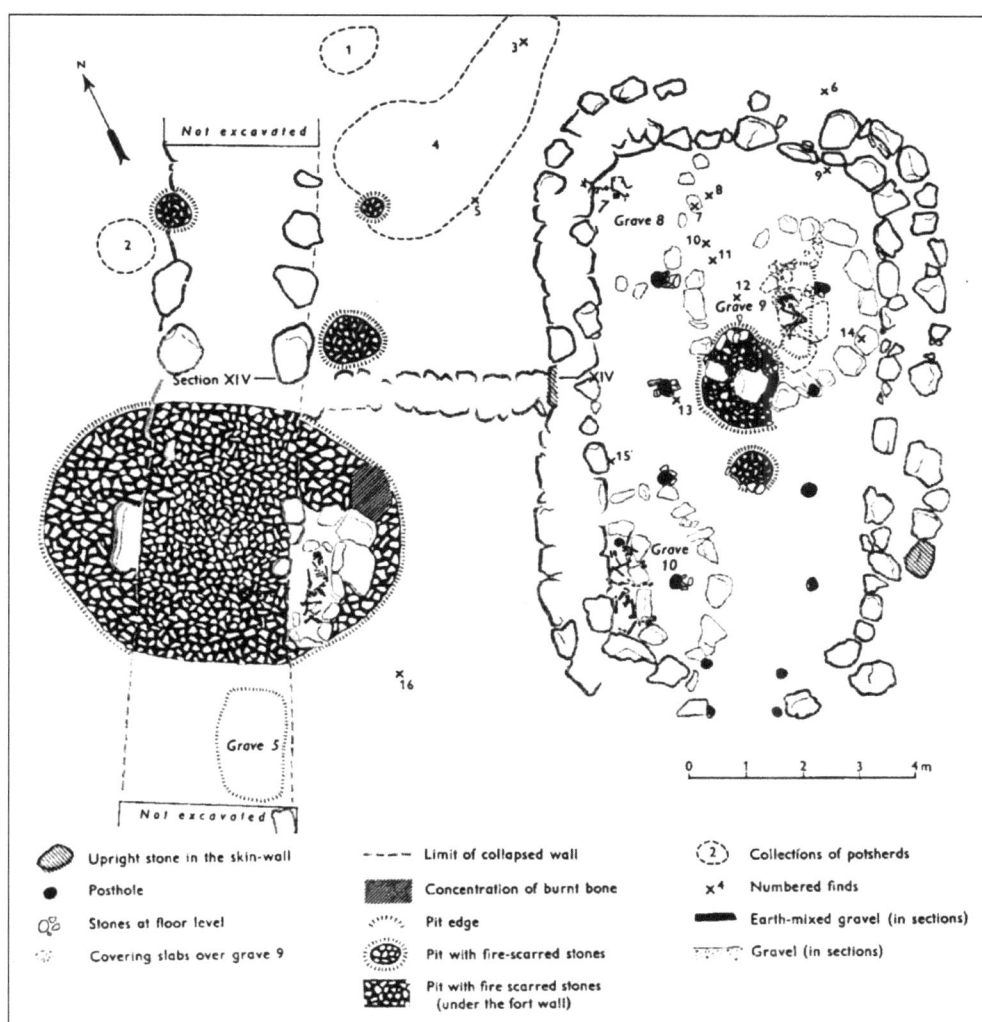

Figure 4.3. Graves and the stone foundation of the house linked with an enclosure to the henge and some of the graves at the Styrmansberget (Partly after Stenberger 1955:619. The figure is partly drawn and edited by the author).

51

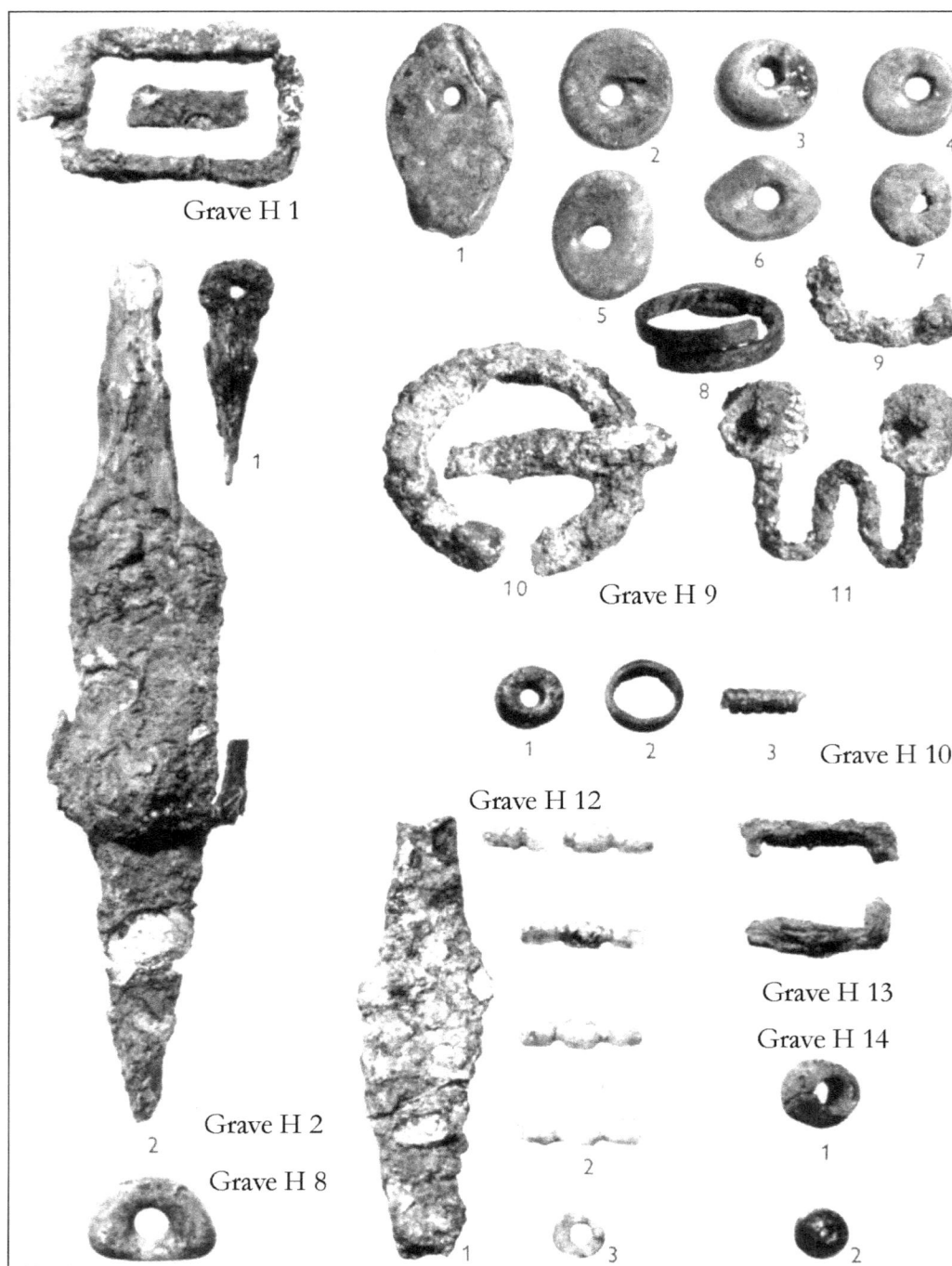

Figure 4.4. Artefacts from the graves at Styrmansberget (After Stenberger 1955:619. The figure is edited by the author).

It is possible to divide the 15 graves at Styrmansberget into two main groups, according to the constructions. The first group consists of seven graves without marking above the surface which were situated, either in the filling of the hedge, or in the rubble layer on the outside of the henge. The graves consist of pits that were covered with only a 10–20 cm soil layer (Lundström, P. 1955:634f). In three of the seven graves, without surface marking, uncremated children and adults were buried (H2, H3 and H5). The second group consists of eight graves with internal limestone cist constructions outside the henge. Some of the graves also had outer stone constructions above the ground surface (Lundström, P. 1955:634f). The house foundation grave (H10, H 8) held three uncremated children and adults. One grave (H11) contained one cremated child. The bones were put in the corner of an adult size cist (1.60). It is the only individual that is cremated among the deceased at Styrmansberget; all the other graves were inhumations. The other graves contained uncremated adults of different age and biological sex.

In comparison with other burials from the same period in Gotland, the artefacts in the burials from Styrmansberget are ordinary objects, neither remarkably "poor" nor "rich" (*Figure 4.4*). In most of the burials the human bones were in disorder. The graves contained remains of women, men and children. The adults were of different ages, spanning from individuals well under middle age to the age of very old. Twelve of the individuals were not able to age consider (Gejvall 1955:740f, 754ff.). The total amount of skeletons, or parts of skeletons at Styrmansberget, make up 7 children, and 22 adults, in sum 29 persons (Lundström, P. 1955:623ff; Gejvall 1955:740f, 754ff). However, in the graves there are also jaws and loose teeth from 43 persons in all (Lundström, A. 1955:781, 784). There are teeth and jaws from 14 adult persons which do not originate from the skeletons in the graves. The teeth and the jaws do not have damages, and therefore they probably were lost post mortem. Only one tooth has a peculiar defect. It has been smoothly polished along the lingual surface. This has probably been caused post mortem (Lundström, A. 1955:781).

Animal bones are relatively common in graves from the Iron Age in Sweden (Iregren 1997). Graves with animal bones from the same period from other areas in Sweden generally contain animal bones of one to three species (Petré 1999b:187, 204; Biuw 1992:255. Several (10) of the burials at Styrmansberget contain lager quantities of animal bones, and some of the graves have bones from 8 different species such as ox, cat, pig, lamb, goat, dog, seal and birds (Lundström, P. 1955:623f.f.). Significantly all child-adult burials at Styrmansberget, contain between 3 and 4 animal species. Another notable piece of information is that the burials contain bones from 17 different birds´ species. The birds could bee divided into three different groups; forest birds, birds found in areas of human habitation and aquatic birds (Lepiksaar 1955:830). In other Iron Age burial context birds occurs in 16,2 % of the graves (Spånga parish in the east middle of Sweden) and the most frequently found birds are gallinaceous bird or a falcon (Sigvallius 1994:78). All child-adult burials at Styrmansberget contained bones of birds and ox. It seems like there are some kind of relation between children-adult, birds and ox at this place.

Child burials in Sweden and in Gotland

The occurrence and percentage of child burials in Sweden vary during different prehistoric periods. For the Iron Age in general, variations are immense. In burial grounds generally supposed to have been used by one or a few farms, the amount of buried children varies between 1–62 % (Welinder 1998:188). Many of the "missing" children probably are buried in other places, other than the traditional burial graves, and archaeologists have not yet

located them (Welinder 1998:188f.). In Gotland, during the Roman Iron Age and the Migration Period, there are only 12 graves that all together contain 15 buried children. The total amounts of excavated and published graves from these periods are about 500–600 (Almgren & Nerman 1923:192; Nerman 1935; Rundkvist 2003). The preservation conditions in Gotland are favourable, due to the soil conditions; therefore the lack of childrens´ remains cannot be dependent on these circumstances. The low amount of child burials may possibly depend on the fact that the majority of the graves were found in the late 19th century and most of the graves were not examined by archaeologists. In modern excavations in Gotland, child burials have been found from other prehistoric periods (Lindquist 1981; Sjöberg 1976; Pettersson 1992; Rundkvist 2003).

The 13 child burials from the Roman Iron Age and the Migration Period in Gotland have been found at different locations. Five of the graves are sited at five different burial grounds, and one grave is located in the middle of a settlement. Four of the periods' children's graves, are single graves and situated at four different burial grounds (Kornettskogen, Västkinde parish, Raä 5913:43; Nygårds, Vallstena parish, Raä 6395:5; Norrbys, Follingbro parish, Raä 10950:38) and northern burial ground at Vallhagar, Fröjel parish, N 20). The mentioned child graves, are not similar to the child-adult graves at Styrmansberget. Most significant, only one of the child graves contains animal bones, but far from the large quantities of animal bones, or the different species or human teeth, found in the graves at Styrmansberget. Only the grave situated in the centre of the Vallhagar settlement, namely grave V1, Fröjel parish, has any similarities with the child-adult graves at Styrmansberget. The grave contains two newborn children, and one man rather old, besides a large amount of animal bones from 5 different species (Almgren, B. 1955:274ff; Gejvall 1955:737).

Interpretations of the burials at Styrmansberget

Stig Welinder (1998) has discussed the low amount of child burials in Gotland during the Roman Iron Age. His argument was based on a seminar paper presented by Anna Adsten (1997). Welinder compares the seven child burials occurring together with 25 adults at Styrmansberget, with the three cemeteries at the settlement of Vallhagar, situated only 2,5 km away from Styrmansberget. In the three grave fields close to the settlement there was only one child grave among the 140 adults (Welinder 1998:191, 196, 200). Welinder's interpretation of the different practises of the children's burials between Styrmansberget and the settlement Vallhagar, is based on the assumption that there was a cultural difference between the people living at Styrmansberget and at Vallhagar. The construction is founded on economical and ecological assumptions based on ideas from Odner (1972), where several groups of people are seen as specialised in various subsistence tasks within a redistributional organisation. According to

Welinder, the landscape around Styrmansberget is not first-rate arable land, but it is on the contrary, an area good for browsing. This quality is emphasised by the occurrence of bones of cattle, sheep, pigs and dogs in the graves, in contrast to the burial grounds at Vallhagar in which animal bones are rare. The author's suggestion is that the population at Styrmansberget had lived and been buried as cattle-herders. The reason why the children at Styrmansberget were buried is that among the cattle-herders, children were useful at an early age in tending the animals (Welinder 1998:192).

I agree with Welinder's idea that there may have been different culturally dependent diversities in child burial practices, in different groups. But I do not think his interpretation of the dualist burial practice between Vallhagar and Styrmansberget is valid, and according to my appreciation, I consider it important to question this dualist separation between herding and farming in the Roman Iron Age and the Migration Period. I assume Welinder apprehends Vallhagar as a farming settlement primarily based on an agricultural economy. Most likely, the farming economies at this time was a mix of agricultural, herding and different forms of gathering as well as to some extent hunting and fishing (Widgren 1982, 1998). Circumstances strengthening this assumption are that the animal bones from the Vallhagar settlement, as well as from other settlements in Gotland, are the same kind of animal bones as those found in the burials in Styrmansberget (Carlsson, A. 1979). These circumstances might imply that the economies in the two different places were not so dissimilar to each other.

Welinder further argues that the cultural perception and appreciation of children between herding and a small-scale agricultural society were unrelated, due to the fact that they were founded in different economic values, for instance the use of child labour (Welinder 1998:191f.). However, I find it difficult to assume that there were great differences between the understandings of children in a herding group, versus a small-scale agricultural group due to economic reasons. Children in a small-scale agricultural society would probably also have been important for their usefulness in the group, if they performed different agricultural tasks, maybe they also attended animals at the farm as herds. According to these arguments the children in Vallhagar should also have been buried.

According to Welinder there was one child burial among 140 adult ones, in the surroundings of Vallhagar (Welinder 1998:191). It is important to note that only a small number of the graves in the burial ground situated to the settlement of Vallhagar, is dated to the same time period as the stone foundation houses of Vallhagar and Styrmansberget (i.e. 0-550 AD). The main part of the excavated graves from the burial grounds near Vallhagar, belongs to the Pre Roman Iron Age (500-0 BC), i.e. to an earlier time. In consideration of this there are three children present; one from the northern burial ground (Nielsen 1955:575-607; Gejvall 1955:718), and two from grave VI in the Vallhagar settlement (Gejvall 1955:736, 707, 737) among 33 adults (22 from the northern- and 9 from the southern burial ground, and at least 2 adults from the settlement graves at Vallhagar) from the Roman Iron Age.

The reversed situation is found at Styrmansberget. According to Welinder there were 15 graves with one adult, one single child grave and 6 double graves with one or two children and one adult at Styrmansberget (Welinder 1998:200). However, it is possible to question the number of persons buried in the graves. According to Anders Lundström who examined the teeth from the graves, there are jaws and loose teeth from 43 adults (Lundström, A. 1955:781, 784). This changes the ratio between adults and children to 7 children out of 43 adults at Styrmansberget. The relative amount of the children and adults buried at Vallhagar and at Styrmansberget respectively, will not be so remarkably large if we consider the teeth at Styrmansberget as representatives of different individuals. The amount of buried children can still be considered as a "high" amount of buried children in a small population. However, I am not convinced that the graves from Styrmansberget should be considered to come from a small population, living in the only building at the place. I do not apprehend Styrmansberget, as an ordinary place, neither to live in, nor to be buried at.

The particular and the general

An important question to ask is what kind of conclusion is it possible to draw about children's position in society, and about the relation between children and adults on the basis of a selected place, a place as out of the ordinary as Styrmansberget? In the material from Styrmansberget there is an ambiguity and a tension between the specific and the general which I find interesting to enlarge on. A way to solve this "discrepancy" between the specific and the general is to use microarchaeology. Microarchaeology is an operative theory of social agency and practice inspired by Sartre's theory of serial collectively (1991), Lacan's psychoanalysis (1988a; 1988b) and the structuration theory of Giddens (1984). It has been introduced by Fredrik Fahlander and Per Cornell (Falhander 2001; Cornell & Fahlander 2002a, 2002b; Fahlander 2003). The aim of microarchaeology is to study the social practice at a local level and to relate the particular to the general (Fahlander 2003:16).

I agree with their line of arguments as well as with their conclusions in microarchaeolgy, even though I have not worked with the material from Styrmansberget with a microarchaeological approach. In michroarcaeology it is argued that the individual actions and particular events generally have some relation to a more general structure (Fahlander 2003:82). Several researchers (Elias 1998; Habermas 1972; Sartre 1991; Bourdieu 1990; Giddens 1979, 1984) have emphasized that there are no clear boundaries between the micro and the macro level.

Numerous of attempts to bridge the dichotomy have been done (Fahlander 2003:18f). One example from archaeology is John Chapman who has observed that the local micro traditions not only are a simple reflection of the global. There also exists a general trend of global structures in the local (Chapman 2002: 161).

A point of departure in microacheology and in my interpretations about Styrmansberget is that it is impossible to place ourselves entirely outside the symbolic order. The structures of the different aspects of society are involved in most of our actions. All of us are unique individuals, but in a similar way. Microarcheology argues that even the unique or the queer only is unique in relation to the actually social normality and they tend to follow certain patterns in our time and social context (Fahlander & Cornell 2002:44).

The place Styrmansberget was probably selected for its topographically extended position and the burials partly have several exceptional characters, which separate them from the ordinary burial pattern of the period. But at the same time the categories from the general pattern in Gotland, also is represented at Styrmansberget, by the house, the stone enclosures, the henges and in some parts of the grave constructions. My suggestion is that the everyday life partly was symbolically incorporated at Styrmansberget, by its similarities with the daily life, by the house constructions, the stone enclosures, the graves and the henges. At the same time the house is not a regular house from the period because it is situated at a henged mountain. The house is connected to the henge with an enclosure (for discussion about the relation between the house, the enclosure and the henge at Styrmansberget, see Cassel 1998:150ff). Styrmansberget is a particular place and at the same time the place was an integrated place in the rest of the society by its special function that it had in society for the persons who used Styrmansberget as a meeting place, ceremonial place, and as a burial ground for some selected persons.

Transformation in life and in death

I interpret the henge of Styrmansberget, as a liminal border where the dead persons buried in the henge, communicated with the spiritual world. They exist in a liminal phase, precisely as young children did in their transformative life course (Scott 1998; Finlay 2000). Children, and especially the lives of young children, consist of numerous phases before they reach the category of adults. These phases are marked socially, culturally and biologically in different ways. Biologically the child gets its teeth at certain ages, looses them, learn to crawl, sit, go and speak. All these phases occur for children in different cultures and they are a form of transformation. The young children in the graves are foetus/neonatal or young children. There were a lot of skills that young children could not manage when they were alive. It is possible that Iron Age society considered them to be in a liminal phase

until they had reached the age of 6–7 years. A child at that age could control the skills of going, running, speaking besides doing a lot of tasks the adults do, and above all they had received their first permanent teeth.

Some of the adult individuals in the graves with the children are represented in form of teeth or jaws. Teeth pass several transformations during the life course. A newborn child has no teeth; at 6–8 months the child receives its first milk tooth, which they start to loose at the age of 5–7 years. At this time the new permanent teeth start to occur and are coming at different intervals up to the late twenties. When old, we often lose our teeth again. My suggestion is that the occurrences of teeth in the burials are as a symbolic expression and a representation of the human life course. The teeth in the graves origin from different deceased adults and in my interpretation they are representations of different individuals and their families, who are not buried at Styrmansberget. I image they were buried in other places in Gotland, after some years when the skeleton was defleshed the descendant opened the graves and took out teeth from their deceased relatives and placed them inside the burials at Styrmansberget. In one case, as mentioned earlier, they even polished a tooth smoothly, post mortem, a piece of effort that can be interpreted as the teeth were seen as a part of a symbolic significance and involved in ritual practises at Styrmansberget.

Many of the animals in the burials also have transformative characters that could be related to a form of life- and dead course. Kristina Jennbert has remarked that the boundary between human and animal disappeared when transformative practices occurred (Jennbert 2002:118). Erika Räf suggests that some mythological selected animal in the Roman Iron Age were help-spirits, which passed the dead from the living, to the afterlife, in a transformation procedure (Räf 2001:16ff). Some of the animals at Styrmansberget could exist in different elements. Possible help spirits could have been some of the animals at Styrmansberget; bird, seal, dog and horse. According to Räf these animals are present both in the mythology of the Iron Age and in the folkloric myths (Räf 2001:22). In this article I can not enlarge on all of the possible symbolic meanings of the animals from the burials at Styrmansberget, but I will give some examples. The seal is a creature that lives in-between the elements, in the water but breaths air and deliver their kids at land or at the ice. In the folkloristic myths the seals and the humans are often mixed (Räf 2001:23), and there have been interpretations about the symbolic mixture of seal and humans in archaeological contexts as well (Storå 2001).

In the Iron Age myths concepts as *"skinn"* (Icel. hamr) and *fylgias* (Icel. fylgia) have connections with birds and the transformation of the human souls (Räf 2001:20). Fylgias are guardian spirits connected to the individual persons or families, and "skinn" (Icel. hamr) was the name of the temporary guise the *hugr* could take for its movements while performing sorcery wizardry (Icel.

trolldómr) (Raudvere 2002:98, 102). Over large geographical areas of the ancient world the conception that the soul can take shape of a bird is spread (Tillhagen 1978:20f; Hagberg 1937:578ff). Birds also are present in the ornamentations of the Migration period. According to Tillhagen (1978) the idea that the migratory birds hibernating in seas, swamps and marshes could originate from the apprehension that the birds are the incarnation of the souls. The earth was the kingdom of the dead and when the birds in the autumn descended down under the earth surface the birds returned to the dead. The arrival of the migratory birds in spring could have held the idea of regeneration (Tillhagen 1978:16, 23). The 17 birds' species at Styrmansberget lived in different environments that could have represented different elements and could have represented different relations and aspects of life and death. Some of these birds could, like the snake, live in "different" elements. The razorbill "flies in the water," and several of the aquatic birds ruffle up their feathers in summer time. This happens at the same time as the birds sit on eggs or have their nestling. During this time the birds cannot fly. It is even possible to capture them with bare hands (for information about hunting of birds that ruffle, see Storå 1968). The ruffle of the birds transforms them for a short time, into birds that cannot fly. These could be interpreted as different forms of transformations and passing of the liminal phases in life and death. The young children were accompanied by one or more adults. It is a possibility to consider the adults as a kind of "help spirits" for the youngsters during the life – death transition (of course it could have been the other way around to).

The snake and the fertility at Styrmansberget

The mythological motifs at bracteates, gold foils, stamps and other figurative artefacts points to a mythological tradition in connection to the Asa mythology from the Migration – Vendel (Merovingian) Period and in some cases it is also possible to connect the artefacts to late Roman Iron Age (Hedeager, Lindberg 1997; Back-Danielsson 1999; Axboe 1991; Solli 1999; Gaimster 1998). In the images of the bracteates there are often different animal attributes that generally are connected with different aspects of the Asa gods. Styrmansberget is situated in Fröjel parish which most likely are named after the Nordic fertility goddess Freja or as she also is named, Fröja (Vikstrand 2001). Presumably one of her cult places were situated in the parish. I suppose there also is a possibility that the worship of fertility and the cult of Freja, or her precursor Nerthus, or some for us unknown goddess was practiced, maybe in a transformed way during the Roman Iron Age and Migration Period at Styrmansberget. Myths, rituals and mythology often have a long dureé even if they transform and change during long period of times.

Childlessness are considered as a great misfortune in many cultures (Tillhagen 1983), and therefore a lot of different conceptions and magic items have been used to improve fertility. In folklore traditions different animals have been used with the aim to increase fertility, i.e. pigs, horses and cats. These because they are apprehended to have an active sexual life, and for this reason, milk from the animals was used to improve an infertile woman's fertility. Other animals that have been used for this purpose are goat rams and dogs (Tillhagen 1983:119). All the child-adult graves contain bones of cattle. The cattle also have fertility connotions in Iron Age mythology. The fertility goddess Nerthus was travelling in a wagon drawn by cows and the cow Audhumbla was the origin of the Nordic cosmology (Jennbert 2002:117). In the Preroman Iron Age cows are often deposited in vessels in Denmark and Germany. The cows are also to be found as images and sculptures on the vessels (personal communication Åsa Fredell 2003-05-23). Åsa Fredell interprets the cow as symbols of fertility which were connected to the creation mythology of the Iron Age (Fredell 2003). The cow is also represented in graves from the Roman Iron Age in form of drinking horns. All of these animals (the cow, the dog, the goat and the cat) are represented in the graves at Styrmansberget.

Bigitta Johansen has interpreted the henges as a snake or a dragon/snake in a comparison with the Norse mythological literature (Johansen 1996, 1997:143ff.). In the fertility ideas the snake is central (Tillhagen 1983:112). One can see this represented at Styrmansberget, through the mythological relation between the henge and the snake. Anders Andrén has followed up Johansen's snake hypothesis, in his interpretation of rune stones (Andrén 2000). Andrén interprets the snakes of the rune stones as a representative of the family, and the snakes express the family's relation to inheritance, ownership, land and territory (Andrén 2000:13). The big snake represents one family and the smaller surrounding snakes represent relations outside the family (Andrén 2000:16). Inspired by Andrén I will make an interpretation of the relationship between the graves, grave groups and the henge in a similar manner.

First I want to emphasize the fact that the concept of *family* is a problematic concept as discussed among gender–critical scholars (for discussion see Arwill-Nordbladh 1998). In this context thus, I do not mean a traditional west European nuclear family. In this paper family is a group of kin related people who were living together in the stone house foundation like a household with extended relations (Svedin 1999). In order to increase the fertility of the family, and maybe even to ensure the survival of the families/kin forthcoming children, they begun to bury their youngest deceased members as well as some adults in the henge/snake. The henge and the house at Styrmansberget were constructed by the group/kin to which the mountain "belonged". This might have been in order for the members of the group to use the house when they were seen as in need to strengthen, or secure fertility with help from the spirits and other forces of fertility active at the place. Possibly some couples stayed and lived for some time in the house and that will explain the every day and ordinary artefacts in the house foundation.

Close to the henge there are three graves. These graves have some similarities with the graves inside the henge. They are not marked above the surface. Adults are buried here and two of the graves contain plenty of animal bones. Furthermore these graves also have similarities (i.e. inner limestone cist) with the graves outside the henge. I imagine that these graves contain deceased that had a very close connection to the family represented in the henge/snake. They might even have been a part of the family, however, at the same time they had a close relation to the group that were buried outside the henge. Therefore they could be seen as a form of mediators and ancestors for different families and their relations in life and death. Probably they were individuals that had been able to both integrate and maintain different spheres.

The stone enclosure running between the house wall and the henge, ties together the house and the henge. When the use of the house ends, they sealed the house by placing three graves inside the house foundation. Two of the graves enclose children. My suggestion is that the graves in the house represent another side of the kin that had close relationship to the family who buried some of their members in the large henge. The graves in the house are constructed with material from the house and have a near contact with the house foundation walls. In this context it seems likely that there was a relation between old constructed foundations and children, this because the children are buried, except one of them, in already constructed foundations, such as the henge and the house foundation. The single graves outside the house foundation, but on the terrace, were placed near the house, because the deceased had a close relation to the family members buried in the house foundation. The single graves outside the constructions (terrace, house and the henge) had some sort of weaker relation to the deceased buried within the structures, their relation were not as close as the person in the graves inside the henge or the house.

Children's life courses and position

In most pre-industrial societies, as well as in current societies, individuals grew into adults in a series of steps from their birth and onwards (Welinder 1998:185, 86). The phases are a part of the child's upbringing by giving them knowledge, working tasks and responsibility (Welinder 1998:185, 86). Passage rites or feasts often marked these stages and sometimes these phases were manifested in the burial practice. It is interesting to note that the children at Styrmansberget were not buried in the same mode. I suggest that this difference between the

child burials depends on the society's apprehension about when the individuals became adult. According to the burial praxis at Styrmansberget, the children's graves are possible to divide into two different social categories.

One group consists of 6 children between the ages of foetus/infants to "young" child. The children were not cremated and they were buried with adults, animal bones and some of these graves also contained teeth. In the other group there were only one young individual at age six to seven years old in grave H 11. The grave is situated outside the henge. This grave contains one cremated child, age considered of 6–7 years old (Gejvall 1955:719). The grave is outstanding in several ways. Firstly, the young individual was the only person at Styrmansberget that was cremated. Secondly, it was the only young individual that was not accompanied by adults. Thirdly, the grave did not contain any animal bones, teeth or jaws as the other child graves did. Fourthly, there are no objects in the grave, as in the other graves with children. Fifthly, the grave also is comparable to the adult graves outside the henge and in the house foundation because the grave has similar inner construction, and the cist had the length of an adult (1.60 m.). The grave is similar in the constructions to the other adult graves that are situated outside the henge and in the house foundation. One possible interpretation is that the cremated young individual culturally was considered as person that had passed the group of "young" child and the social liminal phase in life. By these acts the young child had transformed to another cultural age category, maybe the category of a "young" or "adult", and because of this, the young individual in grave H 11 got a different burial than the other children.

There are two, possibly three, more graves in Gotland, in which children are buried in single graves without adults. In Nygårds, Vallstena parish, grave (Raä 6395:5) dated to IV: 2, contains one cremated child (age not estimated), and buried with one buckle and a knife. The next is a damaged grave (Raä 10950:38) from period V: I in Norrbys, Follingbro parish that contained one inhumated child (no age estimation has been done), and the equipment consists of two needles, bread, one bronze finger ring and ceramics. A grave (N 20) at the northern burial ground at Vallhagar, Fröjel parish, contains the bones from one child between four and five years old; the bones were mixed with coal and soot. There are no objects in the grave; therefore the grave is difficult to date, but most of the burials come from the Roman Iron Age, Vendel and maybe some come from the Viking Age (Nielsen 1955:582, 575). The child graves mentioned above, do not contain animal bones. Some of the graves also hold artefacts. In all of these graves the children were buried alone without adults and possibly they were culturally considered as being an integral part of the category of "young" or "adult".

Children's importance in death and life – children and adults in the same and in different contexts

Finally I will try to draw some general conclusions about children's position in the Roman Iron Age – Migration Period society in Gotland from the case study presented. A case study could be seen as a *situation*. According to microarcheology it is most suitable to study the social interaction in a situation because the situation limits the number of agents, the relative position in their relation, the material context etc. In every act the actors' previous experiences from the society are imbedded (Fahlander & Cornell 2002:44). In the burial act the ancestors and possibly other persons from the society are engaged. Their apprehension about gender, age and social differences in society, as well as norms and the traditions will be expressed in the grave ritual and in the material culture. At the same time when burial rites are preformed norms, traditions and gender apprehensions could be negotiated through the use of material culture.

In this material there are two main groups of child burials. One group consists of single child graves at different burial grounds, with or without artefacts in the burials (H 11, Styrmansberget; Raä 6395:5, Vallstena parish; Raä 10950:38, Follingbro parish). The other group consists of the children that were buried together with adults and with a lot of animals (H2, H3, H5, H8, H10 at Styrmansberget and V1 at Vallhagar settlement). Besides these two groups, there is one single child grave (Raä 5913:43, Kornettskogen, Västkinde parish) which contains one cremated adult and two inhumated children (age not estimated), as well as ceramics and bones from a sheep. The burial is different from the grave H 11, Styrmansberget and V1, Vallhagar, because it only contains bones from one animal and it is located at a "common" burial field.

Let us return to the two different groups of child burials. Among the children that got single burials there are differences in the amount of objects they have received in their graves. Some of them have not got any objects (H 11, Styrmansberget, Fröjel, N 20, Vallhagar, Fröjel). Other has got a burial (Raä 10950:38, Norrbys, Follingbro) with a lot of equipment, like there could have been in an adult's grave. According to my earlier interpretation these children are culturally categorized as "young" or "adults", but in this group there also seems to be other dissimilarities between the children. In the burials these differences are expressed through different amount and quality of the artefacts. It is possible that these differences were dependent on their different culturally ages but there could also be other explanations. My suggestion is that distinctions also could be found between the children of the same cultural age in the society, which could depend on their different social status in the society when they were alive. Their status probably was connected to their position in the kin and their expected forthcoming position in the society when they become adults.

Children and adult in the same burial with a lot of different animal bones occur in two different contexts; at Styrmansberget and at the Vallhagar settlement. In the middle of the settlement of Vallhagar two newborn children were buried together with a male adult (grave VI). It is noticeable that this grave is the only large grave at the settlement and it is placed in the middle of the houses. The burial (V1) at the Vallhagar settlement has similarities with the burials at Styrmansberget through the occurrence of the amount of different animal species'. The burials at Styrmansberget are placed at a special selected place and the grave V1 also is placed in a special selected place in the middle of the settlement. It is not placed at the surrounding burial ground.

It has been suggested that the man was the ancestor and the founder of the inhabitants of Vallhagar (Cassel 1998:127). If the man was the ancestor and the founder of Vallhagar, what meaning did the newborn child in the grave have? Were they also apprehended as ancestors of the village, or did they have some other significance? To try to answer this question I want to focus on the presence of house(s) at both Styrmansberget and at Vallhagar village. Houses with stone foundation from the younger Roman Iron Age are interpreted to be constructed in the purpose of strengthening the old structure of the kin and their kin based landowning properties (Cassel 1998:180). The appearances of children in this context maybe represent the idea of the significances of children and new generations as an integrated part of the daily life and deed at the settlement. At Styrmansberget the burials were partly excluded from the daily life by its special location. At the same time the children and the adults buried there were in a way symbolically integrated in the collective and maybe selective meetings and the rituals that occurred at the place. A conclusion to this would be that children in these aspects were equally considered as adults of different age and sex, as participants in the daily life, the collective meetings and the rituals of the death. I mean that this line of reasoning is at a symbolic level. It is not necessarily so that the symbolic meaning has been the same as the every day life of the living people. The burials and their constructions could be seen as a form of ideas, argumentation and norms of the living in which the children were important as a social bound between the kin, families, the houses and the society.

Another interesting aspects of the graves, especially the children-adult graves at Styrmansberget, is that the children were buried together with adults with ages that varies between below middle age to very old (Gejvall 1955:741f.). My suggestion is that the children and their upbringing was a matter of special concern for the age categories; young as well as old and for men as well as women in the kin group among those who used Styrmansberget. One might even consider the teeth, which originate from different persons, as an extension of this care of the young children beyond the family to other members of the kin, who were associated with the family. This could be interpreted as if the relation between adult and child was seen as important during this period for some families in Gotland.

Summary

To sum up this case study, I have tried to demonstrate that children and adults buried at peripheral locations, do not have to be interpreted as rejected by society. Even though it seems like the burial place is particular, and thus being difficult to draw general conclusions about. I have anyway argued that places like Styrmansberget could have been filled with symbolic meaning. Possibly they could have played an important part in the question of how society constructed their gender relations. These places can be used in order to discuss relations in society between genders, generations, family and kinship. From the burials I also have discussed aspects of the relationship between children and constructions, houses, meetings, ritual life, transformation, life course, death, daily life and status. Of course all of the above mentioned concepts represent wide-ranging areas of discussions. In this article I have not been able to go to the profound of them, but in a forthcoming work I will throw more light upon how gender relations in the society of Gotland in the Late Roman Iron Age – Migration Period society, were negotiated.

References

Almgren, B. 1955. Graves within the settlement. Grave VI. *Vallhagar. A migration period settlement on Gotland/Sweden.* Part I. Ed. Stenberger, M., in collaboration with Klindt-Jensen, O. Copenhagen, pp. 273–276.

Almgren, O. & Nerman, B. 1923. *Die ältere Eisenzeit Gotlands.* Nach den in Statens historiska museum, aufbewahrten Funden und Ausgrabungsberichten im Auftrage der Kungl. Vitterhets-, historie-, och antikvitetsakademien dargestellt. Stockholm.

Adsten, A. 1997. *Barn i Vallhagar.* Institutionen för humaniora, Mitthögskolan, Östersund. Stencil (Seminar paper).

Andrén, A. 2000. Re-reading embodied texts: an interpretation of rune-stones. *Current Swedish Archaeology.* Vol. 8, pp. 7–32.

Ariès, Ph. 1960. (1962). Centuries of childhood : a social history of family life. (Transl. from the French by R. Baldick). New York.

Arwill-Nordbladh, Elisabeth. 1998. Genuskonstruktioner i nordisk vikingatid : förr och nu. GOTARC. Series B, Gothenburg archaeological theses, 9. Institutionen för arkeologi, Göteborg Univ. Göteborg. Diss.

Axboe, M. 1991. Guld og guder i folkevandringstiden. Brakteaterne som kilde til politisk/religiøse forhold. *Samfundsorganisation og Regional variation.*

Norden i romersk jernalder og folkevandringstid. Jysk Arkæologisk Selskabs skrifter. Nr. 27. Eds. Fabech, C. & Ringtved, J. Århus.

Back Danielsson, I-M. 1999. Engendering Performance in the Late Iron Age. *Current Swedish Archaeology.* Vol 7, pp 7-20.

Biuw, A. 1992. *Norra Spånga: bebyggelse och samhälle under järnåldern.* Monografier utgivna av Stockholms stad. Nr. 76. Stockholm University. Stockholm. Diss.

Biörnstad, A. 1955. Previous investigations of Iron Age building remains on Gotland. Herrgårdsklint in Gammelgarn. *Vallhagar. A migration period settlement on Gotland/Sweden.* Part II. Ed. Stenberger, M., in collaboration with Klindt-Jensen, O. Copenhagen, pp. 916–917.

Bradley, R. 1991. Monuments and places. *Sacred and Profane.* Eds. Garwood, P., Jennings, D., Skeates, R. & Toms, J. Oxford University Committee for Archaeology Monograph. No. 32, pp. 135–40.

Bradley, R. 2000. *An Archaeology of natural Places.* New York.

Carlsson, A. 1983. *Djurhuvudformiga spännen och gotländsk vikingatid.* Stockholm Studies in Archaeology. 5. Stockholms universitet. Stockholm. Diss.

Carlsson, D. 1979. *Kulturlandskapets utveckling på Gotland: en studie av jordbruks- och bebyggelseförändringar under järnåldern.* Meddelande B 49, Kulturgeografiska institutionen, Stockholms universitet, Stockholm. Diss.

Cassel, K. 1998. *Från grav till gård. Romersk järnålder på Gotland.* Stockholm Studies in Archaeology 16. Stockholms Universitet. Diss.

Chapman, J. C. 2000. *Tensions at funerals. Micro-tradition analysis in later Hungarian Prehistory.* Archaeolingua Series Minor 14. Budapest.

Engström J. 1984. *Torsburgen. Tolkning av en gotländsk fornborg.* AUN 6. Uppsala. Diss.

Finlay, N. 2000. Outside of Life and Death: Traditions of Infant Burial in Ireland from cillin to cist. *Human Lifecycles. World Archaeology.* Vol 31 (2), pp. 407-22.

Fredell, Å, 2003. Bronze Age imagery: through water and fire. *Current Swedish Archaeology.* Vol. 11, pp. 45-63.

Gaimster, M.1998. *Vendel period bracteates on Gotland. On the significance of Germanic art.* Acta Archaeologica Lundensia Series in 80, 27. Almqvist & Wiksell International. Stockholm.

Gejvall, N. G. 1955. The cremations at Vallhagar. *Vallhagar. A migration period settlement on Gotland/Sweden.* Part II. Ed. Stenberger, M., in collaboration with Klindt-Jensen, O. Copenhagen, pp. 717–719.

Gejvall, N. G. 1955. The hill fort on Styrmansberget. *Vallhagar. A migration period settlement on Gotland/Sweden.* Part II. Ed. Stenberger, M., in collaboration with Klindt-Jensen, O. Copenhagen, pp. 719–723.

Gejvall, N. G. 1955. The skeletons. *Vallhagar. A migration period settlement on Gotland/Sweden.* Part II. Ed. Stenberger, M., in collaboration with Klindt-Jensen, O. Copenhagen, pp. 724–765.

Gilchrist, R. 1999. *Gender and archaeology : contesting the past.* London.

Gilchrist, R. 2000, red. Human Lifecycles. *World Archaeology. Vol. 31 (2).*

Hagberg, L. 1937. *När döden gästar. Svenska folkseder och svensk folktro i samband med död och begravning.* Stockholm.

Hauptman-Wahlgren, K. 2002. *Bilder av betydelse : hällristningar och bronsålderslandskap i nordöstra Östergötland.* Stockholm studies in archaeology, 23. Diss. Stockholm Universitet. Lindome. Bricoleur press.

Hedeager, Lotte. 1997. *Skygger af en anden virkelighed : oldnordiske myter.* København.

Helskog, K 1995. Maleness and femaleness in the sky and the underworld – and in between. Perceiving Rock Art and Political Perspectives. *Proceeding Rock Art: Social and Political Perspectives.* Eds. Helskog, K. & Olsen, B. Oslo, pp. 247–262.

Hegardt, J. 1991a. Gudinge Slott, en märklig gotländsk fornborg. *Tor.* Vol. 23, Uppsala.

Hegardt, J. 1991b. Det patrilaterala samhället, hemliga sällskap och monumentala byggnader. En analys av en gotländsk fornborg. *Tor.* Vol. 23, Uppsala.

Iregren, I. 1997. Why Animal Bones in Human Graves - An Attempt to Interpret Animals Present in Iron Age Cremations in Sweden. In: Smits, E; Iregren, E. & Drusini, A.G. eds. *Proceedings of the Symposium Cremation Studies in Archaeology.* Amsterdam, 26-27 October 1995. Logos Edizioni, s. 9-32.

Jennbert, K. 2002. Djuren i nordisk förkristen ritual och myt. In: Jennbert, K., Andrén, A. & Raudvere, C. eds. *Plats och praxis.* Symposium, Lund 19-21 oktober 2000, pp. 105-133. Lund.

Joyce, R. 2000. Girling the girl and boying the boy. *World Archaeology Vol. 31(2)*, pp. 437-483.

Sellevold, B. J. et al. 1984. *Iron Age Man in Denmark. Prehistoric Man in Denmark.* Vol. III. Eds. Sellevold, B. J. et. al., pp. 207-241. København.

Johansen, B. & Pettersson, I.-M. 1993. *Från borg till bunker. Befästa anläggningar från förhistorisk och historisk tid.* Fornlämningar i Sverige 2. RAÄ. Stockholm.

Johansen, B. 1996. The Transformative dragon: the construction of social identity and the use of metaphors during the Nordic Iron Age. *Current Swedish archaeology 4*, pp. 83-102.

Johnsen, B. & Welinder, S. (red). 1995; *Arkeologi om barn.* Societas archaeologica Upsaliensis: Department of Archaeology, Uppsala University. Occasional papers in Archaeology. No. 10. Uppsala.

Lepiksaar, J. 1955. The bird remains from Vallhagar. Bird remains from the hill fort on Styrmansberget. *Vallhagar. A migration period settlement on Gotland/Sweden.* Part II. Ed. Stenberger, M. in collaboration with Klindt-Jensen, O. Copenhagen, pp. 815–817.

Lillehammer, G. 1986. Barna i Nordens Forhistorie. Drøft Metodegrunnlaget og Kildenes Bærekraft. *K.A.N.* pp. 3-21.

Lillehammer, G. 1989. A child is Born. The Child's World in an Archaeological Perspective. *NAR Vol. 22, no. 2*, pp. 89-105.

Lillehammer, G. 2000. The world of children. *Children and Material Culture.* London and New York. Ed. Sofaer Derevenski, J. pp. 17-26.

Lillehammer, G. 2002. Anthropologie-Geschichte-Kulturvergleich. *Kinderwelten,* eds Alt, K. W. & Kemkes-Grottenthaler, A. Bölau Verlag, Köln.

Lindeberg, M. 1997. Gold, Gods and Women. *Current Swedish Archaeology,* Vol. 5, pp. 99-110.

Lindquist, M. 1981. Mylingar – offer, utsatta barn eller förhistoriska barnbegravningar? *Gotländskt arkiv 53.* Visby, pp. 7-12.

Lundström, A. 1955. An odontological examination of the Iron Age finds at Vallhagar. *Vallhagar. A migration period settlement on Gotland/Sweden. Part II.* Ed. Stenberger, M., in collaboration with Klindt-Jensen, O. Copenhagen, pp. 766–785.

Lundström, P. 1955. The hill fort. *Vallhagar. A migration period settlement on Gotland/Sweden. Part I.* Ed. Stenberger, M. in collaboration with Klindt-Jensen, O. Copenhagen, pp. 610–636.

Meskell, L. 2000. Cycles of life: Narrative homology and archaeological realities. *World archaeology Vol. 31 (2)*, pp. 423-441.

Nerman, B. 1935. *Die Völkerwanderungszeit Gotlands.* KVHAA. 121. Stockholm.

Nielsen, V. 1955. The northern grave-field (graves N 1-N 92). *Vallhagar. A migration period settlement on Gotland/Sweden. Part I.* Ed. Stenberger, M., in collaboration with Klindt-Jensen, O. Copenhagen. Pp. 542–609.

Odner, K. 1972. Ethno-historic and ecological settings for economic and social models of an Iron Age society: Valldalen, Norway. *Models in Archaeology.* Ed. Clark, D. Methuen, London. Pp. 623–651.

Olausson, M. 1995. *Det inneslutna rummet: om kultiska hägnader, fornborgar och befästa gårdar i Uppland från 1300 f. Kr till Kristi födelse.* Byrån för arkeologiska undersökningar. Nr. 9, Riksantikvarieämbetet. Studier från Uv, Stockholm. Diss.

Pettersson, A.-M. 1992. *Ett Gotländskt gårdsgravfält från vendeltiden. En studie av gravar vid ödegården Fjäle i Ala sn.* Stockholms arkeologiska institution. Stencil. (Seminar paper). Stockholm.

Petré, B. 1999a. *Gravfältet Raä 16, Söderby, Lovö sn, Uppland. Ett familjegravfält från yngre järnålder. Rapport, analys, tolkning.* Lovö Archaeological Reports and Studies. Nr. 7. 1999. Department of Archaeology. Stockholm University.

Petré, B. 1999b. *Gravfältet Raä 13, Söderby, Lovö sn, Uppland. Ett gravfält med två familjer från yngre järnålder. Rapport, analys, tolkning.* Lovö Archaeological Reports and Studies. Nr. 6. 1999. Department of Archaeology. Stockholm University.

Raudvere, C. 2000. Trolldómr in Early Medieval Scandinavia. *Witchcraft and Magic in Europe. The Middle Ages.* Vol. 3. Eds. Jolly, K; Raudvere, C & Peters, E. London.

Rundkvist, M. 2003. *Barshalder 1, a cemetery in Grötlingbo and Fide parishes, Gotland, Sweden, c. AD 1-1100: excavations and finds 1826-1971.* SAR. 40. Stockholm University.

Räf, E. 2001. *Krumknivar, kvinnor och kreatur: aspekter på kvinnligt genus under äldre järnålder på Öland; Vad spelar djuren för roll?: Om djur i öländska gravar från äldre järnålder.* Institute of Archaeology, Lund University. Diss.

Scott, E. 1999. *The Archaeology of Infancy and Infant Death.* B.A.R.. International Series 819.

Sigvallius, B. 1994. *Funeral pyres. Iron Age cremations in North Spånga.* Theses and papers in osteology, 1. Stockholm University. Diss.

Sjöberg, A. 1976. Bronsåldersrösen vid Suderbys i Västerhejde. *Gotländskt Arkiv.* Visby, pp. 136–137.

Sofaer Derevenski, J. 1997a. Linking age and gender as social variables. *Ethnographische Archäologische Zeitschrift* 38, pp. 485–493.

Sjöberg, A. 1997b Age and gender at the site of Tiszapolgár-Basatanya, Hungary. *Antiquity.* Vol. 71 (2), pp. 875-889.

Sjöberg, A. 2000. *Children and material culture.* Ed. Sofaer Derevenski, London.

Storå, J. 2001. *Reading bones : Stone Age hunters and seals in the Baltic.* Stockholm studies in archaeology, 21. Stockholm University. Stockholm. Diss.

Storå, N. 1968. *Massfångst av sjöfågel i Nordeurasien:* en etnologisk undersökning av fångstmetoderna. Mass capture of waterfowl in northern Eurasia: an ethnological study of the methods used. Åbo akad. Acta Academia Aboensis. Ser. A, Humaniora. Åbo. Diss.

Solli, B. 1999. Odin the queer? On ergi and shamanism In Norse mythology. *Glyfer och arkeologiska rummen vänbok till Jarl Nordbladh.* Eds. Gustafsson,

A.& Karlsson, H.Gotarc Series A . Vol. 3. Dept. of Archaeology , Gothenburg university.

Strassburg, J. 2000. *Shamanic Shadows. One Hundered generations of Undead Subversion in southern Scandinavia, 7 000-4 000 BC.* Stockholm Studies in archaeology, 20. Department of Archaeology. Stockholm University. Diss.

Svedin, M. 1999. Gender and work at Vallhagar on Gotland during the Early Iron Age: history as fact, fiction or something in-between? *Gender and prehistory.* Ed. Werbart, B. Arkeologiska studier vid Umeå universitet, 7 Dept. of Archaeology and Sami Studies Umeå University, pp. 48-75.

Tillhagen, C. H. 1983. *Barnet i folktron. Tillblivelse, födelse och fostran.* Stockholm.

Tillhagen, C. H. 1978. *Fåglar i folktron.* Stockholm.

Tilley, C. 1994. *A phenomenology of landscape: places, paths, and monuments.* Oxford.

Wall, Å. 2002. Borderline Viewpoints. The Early Iron Age Landscapes of Henged Mountains in East Central Sweden. *Current Swedish Archaeology.* Vol. 10, pp. 95–115.

Wall, Å. 2003. *De hägnade bergens landskap: om den äldre järnåldern på Södertörn.* SAR, Stockholm studies in archaeology, 27. Arkeologiska institutionen, Stockholms universitet. Stockholm. Diss.

Welinder, S. 1998. The cultural construction of childhood in Scandinavia, 3500 BC-1350 AD. *Current Swedish Archaeology.* Vol. 6. pp. 185–204.

Widgren, M. 1983. *Settlement and farming systems in the Early Iron Age. A study of fossil agrarian landscapes in Östergötland, Sweden.* Acta universitatis Stockholmiensis. Stockholm studies in human geography 3. Stockholm. Diss.

Widgren, M. 1998. *Det svenska jordbrukets historia. [Bd 1],* Jordbrukets första femtusen år : 4000 f.Kr.-1000 e.Kr. Eds. Welinder, Stig & Widgren, Mats & Pedersen, Ellen Anne. Stockholm.

Vikstrand, P. 2001. *Gudarnas platser: förkristna sakrala ortnamn i Mälarlandskapen.* Acta Academiae Regiae Gustavi Adolphi, 77. Studier till en svensk ortnamnsatlas, 17. Uppsala. Diss.

Victor, Helena. 2002. *Med graven som granne – om bronsålderns kulthus.* Aun, 30 Institutionen för arkeologi och antik historia, Uppsala universitet. Uppsala. Diss.

Making People Visible; Tapestries from Viking Age Norway

Anita Synnestvedt

Gothenburg University

Abstract

The aim of this paper is to look at material culture from a different kind of view by using Margaret Conkey's method: contexts of action/contexts for power. By investigating different contexts of action scenarios in the material culture and looking for chains of associations between these scenarios and then analysing these contexts of action, it is possible to discover patterns of social activities in the material and hereby discover different contexts for power. As an example of how to use this method I have looked at Viking Age tapestries from Oseberg and Haugen in Norway. The method made it possible to draw somewhat different conclusions and therefore to get a broader picture of the life and work of Viking Age women, - than what is commonly presented.

In 1991 Margaret Conkey developed a method while she was looking at material culture within the Palaeolithic Magdalenian. She named the method *context of action/contexts for power*. In this paper I will give an example of how to use this method further, when looking at material culture. First, I will give you a short explanation as to what the model looks like, followed by a brief historical background of the material used in this case study. Then I will describe the contexts of action scenarios which in turn lead to pictures of contexts for power. Finally, I will present my conclusions and show how this method makes it possible to make people and their relationships visible in the archaeological material. Using this method, also made me able to arrive at somewhat different conclusions, especially about the lives of Viking Age women. Eva-Marie Göransson, among others, claims that the art and crafts of women were much more anonymous in its expression, as well as in the question of production, than that of men. Göransson also says that the female discourse was more anonymous and that it did not have a personal effect on the status of the artist, as it would have had for a man who wrote poetry, for example. Further on, she says that the language of women seems more quiet and collective, even if it corresponds to the structure of that of the poet (Göransson 1999:208-209). In this paper I will question these assumptions and my aim is to prove that there might have been other views on the work, skill, inventions and creative power of the artistic textile work that was probably made by women.

Contexts of action / Contexts for power

Margaret Conkey's method implies searching for chains for associations between different actions and connections, in which different groups can be based upon sex, age and gender. By analysing these contexts of action it should be possible to distinguish different contexts for power. In other words, connections where tensions may have lead to the restructuring of social relationships, or at least to social negotiations in the connections which also include gender (Axelsson 1999:121-122; Arwill Nordbladh 1998:124-125). I would like to use Conkey's own words when she says:

"I will instead advocate using archaeological evidence not as a record of some given predetermined social form, but to elucidate strategies of social action, of social formation, of social production and reproduction. And it will be I suggest in those contexts of action and contexts for power that gender relations (role conflicts, statuses), **as historical forces,** can not only be inferred but also shown to be part of the processes by which the social categories and structures- the ones we usually take as given – are, in fact, constructed." (Conkey 1991:58).

In my work, I have used the fragments of the tapestries from the grave mounds of Oseberg and Haugen in Norway, in my attempt to test this model of interpretation and I have made a model of interpretation to be followed:

- *The tapestries and their possible connections with different spheres of activities* like the growing of flax and working of wool, the sheep industry, tools for weaving, the dyeing of yarn and cloth, the constructions of patterns and the preparations for the tapestries.
- *Social actions* which includes the farm as a concept with space for different activities, the bringing up of children and the matter of passing on knowledge and tradition, craftsmen, trade and social contacts.
- *Social divisions* are about marriage and family, division of labour, the choice of motives in the tapestries and the tradition of storytelling and the question of cult.

- *Negotiations and agreements* include an aristocratic environment, art as a tool for reaching higher status and the function of the tapestries.

Historical background

The area around Oslo, today known as the Oslo fiord, was previously called Viken. On both sides of the fiord there have been finds of Viking ships in grave mounds.

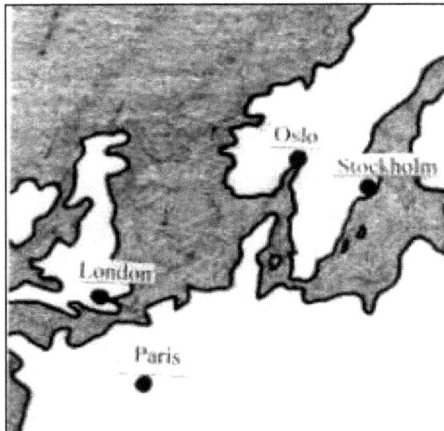

Figure 5.1 Map over Northern Europe.

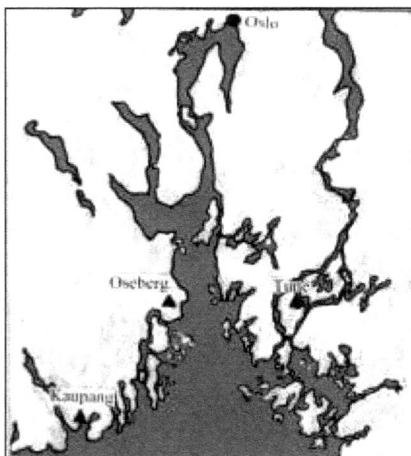

Figure 5.2 Map over the Oslo fiord (Viken)
Drawing by Margaretha Häggström 2003.
Drawing by Margaretha Häggström 2003.

The first one was the Tune ship on the east side of the fiord, excavated in 1867. At the same place, Haugen, there was also a tomb in a mound in which the tapestry of Haugen was found.

A sensational discovery was made in 1904 on the west side of the Oslo fiord, which lead to the excavation of another Viking ship in a grave mound, the Oseberg ship. This would prove to be one of Norway's most important archaeological findings. The grave mound contained an enormous amount of gifts, from the ship itself to furniture, tools, sledges, and horses, all kinds of equipment for the household and many things used in the production of textiles. The gifts were of highest quality and made with great skill. Dendrochronological analyses of the timber in the mound show that it was felled in the year 834 (Myhre 1992:279).

Figure 5.3 A reconstruction of the grave chamber at Haugen where the tapestry was found (After A. W. Brøgger 1921: fig. 11).

Figure 5.4 The Oseberg monument from the excavation in 1904, Photo Th. Larsen, Tønsberg (After Christensen 1992).

There were two women buried in the ship, one aged of 30 – 40 and the other about 50-60 years old. The fact that this rich grave contained the burial of two women was something of a disappointment at the time of the excavation because of the common view about gender roles at the time and the Norwegian out breaking of the Swedish union. It therefore became very important to connect these women to a big chief or a king and for one of them to be the queen, the mother or at least the wife of such a man to mark the nationalistic importance of the finding. The myth that it should be a queen Åsa with her bondswoman was therefore introduced by A.W. Brøgger 1919 and this myth still lives on in many ways.

The commonly presented picture of the Viking Age woman is that her role was the one of mistress of the house and that her domains were those "within". These assumptions are mainly based upon written sources, many of which are about 200 years younger than the actual events they portray. They are also influenced by the new religion of Christianity and its view of women.

the new religion of Christianity and its view of women. The picture of the Viking Age woman as the mistress of the house is of course also based upon our own Victorian tradition (Arwill-Nordbladh 1998:113-115; Mandt 1992:98). I therefore believe that by using Conkey's method when researching the archaeological material, there is a possibility to get a more balanced picture of the ancient people and their lives.

The tapestries

The tapestries I have used in my work may seem very difficult to get a good impression of today, but some of them have been possible to reconstruct and analyse. They are very narrow, about 16-23 cm in width and 1-1.50 m long. They are covered with motives in horizontal rows. The meaning of the pictures seems in most cases to be connected to mythology, the death and rituals of sacrifice. There were probably several weavers working with the tapestries, because there are different techniques used in the different figures. Through the sagas and also in ethnological evidence, you will find that the tapestries probably have decorated the walls in the houses, just above the seats (Ingstad 1992a:185-187).

Figure 5.5 A reconstruction after one of the tapestries, made in watercolour technique by Mary Storm (After Hougen 1940).

The tapestries and their possible connections with different spheres of activities

Anne Stine Ingstad, who has written about the textiles in the publication: *Oseberg-dronningens grav, vår nasjonalskatt i nytt lys* (*The Mound of the Queen of Oseberg, our national treasure in new light*, my translation) from 1992, claims that the Viking Age women had a long and unbroken tradition of making textiles. This long experience has been of great importance and passing on the knowledge from generation to generation has been a determining factor in keeping the traditions alive. The textiles from the Oseberg ship and Haugen indicate that everything must have been carefully planned and that every stage in the preparatory work must have played an important role (Ingstad 1992a:189). It is

also obvious that a lot of the items from the Oseberg ship have been used. They have therefore probably been taken out of their daily use to be put in the grave (Christensen 1992a:85). I will now try finding different chains of associations in the contexts of actions.

Wool and flax were the most important raw materials in the production of textiles. The whole process from raw material to finished product is represented among the tools found in the Oseberg grave. It is also likely that there were a fully developed sheep industry in Norway as early as the Bronze Age. Among the grave goods in the Oseberg burial there was for example a pair of iron shears probably used for cutting wool. Other tools found, connected to this kind of production were wool combs and linen clubs (Ingstad 1992a:189). Susanne Axelsson has made a model of how a year's production of textile work could have looked (Axelsson 1999:129).

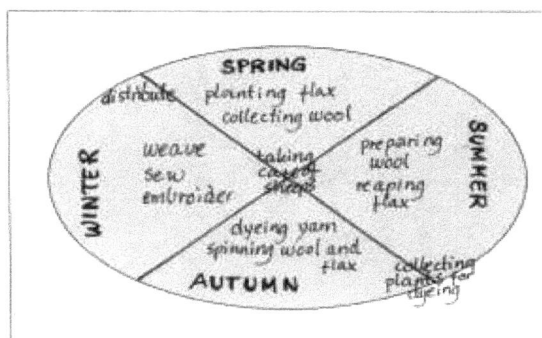

Figure 5.6 A proposed model of the annual cycle of textile production. Drawing by Anita Synnestvedt 2003 (After Susanne Axelsson 1999: fig. 4).

Both flax and wool had to be spun and this was the kind of work that could be done by old as well as young people. It could also have been carried out in different places on the farm, for example when herding the sheep, goats and cows. The daylight was not that important either, as it was in the process of weaving (Grenander–Nyberg 1976:100; Arwill- Nordbladh 1998:206). The spinning tools found in the Oseberg burial was whorls with and without attached spindles and several loose spindles. A pair of carved wooden pieces may also have been used to attach the wool to, during spinning. Other tools found for weaving were some smaller looms, one of which appears to have been a tubular loom and two others were braid looms. There were also a number of small square tablets for tablet weaving. It seems like most of the tools have had some connection with tapestries or finer tablet weaving (Christensen 1992a:131-133).

The wool used in the tapestries has of course been dyed before it was used in the weave, but whether this has been done on the farm or bought at a market, is hard to say. There are fragments in the textile material probably dyed with madder, as the colorant alizarin was found in it. It is of very high quality and therefore probably an imported product (Ingstad 1992a: 193-208). In a bucket in the Oseberg ship there were also seeds from woad which produces a blue colour (Brøgger 1917: 71).

The patterns of the tapestries must also have been planned in detail and exactly how people would solve this we don't know. But they must have had a great knowledge and feeling for both the different quality of the threads, colours and consumption of both colours and tread (Arwill-Nordbladh 1998:208). We don't know if the patterns were used by many weavers, so that the stories they told could be spread, or if each tapestry had its own special design.

should be done, by whom, with whom and when this work should be done.

Figure 5.8 The tapestry from Haugen, reconstructed drawing by Sofie Krafft (After A. W. Brøgger 1921: fig.17).

Social actions

Another part of the production process is the social actions that are part of people's lives. These include contacts, thoughts, traditions, ideas, dreams, aspirations and people's place in society. In all of these locales, you can find social actions functioning as a constant movement that pushes people and action forward. In these meetings and actions you will also find negotiations and compromises, connections where tensions may have lead the reconstructing of social relationships, or at least to social negotiations.

Bringing up children for example, includes a lot of opportunities for negotiation regarding who should be responsible for children's education and pass on the knowledge, and also what kind of knowledge should be passed on. In Iron Age society, children probably had to take part in the daily work from an early age, both outdoor and indoor. The common view is that there existed a division between female and male activities. Girls were supposed to learn about everything that concerned the household and boys should learn about hunting, fishing, farming, crafts like ironwork and woodcraft, treating weapon and learning the laws. It was also important to learn about culture and rules of conduct (Meulengracht Sørensen & Steinsland 1990:42-45). Was this really how it was? It is difficult to know for sure, but we have to be aware of our own values and preconceptions concerning gender rules.

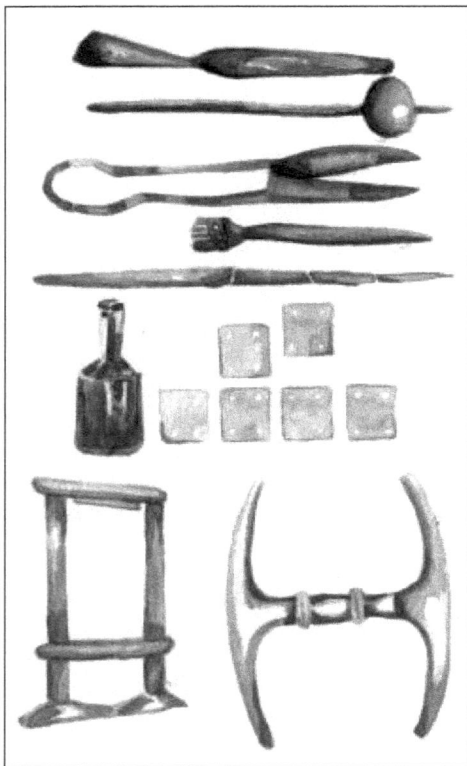

Figure 5.7 Different textile tools found in the Oseberg ship. Drawing by Margaretha Häggström 2003.

As I have shown here a lot of craftsmen are required, as well as different specialists within many areas, to produce both ordinary fabric as well as something as specialised as a tapestry. It is therefore not only the weaver who plays an important part in the procedure, but the whole chain of activities must function, from the farming of the sheep to the spinning of the wool and the weaving itself. It is therefore obvious that in the production of textiles a lot of interfaces are required. Also, groups of people who change in structure, connection or context may have been in conflict with each other. There may at least have been social tensions in discussions in what kind of work that

The farm as a concept is also a place where many different interests and gender groups meet, giving rise to many different kinds of negotiations. During the time we call the Viking Age, there is big change in the construction of houses. From the long houses used by both people and animals, you will now find different houses on the farm for different purposes (Christensen

1992c:171). In Nordic mythology you may find that the whole world is described in terms of different farms: *Utgård, Midgård and Asgård* (Varenius 1998:103ff). The farm is therefore a place for different kinds of dwellings, big as well as small, divine or human.

Figure 5.9 Wood work from the Oseberg wagon, reconstructed drawing by Mary Storm (After A.W. Brøgger1937).

Through trade and faraway travels, you may find room for negotiations about which people to trade with and with what kind of goods. Trade was an important and dominating part of Viking Age society and contacts between Viken and foreign countries were good. Import and export of luxury goods were frequent (Christensen 1992c:175). Another aspect of trade is that it was not only goods that were imported, but people were also a commodity. These slaves in turn brought new ideas, thoughts and traditions that could have had an impact on society and lead to negotiations, conflicts and changes. In these circumstances, you may also find constructions of gender relationships where there may exist different interests in both what to trade and with whom. Surely, there have been tensions in meeting with people from other countries, including trading with slaves. Finally, the pattern of contacts also includes tensions, reconstructions and negotiations of social relationships. During rituals, for example, different people have been given different roles and there are several examples of these kinds of tensions in the saga literature.

On farms like Oseberg and Haugen, there would probably have been big gatherings in connection with cultic events in winter, spring, summer and autumn. These events made it possible for people to gather and discuss news and daily problems. They could share new inventions, for example in house constructions and they could listen to stories from faraway travels, exchange gifts and show off new items (Christensen 1992c:175).

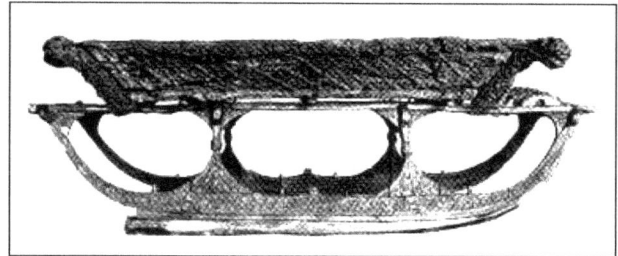

Figure 5.10 One of the sledges, found in the Oseberg ship (After Shetelig 1930).

Tensions may also have arisen on the farm between different craftsmen. This may have included the area "outside" the farm, for example in a competition about what kind of tools to make, depending on what seemed most important at the time or possessed a higher status. There may also have been tensions concerning the use of different areas of the farm. Some craftsmen might have worked on the farm, others might have moved around and there were probably different levels of status connected to different kinds of handicraft production. Eldrid Straume discusses the Iron Age smith and whether the smith had a high or low status and how this can be discovered in the grave material. She also deals with the question about people being domiciled. Her conclusion is that there were two kinds of smiths; the peasant smith that was connected to the farm and the specialised smith that worked on behalf of kings, chiefs and wealthy people (Straume 1986:45-58). I believe that a lot of these assumptions are also applicable on the production of textiles. There might have been a specialised production of finer cloth, tapestries and tablet weaving, as well as production of the "everyday" cloth, not forgetting the production of sails, which must have occupied a great deal of people.

Social divisions

In every society, independent of time or political structure, you may find hierarchies within areas like work, family and in all kinds of interaction between people. We might speculate about who was in control of the textile items, who chose the motifs fore the tapestries and who was in charge of and controlled the pieces when they were completed. Within these areas, there can be many situations where tensions may have arisen, concerning family and other issues such as marriage, travels, household influences, the treatment of slaves, the buying of new slaves.

The most important family constellation during the Viking Age was not the nuclear family but the clan. This family constellation was a lot bigger and could include people from many generations. You were a member of this family group, but not necessarily totally loyal to the whole group. The loyalty was chiefly directed to the immediate family (Meulengracht Sørensen & Steinsland 1990:17-18). There was in the Viking Age society a differential in gender rules, but these rules might also have been possible to transcend. Also, there seems to have been little suspicion against the capability of women in this society (Sawyer 1992:77).

In the division of labour, you would find tensions not only in the social division between husband and wife, but also between servants and slaves, and between different kinds of gender. The principle of the division of labour in Viking Age society is built upon a system of slaves. There also existed a social differentiation between slaves and in big households one slave could be responsible for watching the other slaves (Zwilgmeyer 1986:71). There is therefore room for different contexts for power to manifest, both between different women and also between women and men, concerning the working areas that were given priority and how well the work should be done. The working division between craftsmen is often presented as a division in making products for either common or artistic purposes. Against this view stands the fact that common items often are decorated artistically and there might have been other important divisions of labour than those we discuss today. Therefore, there might have existed contexts for power scenarios where craftsmen could win or lose influence over the common area or the holy area and where different genders could have held different positions.

The choice of motif in the production of tapestries was probably in the hands of the one who was responsible for the work. Also, we can assume that there might have been possibilities here for tensions, when the men, for example might have wanted special kinds of motifs that would increase their status. Women on the other hand, might have made other choices in their selection of motifs. Here you might find the tradition of storytelling a determining factor.

The choice of motif for the tapestries is probably a question about in the purpose in which the tapestries would be used. In the sagas, you can find stories about women weaving men's heroic actions. But what we actually can see in the fragments is stories about cultic events, women and mythology (Göransson 1999:135). In the oldest of the sagas, the Edda poems, you could get the impression that women were the bearers of the storytelling tradition (Mundal 1992:69-84). If women's stories were passed on from one generation to another, it would seem natural to also picture the stories in the tapestries.

Both the female and the male cult would also have been the scene for negotiations and tensions in the matter of both space and influence. In the prehistoric Nordic society, religion and daily life were connected and not separated. Rituals were part of everyday life. Women could have the opportunity to reecive high status as a priestess in the cult (Steinsland 1986:31-34). Anne Stine

Ingstad suggests that the "Oseberg queen" was a priestess of Freya and that many of the items in the ship were part of her cultic equipment (Ingstad 1992b:224-256).

Figure 5.11 Detail from one of the tapestries found in the Oseberg ship, reconstructed drawing by Mary Storm (After A.W. Brøgger 1937).

Negotiations and agreements

Why and for whom have these objects been made? Were they used as gifts? For exchange? In what kind of social context would they be found? Is it possible to discover different kinds of gender in this material?

These questions may raise speculations about how different constellations of gender have functioned and what tensions and meetings that may have given rise to the social renegotiations and agreements.

In most societies, items are used as a mark of social and economic status. The chiefdoms can be observed through the ideals shown in rune stones, in the sagas and in the material culture. Prestige was not the collection of wealth, but a matter of giving. The gift was the most important thing that made it possible to manipulate personal status. The gift had to be of high quality and generous enough to be of importance to the giver, so it would give him respect. The demand for quality should therefore be a ruling factor in producing material culture (Varenius 1992:29-33).

A tool for reaching higher status could have been to connect "artists" to important centres or big households. The high artistic quality of the items in the Oseberg ship has often been discussed, but the discussions have mostly focused on the wood work and not the textiles as something specifically artistic. The craftsmen that carved the wooden objects have later been given names like the baroque master and the academic (Christensen 1992b:154-164). The textile workers are rarely discussed in terms of artists and their work is not considered a piece of art in the same way as the wood and metal work. Instead it is mostly discussed as a matter concerning the household.

In the sagas you may find many places where tapestries are used to "dress" a room, to make the room worthy of prominent guests, often spoken of as royal. In many of the Icelandic Sagas you may find descriptions of heathen buildings decorated with tapestries, in several places (Salvén 1923:11-13). Arwill-Nordbladh also discusses how important it is to arrange a feast correctly. She mentions the saga of Gisle Sursson as an example of how the tapestries could play an important part in forming a social situation (Arwill-Nordbladh 1998:159-171).

It is possible to state that tapestries have existed within an aristocratic environment were they were objects that increased both wealth and status of the owner. They may also have played an important role as gifts, where high quality and artistic skill have been of great importance.

I have on this arena; put the tapestries in the centre. In this centre you may find negotiations in the contexts of action, the social actions and the social divisions. These negotiations will in turn lead to interpretations of renegotiations and agreements, which mean scenarios from contexts of action to contexts for power.

Figures 5.12-5.13 Wood work from, the wagon found in the Oseberg ship, reconstructed drawing by Mary Storm (After A.W. Brøgger 1937).

Discussion and Results

What are then my conclusions after using Margaret Conkey's method, like this?

By investigating the contexts of actions in the textile work which I have chosen, it is clear there were many places that involved opportunities and space for negotiation, concerning the changing of gender constructions. Opportunities were also offered when it came to areas where tensions arise which made it possible to question well known patterns.

My opinion is therefore, that because of the high status the textile work was given in the Oseberg grave, it seems that the buried persons were given this enormous burial, not necessarily because they were connected to an important man, but because of their own power. Through revealing the contexts of action and contexts for power scenarios, I believe that the production of textiles in this case has been of greater significance than just a production for household requirements. If they were only made to satisfy the household requirements, it would have seemed enough if just the mistress of the house had been involved in this work. It would not have been the work of many hands, which the tapestries probably are. In a big household, there would have been enough work to occupy everybody with the making of "everyday" textiles. It should therefore indicate something out of the ordinary if several women could be occupied with making tapestries. This kind of work demands skill and time as well as light. It therefore seems possible that it was a production connected to gifts with high status or trade that would have been of great importance in Viking Age society. Most of the weaving tools in the grave are connected to the weaving of tapestries and finer tablet weaving.

In the sagas, you may find a lot of places where the tapestries are mentioned with great respect, for example in the Gisle Sursson Saga where Gisle mentions tapestries as "items of great value". This could be a sign that these objects were demanded and highly desirable, which also means that they were something that was made for the public scene (Gisle Sursson Saga).

In the grave chamber at Haugen you will find no connection to any textile production. In this case, you can probably notice an example of the status of the tapestry. It was worthy decorating a tomb dedicated to a male chief. Tapestries therefore seem to be of importance to both men and women. Tapestries were probably taken good care of and used for many generations. Erling Johansen has speculated that the fragment from Haugen could be a depiction of the burial of the Tune ship (Johansen 1986:151). I would instead argue for the possibility that the fragment shows the burial at Oseberg. Facts, which I will base upon indications like the lack of weapon in the picture, the years that have passed between the burial in Oseberg and Tune, the close connection between the two places and their similarities as possible central places. The burial at Oseberg must have been a great event spoken about for generations afterwards. Therefore, such an event seems natural to make pictures and stories about.

Ellen Høigård Hofseth, among others argues that women could have had other roles beside the one most commonly presented; the mistress of the household. Høigård Hofseth says that women could have had important roles in trade, arguments which she bases among burial evidences from the trading place of Kaupang, where you can find a range of women's graves of the same status as men (Høigård Hofseth 1999:101-128). I also believe that women could have possessed other roles than the mistress of the household and roles involved with the cult. I will therefore argue for the additional role of artistic craftswomen of first rank. These assumptions are based upon the high status and great importance of the textile work in the Oseberg burial and the contexts of action and contexts for power scenarios I have drawn up. I therefore assert that the "Oseberg Queen" may have been a woman (or both) that was valued because of her crafts work and artistic quality, as an important person respected for her own qualities and not necessarily related to a man. - An important person who brought her family and estate high status, wealth and a lot of prestige. She or both of the buried women may have been respected because of this and not because they only had the role of the "mistress of the house", the wife of a king or a big chief, or at most a priestess connected to the goddess of Freja.

Summary

I have now given you a glimpse of how I have used Margaret Conkey´s method, context of action/ context for power in my work with the 8th- 9th century tapestries from Oseberg and Haugen in Norway. I have given you a brief historical background to the findings. I showed you, further on, how I have used Conkey´s method with a model in which I divided the material into different spheres with subheadings. The conclusion I drew from this is that it is possible to identify other roles played in the lives of Viking Age women different from the one of the mistress of the household or the Freya priestess. I have argued for the idea of the Viking Age woman as an artistic craftswoman with power beyond the areas "within". Also, I would like to claim, in contrary to others, that the art and craft of women were **not** anonymous in its expression, in the production or in the female discourse.

Finally I would also like to advocate the interpretative model of Margaret Conkey which I believe has great potential and presents us with a great challenge.

At last, I will give you some words of wisdom from the people on the Oseberg ship. These runes were written on an oar found on the Oseberg ship:

Humankind knows little.

Figure 5.14 Runes found on an oar on the Oseberg ship, collage by Anita Synnestvedt 2002

Acknowledgements

First of all I would give many thanks to Tove Hjørungdal for inviting me to her session in EAA in Thessalonica 2002 and for her support, good advices and interest in my work. It gave me a memorable experience, both in participation in the session and contributing in this volume. Thanks, also to the Institution of Archaeology in Gothenburg and Kristian Kristiansen, who gave me possibility to join the EAA conference. Many thanks to my friend Margaretha Häggström who so kindly made maps and drawings for this paper and also, I am very grateful to Victoria Holmqvist for her generous help with the English translation and good advices writing grammatically correct.

References

Arwill Nordbladh, E. 1998 *Genuskonstruktioner i nordisk vikingatid: förr och nu.* Göteborg.

Axelsson, S. 1999 Att befolka forntiden - människor på järnåldersgården vid Sund. *In Situ.* pp. 19-131.

Brøgger, A. W. 1917 Osebergfundets historie. In *Osebergfundet I*, eds. A. W. Brøgger, Hj. Falk & H. Schetelig, pp. 1-119. Kristiania.

Brøgger, A. W. 1920-21 *Rolvsøyætten. Et arkeologisk bidrag til vikingtidens historie.* Bergen.

Brøgger, A. W. 1937 Gullalder. *Viking I*: pp. 137-196.

Christensen, A. E. 1992 a Kongsgårdens håndverkere. In: *Osebergdronningens grav. Vår nasjonalskatt i nytt lys*, red. Ingstad, A. S. & Myhre, B., pp. 85-137. Chr. Schibsted forlag A/S. Oslo.

Christensen, A. E. 1992 b. Dronningens kunstnere. In: *Osebergdronningens grav. Vår nasjonalskatt i nytt lys*, red. Ingstad, A. S.& Myhre, B., pp. 154-166. Chr. Schibsted forlag A/S. Oslo.

Christensen, A. E. 1992 c. Livet på kongsgården. In: *Osebergdronningens grav. Vår nasjonalskatt i nytt lys*, red. Ingstad, A. S. & Myhre, B., pp. 167-175. Chr. Schibsted forlag A/S. Oslo.

Conkey, M. W. 1991 Contexts of Action Contexts for power: Material Culture and Gender in the Magdalenian. *Engendering Archaeology. Women and Prehistory,* eds. J. Gero & M. Conkey, pp. 57-92. Blackwell. Oxford.

Gisle Surssons saga (n.d.) Översättning (translated by) M. Malm, Stockholm.

Grenander Nyberg, G. 1976 *Så vävde de. Handvävning i Sverige och andra länder.* LT:s förlag. Stockholm.

Göransson, E.-M.,Y. 1999 *Bilder av kvinnor och kvinnlighet, -Genus och kroppsspråk under övergången till kristendomen.* Stockholm.

Hoftun, O. 1995 Jernaldersamfunnets kvinnlighet. *K.A.N. Kvinner i arkeologi i Norge,* Vol. 19-20, pp. 99-114.

Hougen, B. 1940 Osebergfunnets billedvev.*Viking* IV, pp. 85-124.

Høygård Hofseth, E. 1999 Historien bak handelskvinnen på Kaupang. Kvinnegraver fra vikingtid langs Vestfoldkysten. *Viking* LXII, pp. 101-128.

Ingstad, A. S. 1992 a Tekstilene i Osebergskipet. In: *Osebergdronningens grav. Vår nasjonalskatt i nytt lys,* red. Ingstad, A.S. & Myhre, B., pp. 176-208. Chr. Schibsted forlag A/S.Oslo.

Ingstad, A. S. 1992 b Oseberg- dronningen- hvem var hun? In: *Osebergdronningens grav. Vår nasjonalskatt i nytt lys,* red. Ingstad, A. S. & Myhre,B., pp. 224-256. Chr. Schibsted forlag A/S. Oslo.

Johansen, E. 1986 Billedveven fra Haugen – en arkeologisk åpenbaring i farger. *Viking* XLIX, pp. 147 -152. Oslo.

Zwilgmeyer, V. 1986 *Viking kvinnen: liv. lov. virke.* Tiden. Oslo.

Mandt, G. 1992. Hva styrer våre valg av tolkningsmodeller? Om framveksten av ett nytt perspektiv i arkeologisk forskning. *K.A.N. Kvinner i arkeologi i Norge,* vol. 13-14: pp. 78-113.

Meulengracht Sørensen, P. & Steinsland, G. 1990 *För kristendommen. Diktning og livssyn i vikingetiden.* Gyldendal forlag. København.

Mundal, E. 1992 *Fokus på kvinner i middela derkilder,* eds. Sellevold, B., Mundal, E. & Steinsland, G. Viktoria förlag. Skara.

Myhre, B. 1992 Kildeproblem ved bruk av arkeologisk materiale, In: *Osebergdronningens grav. Vår nasjonalskatt i nytt lys,* red. Ingstad, A. S. & Myhre, B., pp. 279-285. Chr. Schibsted forlag A/S. Oslo.

Salvén, E. 1923 *Bonaden från skog. Undersökning av en nordisk bildvävnad från tidig medeltid.* Stockholm.

Sawyer, B. 1992 *Kvinnor och familj i det forn- och medeltida Skandinavien.* Viktoria förlag. Skara.

Shetelig, H. 1930 *Det norske folks liv og historie gjennem tidene: Fra oldtiden til omkring 1000 e.Kr.* Oslo.

Steinsland, G. 1985 Kvinner og kult i vikingetid. *Kvinnearbeid i Norden fra vikingtiden til reformasjonen, foredrag fra et nordisk kvinnehistorisk seminar i Bergen 3-7 August 1983,* pp. 31-42.Bergen.

Straume, E. 1986 Smeden i jernalderen, bofast- ikke bofast, høy eller lav status. *Universitetets Oldsaksamling, Årbok 1984/1985,* pp. 45-58. Oslo.

Varenius, B. 1992 *Det nordiska skeppet, teknologi och samhällsstrategi i vikingatid och medeltid.* Stockholm studies in archaeology, 10. Stockholm.

Folk belief and society
An example from Northern Sweden

Lillian Rathje

Västerbotten Museum, Umeå, Sweden

Abstract

This paper reflects on how relational analogies, and especially notions of folk belief, can be used in order to comprehend prehistoric societies. For a case study the Late Iron Age and Early Medieval Periods in coastal Västerbotten, Northern Sweden, are chosen. By putting together different kinds of materials one can create a contextual model for such entities as ideology, economy, social relations, and the relations between these entities. A general conclusion of this study, is that coastal society in Västerbotten could be said to actively emphasize society's social structure as relatively egalitarian in early historic times, without stressing any particular social category or gender.

Introduction

The aim of this paper is to reflect on how relational analogies, and especially notions of folk belief, can be used in order to comprehend prehistoric societies. In order to recognize how people lived their lives, one has to try to understand how they were organized on different levels, concerning mutual relations as well as relations to the surrounding world.

A prehistoric society can be dealt with on different levels, from the level of the individual to the society as a whole. The different levels demand different analytical tools and offer different materials. By relations between these different levels, society can be specified and understood (cf. Crumley 1994). One or more levels can change at an uneven rate and some cultural dimensions change faster than others. When culture is viewed as an abstraction it is easy to forget the fact that we are dealing with humans as actors in an ongoing process. It is not cultures that meet but people who are engaged in both cultural meetings and in cultural conflicts. People are creating and recreating their being in the world from contextual premises (Svanberg 1999:15). This does not mean that I view society as just the sum of individuals; it is more than that. The social system of which the individual is part, must be understood with a point of departure in the whole (Durkheim [1895] 1978). The best way to begin to create a model of society is thus to take a point of departure in social relations and social structures on a local level, rather than in ecological and technological structures, when investigations of the cultural expression of society are aimed at (Nordquist 2001:21). This approach would enable us to see the complexity of social conditions. Together with a broader perspective, a positive interpretational spiral can be created (Forsberg 1999:281). One way of doing this is to use ethnographic and historical sources rather close in time and place to the archaeological material one tries to understand. This kind of material can be used to create new insights and to give a starting point for a thick description of society (cf. Geertz 1993:10). I want to reflect on how folk belief and

traditions can contribute to a model better in line with material and social relations as reflected in early historic and probably in prehistoric societies. The central feature in belief concepts is to conserve the prevailing structure of society.

A better part of Swedish folk belief material shows that there is a clear distinction between northern and southern parts of the country. I interpret this distinction as an indication of differences between the regions, in conceptions of the world and in structures of society as well.

To illuminate this, I will comment on concepts of two distinct subjects to folk belief, namely on concepts about causes of illness in folk medicine, and on concepts about the whore. Folk belief is active in a context, and thus I think that folk belief in the northern parts of Sweden can be seen as part of the egalitarian strategy that was at work in there during the late Iron Age. This is communicated in such various social phenomena as on the one hand simple graves, and on the other hand the practice of teamwork. As a contrast, folk belief and the evidence of Æsir-beliefs in the southern parts of the country, together with the character of the physical remains, reflect a more hierarchical structure.

The land of the Amazons

As a case study I have chosen the Late Iron Age and the Early Medieval Period in the coastal area of Västerbotten, Northern Sweden (*Figure 6.1*). By piecing together different kinds of materials one can create a contextual model for such entities as ideology, economy, social relations, and the relations between these entities. In a contextual model the material culture is viewed as active in social strategies and as part of the construction of both the material and the immaterial aspects of daily life (Hodder 1986). The material remains can thus, together with other sources, make up a foundation for questions about the way humans lived in, acted in, and imagined the world. The use of this kind of material has however to be carried out with caution; there is a long time span between the Iron Age and the earliest historical records from the 16th century, dealing with economy and settlement structure. Besides, the material on folk culture and popular beliefs are mostly from the 17th to 19th century. And even if the ethnohistorical material is close in time to the material sources, they should not be used without critical evaluation. One of the most obvious flaws with the methodology is that it is produced without a gender critical analysis. Something that often is missing in models about prehistoric societies is the relation between different sex/gender categories as well as differences within categories along with the meaning of socialization in the keeping and changing of cultural patterns (Rathje 1999, 2001). The area of investigation, has by the Finnish ethnologist Helmer Tegengren (1965), been suggested to be the land of the "Amazons". This label corresponds to a reference from Adam of Bremen and his descriptions of the Nordic islands around AD 1080. Adam's narration says that north of the vast area ruled by the Sveones, was the land of the females. Tegengren suggests that this is not a fable but has a factual background. He believes that the notion can be connected with the late winter coastal economy that left farms populated by women while the men were all out on the ice for sealing.

Figure 6.1. Area of investigation

According to earlier interpretations, the coastal area of Västerbotten was sparsely populated and lacking sedentary settlement during the Iron Age. This period was characterized by a marked border that parted two areas of very different character as concerns antiquities. South of the border there was a hierarchical system, marked by grave mounds and three-aisled long houses (Ramqvist 1983, 1998). In the area of the present investigation, no

houses have been found, but with respect to other ancient monuments, especially the occurrence of stone settings and hut foundations in the same geographical area, a cultural zone can be delimited, which stands out from the surrounding areas.

Figure 6.2 Map drawn from the writings of Adam of Bremen c. 1080 AD (After Lund 1978:21).

During early historic times, the coastal area of Västerbotten was a relatively homogeneous farming society. The dominating settlement structure was small farms. The large farms and estates that were common in other parts of the country, were absent. In the late the Middle Ages, there was a well-established rural community in the coastal area. The 161 villages mentioned in tax records from the middle of the 16th century, probably have their roots so far back in time. The population in these villages were versatile and the villages often self-sufficient, with an economy based on fishing, seal hunting, and husbandry, and to a lesser degree on agriculture. The lack of available men that were not themselves landowners, also promotes the picture of a society that lacks hierarchical structure (Ahnlund 1955; Hellström 1917; Jonsson 1971; Olofsson 1962a & b; Vikström 1994a & b).

The Late Iron Age economy was probably mixed, including stock breeding, agriculture, and seal hunting. Pollen diagrams from this area show that barley and rye, as well as flax and hemp were cultivated from AD 400–500 and that cattle breeding was of importance, though datable remains are scarce (Broadbent 1982:157; Engelmark 1976:99 ff.; Engelmark & Wallin 1996:1f.). The plenty of hut foundations along the coast, dating from AD 400 to the Early Medieval Period, and mostly to the Viking Age as well, prove the importance of seal hunting (Broadbent 2000).

Figure 6.3 Different building traditions in northern Scandinavia during the Iron Age.
According to Ramqvist (1992: 74) there is an empty space, void of settlement, in the coastal area of Västerbotten.

A model for the relationship between the Iron Age seal-hunting camps, presumably used for collective hunts, and contemporary settlement based on where there is arable land today, has been put forward by Noel Broadbent. Hunting huts are grouped regionally, and the grouping of 3–5 huts suggests a hunting team with the same construction as historically known fishing teams. The same structure can be discerned from tax records on maps from the 16th century and from recordings on fishing camps from the 19th century (Broadbent 1988:153 ff.,1991). The similarities in the structure of sealing, together with the fact that the social structure seams fairly unchanged from the oldest tax records on to the 19th century, make it possible to use relational analogies in order to make an explanatory model for this society.

Such models ought to be contextual and cannot be based solely on archaeological material. If we only use the visible archaeological material known to us today, we would be left with a picture of a society where seal-hunters, supposedly male, expressed their identity in the hunting areas, and a burial tradition that supposedly played down the markings of identity. That, I think, is not especially interesting or illuminating for the understanding of the community in the coastal area.

The archaeological features, together with the traces of agriculture and husbandry indicate the presence of a settled population expressing their own cultural identity, in many ways different to the ways of their neighbours to the south.

The context of gendered action

All kinds of work are part of the creation and strengthening of social relations and thereby social processes that mirror and symbolize other aspects of society. Sex/gender categories can be viewed as structuring elements in the material and social life of a society. To these categories are attached to different sets of rules, norms, and expectations about the behaviour within, and relations between the categories. Because of this, individuals' actions are limited according to culturally defined norms. This affects the individual's sense of self as well as sense of other.

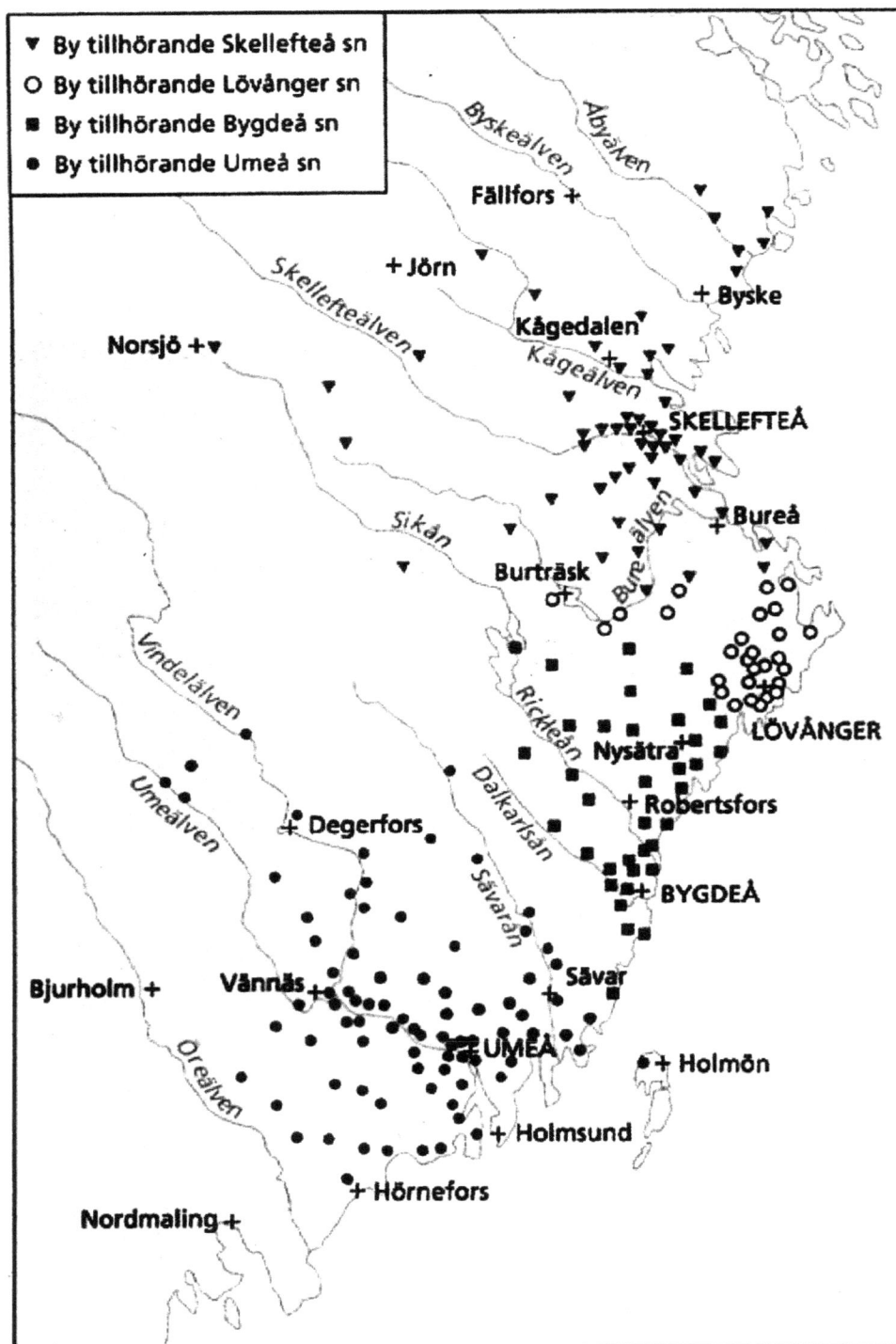

*Figure 6.4 The same area as in Figure 6.3; in the beginning of the 16th century,
it had a number of 161 villages
(After Vikström 1994b: 58).*

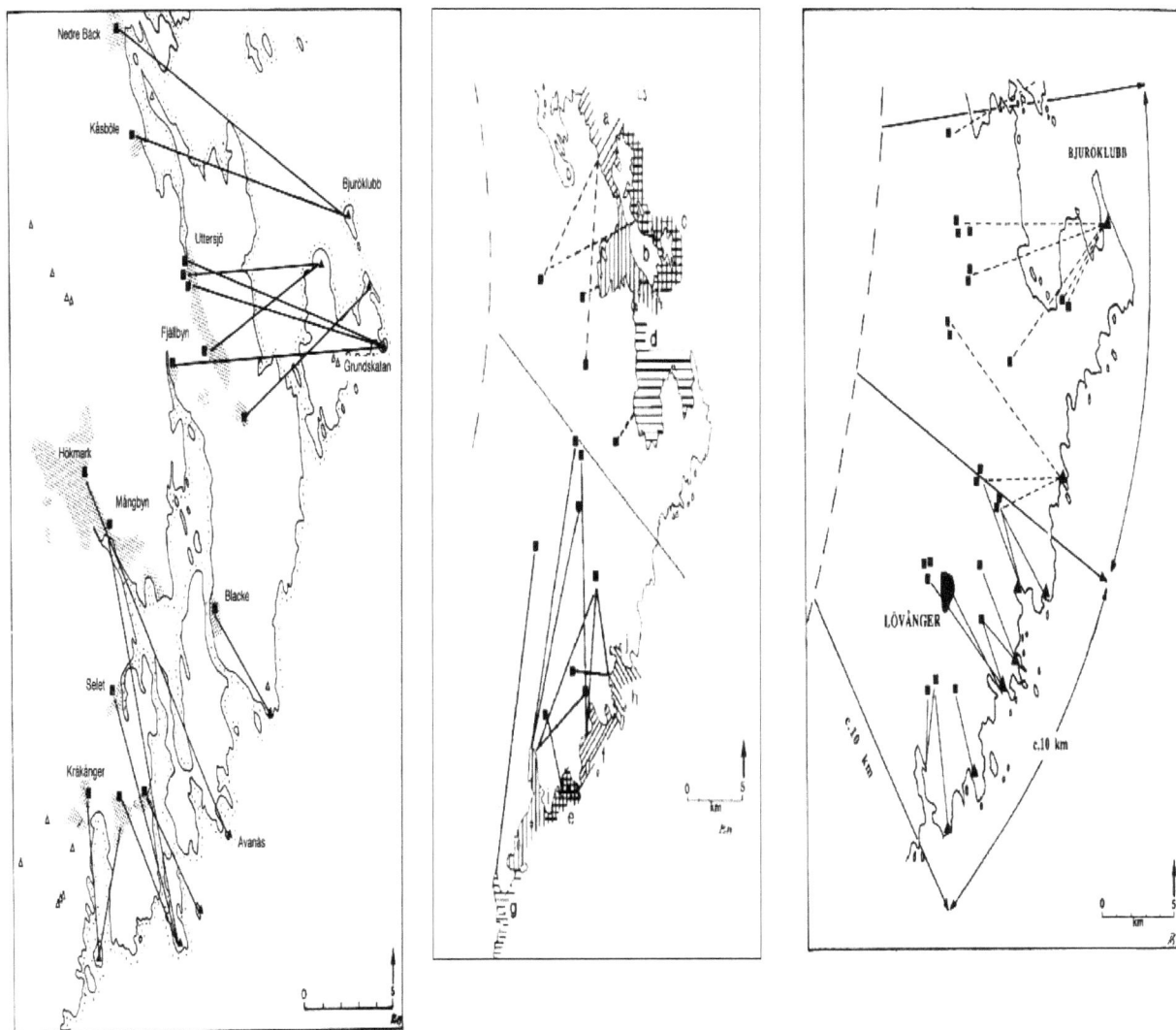

Figure 6.5. Seal hunting during Viking Age (with supposed settlement areas) and Medieval Age (with connection to villages according to taxations from the 16th century) and fishing during the 19th century have in large the same structure (After Broadbent 1991:230, 226, 227).

Figure 6.6 One of the main archaeological features in the region are hut foundations (Photo: Västerbottens museum).

The categories are thus always situational and dynamic. They are not fixed through time or from place to place (Arwill-Nordbladh 1998:174 f., Conkey 1991, Moore 1994:8 ff., Ortiz 1994:893 ff., Rasmussen 2001).

Humans are not, I think, independent bodies that can perform what any acts they wish. Culture has to be taught, with its possibilities and restraints. The direction our actions take is then a mixture of different kinds of knowledge from within our own society and knowledge from outside. The choices we make are dependent upon our view of the world, which is not always, if ever, logical in the western philosophical sense. It is important to recognize that contemporary culture and society are constituted historically, locally, and willfully. At the same time that the existing normative discourses influence the individuals' behavior, it also creates the basis for change (Liliequist 1999:38 f.). One way to view the cultural expressions of a society is to view them as a process where stories are the basis of interpretation of reality and thereby for action in different circumstances.

If we look at the historical records, division of labour have been strictly divided and assigned to teams of one sex/gender category. Male teams performed seal hunting, and contrary to other parts of Europe, husbandry was performed by female teams. These teams were probably strongly traditional, rooted in the local community and characterized by a non-hierarchical structure.

Figure 6.7. The seal hunting teams were organised in groups of men who where neighbours and/or related to each other. The age of the participants varied from seven to over seventy years (Photo: Västerbottens museum).

In the coastal area of Västerbotten there are no evidence for more than two institutionalised and normative sex/gender categories (cf. Nanda 2000:1 ff.), which seasonally acted in different contexts. These contexts have separate local settings, the archaeologically visible seal-hunting camps (and the not visible ice-hunt camps as in *Figure 6.7*) and the not yet archaeologically detected places for husbandry — possibly the shielings or summer farms.

The matter of belief

Cultural identity is expressed by material culture, and there are visible differences between the investigated area and the neighbouring areas. The immaterial differences in cultural identity are harder to come by. These expressions can be indicated by ethnographic material, for example the notions on folk belief.

Folk belief should be viewed not as a system, but as a process, and therefore in a continuous change. The beliefs are diversified and can for that reason only be described in fragments, in their observed, social and conceptionalist manifestation. In order to make it possible to understand the belief system, one has to put the fragments together

into a wholeness and at the same time do justice to contradictions and dynamics (Rydving 1993:10).

Figure 6.8 The local setting of gender separated working teams often excluded the other normative gender category, as seen in this picture. It is obvious that small boys and girls, not yet part of the normative sex/gender category, had their place in the shieling. But if you look at the man to the left, it is obvious that he is present in the shieling just for the photographic session (Photo: Västerbottens museum).

Religious expressions of society can be found on different levels, expressing everything from the religion of an elite to more popular beliefs (Larsson 1999). These levels can further have different extensions in space as well as in time. It is probable that the concepts of folk belief are more obsolete and less subject to change here, and therefore may find themselves as part of a long process in which old beliefs may linger for a long time in daily social processes.

Our conceptions of reality are culturally specific and vary with time, place, and social environment. Popular beliefs in different areas reflect to a certain degree the prevailing social order (Leach 1976). I think therefore, that there is a need to emphasize the northern folk-beliefs and traditions in order to build a model that is better in line with material and social relations as reflected in early historic and probably late prehistoric societies along the coast of Västerbotten.

However, I think that the often-used analogies with Æsir-beliefs, when addressing questions about Iron Age society in the Nordic countries, are not useful in this area. There is no material evidence, neither Thorshammers nor grave mounds, which can be connected with that belief-system. Instead I will use the folk belief found in the Northern regions during historic times.

Anthropologists have long claimed that people's religious conceptions and their social organization are closely related. In different studies it has been shown that the supernatural order is a kind of projection of human social relations (Godelier 1977, Keesing 1998). With this in mind one can look at folk belief as a kind of mirror or projection of the human world.

This is of course not a direct reflection, but by looking at what kind of supernatural beings that exist in a society, one can to a certain degree see the scale of that society's political organization. The popular beliefs cannot be seen as separated from everyday life, but as active in social processes and can thus not be viewed as independent from other parts of society.

Conceptions of folk belief affect people's actions, to a greater or lesser degree, but they are also an analogy of how society ought to be constituted. The central feature in belief concepts is to conserve the prevailing structure in society. Accusations of crime against behaviour laws of a society, for example accusations about witchery or whoredom, are commonly directed downwards in a hierarchical society. Thereby they do not threaten the prevailing structure (Douglas 1966:3). It might be said that greater changes in people's conceptions of the world are slower in non-hierarchical societies, but when society develops hierarchies, changes occur as well in concepts of the world.

Our conceptions of reality are culturally specific and vary in time, place and with social environment. This culturally specific conception of reality generates specific mental pictures of reality, pictures that affect our categorization of reality and the structure by which we determine our categories. Our cognitive model of reality is thus based on our physical, mental and emotional experience of the world and on our conceptions. Our way of interacting with the world is thus of great importance to our way of structuring our categories (Westum 1999:217).

Folk belief as a norm giver

A better part of Swedish folk belief material, from the 17th century and onwards, shows a clear distinction between the northern and the southern parts of the country. I interpret this as an indication of differences in conceptions of the world and in social structure between these areas.

If the point of departure is the individual and the individual's relation to other individuals in different positions in society, the perspective has to be directed to integration rather than variation and to content rather than to form. One should not, as in earlier research, make a distinction between humans' spiritual world, ritual behaviour and the society in which this phenomenon occurs.

The main focus in the analysis of folk belief is thus to be based on society's structure and on the norms that maintained and defined this structure. A consequence of this, is that folk belief has to be studied both in its context and in a wider cultural perspective. In order to gain a deeper understanding of the structure, one also should look at different material fields of action, i.e., the social activities that involve the use and creation of material culture. These fields of action can be seen as fundamental components in society's social structure, and life in society can be said to be constituted by various partly coincidental fields of action, where matter to different degrees is transformed into material objects characterized by human action and intention. In analysis of the relations between these fields of action, we can gain a deeper understanding of imbedded conflicts, both between the perspectives of social groups as well as between the social reality and the ideological representation (Nordquist 1999:23). The theoretical notion that one single subsystem could be viewed as representation of the whole system cannot show the conflicting concepts existing for example in folk belief.

To illuminate the difference in folk belief between the southern and northern parts of Sweden, I will comment on concepts about causes of illness in folk medicine, and on concepts about the whore.

Words and categories do not arise from a cultural vacuum but can be viewed as more or less clear mirrors or vague silhouettes of the culture in which they have raised. In order to understand the semantics of popular categories and how these categories are connected, it is important to emphasize the popular concepts of the world and, in accordance with this, the mental historical connection where it has its natural position (Westum 1999:10). In the same way that Durkheim claimed that humans were a reflex of social experiences and institutions, Young claimed (1976) that popular notions about diseases explain and confirm important truths about society and its social relations (Frykman 1977:5 ff)

Disease, cure and cause

Within the field of folk medicine, there are many concepts of belief that has long traditions. Access to academic medicine is a late phenomenon in the northern parts of Sweden. The first barber came to Västerbotten in 1648. In the year 1781, there was one doctor's office in Umeå. In the middle of the 19th century there were 5 hospitals, but they were small. In Umeå, for example, there were only 8 beds for the sick. In light of these circumstances, it is not hard to understand that traditions of folk medicine have had a strong hold on people up to historic times (Rathje 1983).

One of the diseases that were threatened within folk medicine was *skäver/riset*, a disease that within academic medicine is commonly referred to as rickets, but a disease that was viewed as having many different causes and treatments in folk medicine. In light of the discussion above, this disease could be viewed as a symptom of the society, rather than a disease by today's meaning, and thus may mirror something fearful in relation to the surrounding world. In this light, the child itself is rather like a minor character (Frykman 1977:26). Within folk medicine illness is classified by cause rather than by symptom, and this explanation sometimes had the characteristic of role instructions for the mother-to-be about how she should behave in different situations.

In south-western Sweden diseases have been seen as caused by humans, whom one actually knew and who lived in the neighbourhood, who could not or would not be allowed to adjust to the moral norms and lifestyles in society. These persons were thus viewed as a threat to society and the normative lifestyle. In southern Sweden there was a greater population density and a more stratified social structure, and fears were channelled to people who did not fit in. Research on the concepts of *skäver* has shown that more and more marginalized groups were mentioned in the naming of the diseases, which in its turn could be interpreted in terms of more insecure surroundings (Stattin 1991). The diseases in this area were explained as caused because the mother-to-be had met some of these "unclean" persons. It was thus these socially marginalized persons who were seen as dangerous, as "unclean", and this created a way to keep different classes of people separated. Accusations of "uncleanness" were a way to conserve the ruling social order in this farming society. *Skävern* could be used as a corrective, as a way to make the wrongdoer adjust in conformity with the norms. Gypsies, *rackare* (horse butchers) and beggars were seen as more dangerous than for example *löndahoror* (whores that had hidden their shame); these categories could actively cause the illness. Everything that did not have a part in daily life was dangerously strange. The risk for a child to die during the first weeks of life was also a harsh reality. The more concepts about rickets that are studied, the more obvious it is that the concepts bear witness to the way in which people categorized their surroundings (Frykman 1977:52).

The relatively egalitarian structure of society in northern Sweden is on the other hand visible in the fact that the division into different classes was rare north of the so-called *Limes Norrlandicus* (that is the old border between Southern and Northern Sweden). The background to prejudices against for example *rackare* was thereby missing. In other parts of the country, horse butchers were marginalized and ordinary people did not want to have anything to do with them (Egardt 1962). In northern Sweden, the structure of society was different, and the fears and explanations of causes were instead transferred to supernatural beings. In this area it was the people themselves who through their own doing, conscious or unconscious, in relation to the *vittra* (the common being in the north) caused the problem. *Vittra* was a being that in conformity with people lived in family groups; they also had the same modes of subsistence that other groups in the north, such as engaging in stockholding or herding reindeer (Dahlstedt 1983). Diseases were in this area thus not seen as caused by marginalized people. Another difference

between the southern and northern parts of Sweden in the attribution to rickets, *skäver/riset*, is that in the former area it often referred to cause while in the later area it instead refereed to symptom (Westum 1999:173).

For both areas there were also many conceptions of the way in which a mother-to-be could cause illness for her child; if she for example was looking at a fire the child got birthmarks in form of fire marks. This kind of explanation does not have much to say about the structure of society, but about how the woman should behave according to norms.

To view the mother as directly causing the child's illness is not reasonable. It is not the mother that is evil; she is only the medium used by supernatural powers to harm the child. She is also the one who can take preventive measures by avoiding certain situations and actions. This is her responsibility. The fact that the mother can be seen as the mediator can be explained by the term "liminality". As with the unborn child, the mother is in a liminal state; she is in that way closer to the supernatural and thereby also more susceptible to the influence of such powers.

The matter of sexuality

There is also a difference between the north and the south in views on sexuality and marriage, with the tradition of *nattfrieri*, courtship at night, in the north and the more rigorously arranged marriages in the south. According to Jonas Frykman (1977:14 ff.), the problem of sexuality should be attacked from a socio-cultural angle. The actual intercourse could be viewed from three different interrogative sentences, which have to do with norms, relations and the situation.

These sentences are:
• What cultural norms exist for sexual actions?
• What are the social status of the involved and their status in the social landscape?
• What time and place is at issue?

From these kinds of questions the northern tradition can be interpreted as a symptom of an non-authoritarian relationship between youth and elders – but it does not necessarily bear witness to an open-minded attitude to youths' sexuality (Frykman 1977:15). In line with this the view of the whore (the unwed mother) also varied between different parts of the country.

The whore was only dangerous in her direct relation with other women; at a distance she was no threat. Her danger could be seen in both the public and the private sphere, and there was a significant difference between these areas, each with its own specific character and function. In the public sphere she had to mark herself with *horluva* (a specific cloth on her head), which immediately signalled her potential dangerousness and thus regulated her relation with married women.

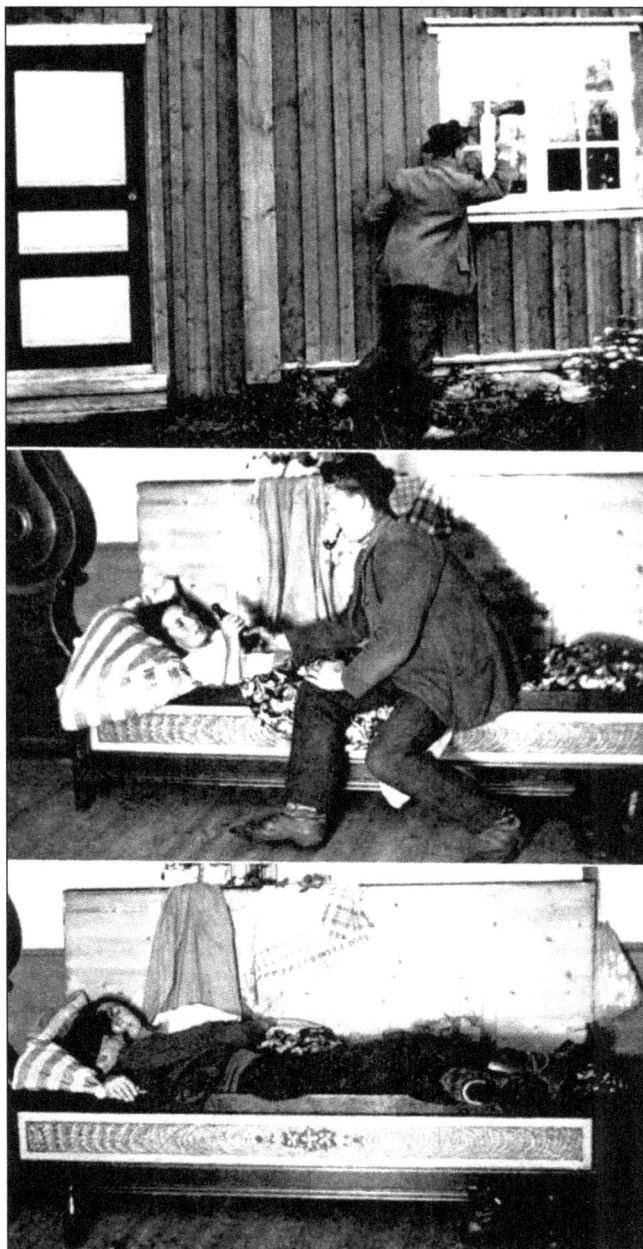

Figure 6.9. Arranged pictures of nattfrieri the courtship at night. The younger men go around in groups to younger women in the area, and one of them stays when invited. He then presents her with some gift, and lie down besides her, but he is seldom invited under the blanket. If he comes down to coffee in the morning, marriage is considered a possibility (After Hellspong and Löfgren 1977:257).

The region in which she was seen as causing illness to children encompasses to a great extent the same area where women almost up till today had fewest children outside marriage, and where there thus were few obvious whores. The concept of whore-*skäver* is thus in its essence a way of expressing a society with a structure with provable and restrictive moral control (Frykman 1977:73 f.).

As dangerous as the whore was in the female sphere, as lucky she was in the male sphere. To meet a whore on the way to fishing or hunting gave good luck. On the other hand, to meet a honourable woman was bad luck, because to meet such a woman out alone was an anomaly. The men were thus not threatened and not the ones who made sanctions against the whore. The whore's actual possibilities to work were often limited to work that normally was considered males' work. This work was in most cases outdoors (Frykman 1977:87).

Common roads were places in which whores had full legitimacy to be present, but where married women ought to be seen only in company with her husband. This was a way to keep married women off the roads. Odd Nordlander (1956–57) has given one of the Norwegian pregnancy prohibitions an explanation that is coherent with this. The concept that pregnant women were a much-sought prey for the bears could be derived from the fact that the husband had few means to control his wife's decency. This was especially true in the north where women spent the summers in shielings.

In the south folk belief included different ways to cast spells in order to make "loose" women pregnant. In the northern parts, on the other hand, the only occasion when means of conception are discussed in folk belief is as a means to promote pregnancy within marriage (Frykman 1977:105). Children outside marriage have existed in both these areas, but the sanction-givers were of different social status. In the south, it was the collective of married and honourable women who sanctioned the unwed mother; in the north it was the youth who ridiculed both the mother and the supposed father. It was also much easier to become honourable again in the northern parts of the country.

There are, besides the above-mentioned concepts in popular culture, other concepts in folk belief that mirror these differences between the north and the south. While the *vittra* affect all people, in good or bad ways, there are beings that have their primary existence in the south that are more gender-specific. These are *näcken* (the water man) and *skogsrået* (the forest woman) whose dangerousness primarily was directed towards the opposite sex.

Conclusion

Folk belief has acted in a context, and I think that the notions on folk belief, in connection with the simple graves and the presence of teamwork, can be seen as part of the egalitarian strategy that was at work in northern Sweden during the Late Iron Age. The lack of permanent marginalized persons and the view of supernatural beings as the cause of sickness in the north make it possible to conclude that the society along the coast of Västerbotten in early historic times could be said to actively emphasize society's social structure as relatively egalitarian, without stressing any particular social category or gender. The tradition of *nattfrieri* can also point in this direction and be viewed in connection with the neolocal reproductive strategy, as opposed to the arranged marriages in the southern Sweden, which instead can be seen in the light of a continuity strategy (cf. Blanton 1994). It is probable that the church's claim for power and authority, and a hierarchical vision of society did not yet have domination

in all areas when the concepts of the folk belief were written down.

References

Ahnlund, N. 1955. *Västerbotten före Gustav Vasa*. Umeå.

Ambrosiani, B. 1971. *Arkeologisk undersökning 1966. Hornslandsudde, Rogsta socken, Hälsingland*. RAÄ-rapport 1971 B. Stockholm.

Arwill-Nordbladh, E. 1998. *Genuskonstruktioner i nordisk vikingatid. Förr och nu*. GOTARC Series B. No. 9. Göteborg.

Blanton, R.E. 1994. *Houses and Households. A Comparative Study*. New York & London.

Broadbent, N. 1982. *Den förhistoriska utvecklingen under 7000 år*. Skellefteå-bygdens historia 3. Skellefteå: Skellefteå Kommun.

Broadbent, N. 1988. Järnålderns och medeltidens säljägare i övre Norrlands kustland. In: Baudou, E. (ed.): *Arkeologi i norr* 1, pp.145–165. Umeå: University of Umeå, Department of Archaeology.

Broadbent, N. 1991. Järnålderns sälfångst i Bottniska viken. Om ett nordligt socioekonomiskt och kognitivt system. In Wik, B. (ed.): *Sentrum–periferi. Sentra og sentrumdannelser gjennom førhistorisk og historisk tid. Den 18. nordiske arkeologkongress, Trondheim 28.8.–4.9.*

Broadbent, N. 1989. Gunneria 64. Wik, B. (ed.): pp. 223–231. Trondheim: Universitetet i Trondheim Vitenskapsmuseet.

Broadbent, N. 2000. Seal hunters, labyrinth builders and church villagers. The seal hunting cultures project. In: Lindgren, B., Nordquist, P. & Rathje, L. (eds.): *Tidsperspektiv. Tidskrift för arkeologisk samhällsanalys* 1/2000, pp. 7–21.

Conkey, M. W. 1991. Context of action/contexts for power. Material culture and gender in the Magdalenian. In: Gero, J.M. & Conkey, M.W. (eds.): *Engendering Archaeology*, pp. 57–92. Oxford: Basil Blackwell.

Crumley, C. L.(ed.): 1994. *Historical Ecology*. Santa Fe: School of American Research.

Dahlstedt, T. 1983. Tro och föreställningar kring vitra i Övre Norrland. In: Dahlstedt, T. & Arvidsson, A. (eds.): *Vitra och bäran. Två studier i norrländsk folktro*. Skrifter.

Serie C. Folkminnen och folkliv, No 3, pp. 1–77. Umeå: Dialekt-, Ortnamns- och Folkminnesarkivet.

Durkheim, É. [1895] 1978. *Sociologins metodregler*. Göteborg: Bokförlaget Korpen.

Douglas, M. 1966. *Purity and Danger: An Analysis of the Concepts of Pollution and Taboo*. London: Routledge & Keagan Paul.

Egardt, B. 1962. *Hästslakt och rackarskam: En etnologisk undersökning av folkliga fördomar*. Nordiska museets handlingar 21. Stockholm: Nordiska museet.

Engelmark, R. 1976. The vegetational history of the Umeå area during the last 4000 years. In:

Engelmark, R. (ed.): *Paleo-ecological Investigations in Coastal Västerbotten, Northern Sweden*, Early Norrland 9, pp. 75–111. Stockholm: Almqvist & Wiksell International.

Engelmark, R. & Wallin, J. E. 1996. Naturresurser och odling i norra Västerbottens kustland från sen vikingatid till nutid. Resultat av pollenanalys. Unpublished paper. Umeå: University of Umeå, Department of Archaeology. Forsberg, L. 1999. The Bronze Age site at Mårtenfåboda in Nysätra and the settlement context of the cairns on the coast of North Sweden. In: Hurre, M. (ed.): *Dig It All. Papers Dedicated to Ari Siiriäinen*, , pp. 251–285. Helsingfors: Finnish Antiquarian Society.

Frykman, J. 1977. *Horan i bondesamhället*. Lund: LiberLäromedel.

Geertz, C. 1993. *The Interpretation of Cultures*. London: Fontana.

Godelier M. 1977. Economy and religion. An evolutionary optical illusion. In: Friedman, J. & Rowlands, M. (eds.): *The Evolution of Social Systems*, , pp. 3–12. London: Duckworth.

Hellspong, M & Löfgren, O. 1977. *Land och stad. Svenska samhällstyper och livsformer från medeltid till nutid*. Lund: LiberLäromedel.

Hellström, P.1917. *Norrlands jordbruk*. Norrländskt handbibliotek IV. Uppsala.

Hodder, I. 1986. *Reading the Past. Current Approaches to Interpretation in Archaeology* Cambridge: Cambridge University Press.

Jonsson, I. 1971. *Jordskatt och kameral organisation i Norrland under äldre tid*. Kungl. Skytteanska Samfundets Handlingar 9. Umeå.

Keesing, R. M. 1981. *Cultural Anthropology. A Contemporary Perspective*, 2nd ed. New York: Holt, Rinehart and Winston.

Larsson, T. B. 1999. Symbols, divinities and the reproduction of social inequality. In Goldhahn, J. & Nordquist, P. (eds.): *Marxistiska perspektiv inom Skandinavisk arkeologi*. Arkeologiska studier vid Umeå universitet 5, pp. 49–84. Umeå: University of Umeå, Department of Archaeology and Sami Studies.

Leach, E. R. 1976. *Culture and Communication. The Logic by Which Symbols Are Connected*. Cambridge: Cambridge University Press.

Liliequist, M. 1999. Socialisation från vaggan till graven. In: Ehn, B. (ed.): *Kultur och erfarenhet. Aktuella teman i svensk etnologi*, pp. 11–39. Stockholm: Carlsson.

Lund, A. A. 1978. *Adam af Bremen. Beskrivels af øerne i Norden. Oversat og kommenteret af Allan A. Lund*. Højbjerg: Wormianum.

Moore, H. L. 1994. *A Passion for Difference. Essays in Anthropology and Gender*. Cambridge: Polity Press.

Nanda, S. 2000. *Gender Diversity. Crosscultural Variations*. Prospect Heights: Waveland Press.

Nordlander, O. 1957. Mannbjørn. Ein studie i heimfestningsproblemet ved vandresegn. In: *By og bygd* 1956–1957, pp. 133– 156.

Nordquist, P. 2001. *Hierarkiseringsprocesser. Om konstruktionen av social ojämlikhet i Skåne, 5500–1100 f.Kr.* Studia Archaeologica Universitatis Umensis 13. Umeå: University of Umeå, Department of Archaeology and Sami Studies.

Olofsson, S. I. 1962a. Övre Norrlands medeltid. In: Westin, G. (ed.): *Övre Norrlands historia* 1, pp. 123– 251. Umeå: Norrbottens och Västerbottens läns landsting.

Olofsson, S. I. 1962b. Övre Norrlands historia under Gustav Vasa och hans söner. In: Westin, G. (ed.): *Övre Norrlands historia* 1, pp. 253–516. Umeå: Norrbottens och Västerbottens läns landsting.

Ortiz, S. 1994. Work, the division of labour and cooperation. In: Ingold. T. (ed.): *Companion Encyclopedia of Anthropology. Humanity, Culture and Social Life*, pp. 891– 910. London & New York: Routledge.

Ramqvist, P. H. 1983. *Gene. The Origin, Function and Development of Sedentary Iron Age Settlement in Northern Sweden*. Archaeology and Environment 1. Umeå: : University of Umeå, Department of Archaeology.

Ramqvist, P. H. 1992. Building traditions in northern and north-eastern Europe during the Iron Age. In: Hårdh, B & Wyszomirska-Werbart, B. (eds.): *Contacts Across the Baltic Sea during the Late Iron Age (5th–12th centuries). Baltic Sea Conference, Lund October 25–27, 1991*. Report Series No. 43, pp. 73–83. Lund: University of Lund. Institute of Archaeology.

Ramqvist, P. H. 1998. *Arnäsbacken. En gård från yngre järnålder och medeltid*. Umeå: Prehistorica.

Rasmussen, S. 2001. Pastoral nomadism and gender. Status and prestige, economic contribution, and division of labor among the Tuareg of Niger. In: Brettell, C. B. & Sargent, C. F. (eds.): *Gender in Cross-Cultural Perspective*, pp. 280–293. Third Edition. Upper Saddle River, New Jersey: Prentice Hall.

Rathje, L. 1983. *Norrländsk folkmedicin. Sammanställning av folkmedicinskt arkivmaterial*. Skrifter. Serie D. Meddelanden, No 3. Umeå: Dialekt-, Ortnamns- och Folkminnesarkivet.

Rathje, L. 1999. Husbandry and Seal Hunting in Northern Coastal Sweden: The Amazon and the Hunter. In: Wicker, N. L. & Arnold, B. (eds.): *From the Ground Up: Beyond Gender Theory in Archaeology. Proceedings of the Fifth Gender and Archaeology Conference*. BAR International Series 812, pp. 103–106. Oxford: BAR Publishing.

Rathje, L. 2001. *Amasonen och jägaren. Kön/gender-konstruktioner i norr*. Studia Archaeologica Universitatis Umensis 14. Umeå: University of Umeå. Institute of Archaeology.

Rydving, H. 1993. *The End of Drum-Time. Religious Change among the Lule Saami, 1670s–1740s*. Acta

Universitatis Upsaliensis. Historia Religionum 12. Stockholm: Almqvist & Wiksell International.

Stattin, J. (ed.): 1991. *Det farliga livet. Om avund, rädsla, rykten och fördomar.* Stockholm: Natur och kultur.

Svanberg, I. 1999. *Hästslakt och korgmakare. Resursutnyttjande och livsstil bland sockenlappar.* Skrifter utgivna av Johan Nordlander-sällskapet 21. Umeå.

Tegengren, H. 1965. Hunters and amazons. Seasonal migrations in older hunting and fishing communities. In: Hvarfner, H. (ed.): *Hunting and Fishing,* Luleå: Norrbottens museum.

Westum, A. 1999. *Ris, skäver och skärva. Folklig kategorisering av några barnsjukdomar ur ett kognitivt semantiskt perspektiv.* Skrifter utgivna av Dialekt-, ortnamns- och folkminnesarkviet i Umeå.

Serie A. Dialekter. Nr 13. Diabas. Skrifter från den dialektgeografiska databasen inom Institutionen för nordiska språk vid Umeå universitet. Nr 5. Umeå.

Vikström, E. 1994a. Västerbotten genom tiderna. In: Sundin, B. (ed.): *Västerbotten genom tiderna,* pp. 10–23. Acta Bothniensia Occidentalis 14. Umeå: Västerbottens läns hembygdsförbund.

Vikström, E. 1994b. Medeltiden. In: Sundin, B. (ed.): *Västerbotten genom tiderna,* pp. 54–63. Acta Bothniensia Occidentalis 14. Umeå: Västerbottens läns hembygdsförbund.

Young, A. 1976. Some implications of medical beliefs and practices for social anthropology. *American Anthropologist* 78, pp. 5–24.

Female Saints, their Altars and their Offerings
Popular Social Practice in 21th Century Argentina

Per Cornell

Department of Archaeology, Gothenburg University

Abstract

In this article, an important intention is to point at a type of material trace in the contemporary, which merits much more attention. These are the several non-official saints in Argentina, and a range of these are accompanied by cults, centred on small altars and related offerings, spread over the countryside. The archaeological analysis itself has not been made. Perhaps, this article will help to demonstrate the potential in, and the importance of addressing this type of social trace in an archaeological frame.

Introduction

There are several non-official saints in Argentina, and several of these are accompanied by cults, centred on small altars and related offerings, spread over the countryside. The aim of this article is twofold. In part, it aims at demonstrating the existence of such cults, and in particular two traditions, related to female cults. These two female saints exhibit very different characteristics, there are actually striking differences. At the same time, this article is concerned with the possibilities for a future archaeological contribution to the study of this type of social practice.

Social materiality studies are a broad field, and there has been a significant increase in this area of study during the last 15 years or so. It will make no sense to quote the extensive bibliography. Suffice to mention the work of the French sociologist Bruno Latour (1999), and his elaboration on the concepts of actant and symmetry, and some other, perhaps less rigid contributions (cf. Riggins 1994; Andrén 1997; Dant 1999; Graves-Brown 2000; Cornell & Fahlander 2002a; Cornell & Fahlander 2002b). The study of materiality has become relevant for sociology, anthropology, ethnology, and other branches (cf. McDannell 1995). If traditional sociology (cf. Parsons 1951) deemed *things* to have no direct effect on humans, there has been a renewed interest in recent years. Archaeology, thus, is not alone in coping with materialities, but it is a particular way of coping with materialities, with a large and dynamic tradition.

It may prove productive to understand *archaeology* as the study of time and materiality, in the realm of the social. The social is here the human condition, the "collective" character of all human making, the impossibility of non-social perception. Time, because it is another basic aspect of the human condition, and materiality, since there is no social world in which materiality is not operative, as discussed by Sartre (1960).

In this understanding, archaeology operates both on "prehistory" and history. When addressing prehistory, the scholar is almost exclusively restricted to material traces. But when the scholar addresses history, in the traditional understanding of the term, there are several different types of sources available. For contemporary studies (and we will discuss this term below), the scholar may be living close to, or inside, the "object of study", and may make what can be called "direct observation", which allows for several preliminary estimates. There are people to ask, and oral sources may be established. And there are written sources of different kind available, and possibly images, like filmed material. But, still, there are also material sources and material traces. And if *archaeology* is to contribute to contemporary studies, it should be by means of materiality studies.

The archaeologist working on prehistory is, in Lubbocks words, "relieved from the embarrassing interference of tradition" (1872:427). Lubbock himself did not, however, work by this standard, introducing, at large scale, Victorian ethnography into archaeology, reflecting, of course, human tradition. At the same time, of course, the archaeologist working on prehistory is the prisoner of given material traces; there is nothing else available, her or his view is restricted, bound.

Working on the contemporary, the available information is, at times, overwhelming. The process of exteriorisation of memory, the "liberation of memory" to speak with Leroi-Gourhan (1965), has achieved extremely complex forms in a world of satellites and digital memories. As discussed by Derrida, humans can put ever more information on the *reserve*, and it can be introduced again, at different geographical and chronological points (Derrida 1967). Still, this seemingly ever increasing amount of information is not only a blessing, it also creates problems of many kinds. There is no space to discuss these problems here. Only one of them will be mentioned, the difficulty to scan and evaluate information. Even specially trained bodies, such as the US agency CIA have been proved to have great difficulties in scanning and evaluating information. The amount of data is simply overwhelming, and there is, it seems, no simple means to solve these problems. Now, I (as signing this article), am not entirely unhappy with this situation. Orwell's Big Brother scenario seems far away. Rather, lack of information, and above all, difficulties in handling information, restricts control even for those amassing wealth and power. Making managerial or political decisions is no simple task, and most current models on decision making seem quite out of date, at best.

While the amount of information grows steadily, our ways to cope with social problems do not grow in the same way. In a sense, we are partially "choked" by a massive information attack. However, the growth of information counts mainly for filmed material, written texts and lists etc. The knowledge of contemporary daily life's social materiality is relatively restricted. Strange as it may seem, what is less well documented is thus contemporary garbage and non-institutional materiality. Following from this, our image of the world is not that of what people generally live, even if such images may occur now and then in the massive wealth of information circulating.

Archaeology has engaged with these problems. Rathje and his followers have made a fundamental contribution in their studies on contemporary US garbage. Rathje also informs on the lack of correlation between direct data from informants and the evidence from garbage. People often give numbers for their beer or sugar consumption, for example, sub-estimating the amount as indicated in the garbage they have produced (Rathje & Cullen 1992). This is probably not a question of people lying. Some people may lie about their consumption, but in most cases it is rather a question of trying to adapt to cultural standards, to try to follow imagined norms. In a sense, the *discrepancy* between the data as achieved from the informant respectively the garbage, demonstrates important aspects of social life, far beyond the information from any singular source.

Rathje speaks about "the archaeology of us", when addressing the garbage project. Much archaeology carried out under the name of ethnoarchaeology similarly addresses contemporary daily-life social materiality, and is thus of greatest value for contemporary studies. As discussed by Gosden (1999), the term "ethnoarchaeology" should be avoided, since it implies a sort of racism, a strong idea of "we" and "them". Actually, the Nunamiut, as studied by Binford (1978), lived in the same "contemporaneity" as the citizens of Tucson, studied by Rathje (cf. Fabian 1983).

But "contemporaneity" is a difficult term. And it is yet more difficult to speak about the "present". This topic can neither be addressed in detail in this connection. Suffice to mention Benedict Anderson and his discussion on the "Imagined Communities" (1983). Anderson demonstrates that the idea of loving the same "present" has not always

been existent. It is rather a quite late modern construct. While it can be argued by Newtonian physics that there is a global sequence of "now", this does not necessarily apply to social lived human experience. All particular social clusters do not necessarily always have effects on each other. There is no empirical evidence to sustain such a generalised and extreme systems-theory "functionalist" argument. While there are – often – effects from one cluster on another, there is not always, or necessarily, an effect on all social clusters from all possible occurrences in all social clusters. Some happenings have effects only in certain limited areas, or even only on some particular people. Thus, "now" is not always a good category in discussing social life.

Actually, our knowledge of social events and happenings around the globe in our "contemporaneity" is limited. And many series of "happenings" or "occurrences" start at different points in time, and end at different points. There are no complete, smooth, generalised chrono-logics of all action in all social spheres at all places. The reader may at this point, and justly so, find this a boring repletion of the obvious. The problem is that the idea of the opposite seems to govern several approaches to social analysis in archaeology. It is quite common, for example, to find statements like the following: "It is impossible to study the past, because the only thing we know is the present, and everything we say is of the present". Such a statement takes for granted that the "present" is simple and straightforward, while the past is difficult and obscure. It may well be argued that "the present" is at least as difficult a concept as "the past". And, what interests most in relation to this "present" text, the present is not necessarily "easier" to cope with than is the past.

Archaeology can certainly contribute constructively to the study of the "contemporaneous". But this field remains little developed, and we may (opting for a not very suitable metaphor) say in its "infancy". Archaeologists must, for one part, be much more open to collaboration with other scholars working the contemporaneous, including sociologists, anthropologists, geographers, biologists, geologists and many other disciplines. At the same time, archaeologists must refine and develop their own methods, and contribute to the development of relevant social theory. Archaeologists will only contribute if they do so from the point of view of their particular source - material traces – and from archaeological methods. At times, it may be useful to forget, temporarily, in the research process, the heavy burden of tradition, as discussed by Lubbock.

Non-Official Altars

In this article, an important intention is to point at a type of material trace in the contemporary, which merits much more attention. It will only be a short and sketchy discussion on an example from Argentina, South America, which will have to suffice. The archaeological analysis itself has not been made. Perhaps, this article will help to demonstrate the potential in, and the importance of addressing this type of social trace in an archaeological frame. It is of little use to discuss here if this social practice is a religion or not. There is no dogma related to it. At the same time, its practice resembles religion in some ways. Neither the word "cult" is of major interest. It is, generally, of little operative value.

In contemporary Argentina, in a tradition going back at least hundred years, there are small altars spread over the landscape, dedicated to non-official saints, i.e. saints not proclaimed by the roman-catholic church, or other institutionalised religious orders, for that matter. This type of altars has existed over a hundred years or so and are related to particular non-official saints, and there are frequent offerings deposited at the altars. The term "popular religion" has often been used in this context. The question whether this concept is suitable for discussing non-official altars or not, is an open one.

What may be of importance to remark is that it is not an "official" practice of Roman Catholic Church, neither a distinct different Christian congregation, such as e.g. the Pentecostals. There is no dogma, no formal institutional body of priests, or officiates whatsoever, related to this cult. It is not even similar to less formal, but still organised traditions of faith, such as brands of occultism or spiritism, which were frequent in Argentina some hundred years ago; when several of the traditions related to non-official altars were initiated. While much more has been written on Israelites in Peru, or about the Pentecostals in different areas of Latinamerica (cf. Boudewijnse, Droogers & Kamsteeg 1998), or on occultism and spiritism (cf. Santamaría et al. 1992), there has been relatively little written about non-official altars in Argentinean social practice. There is also a stark contrast to other contemporaneous sects or cults, more intellectual and more weboriented, such as the cult to KnightTemplars (cf. for example www.members.es.tripod.de/Nuevoshallazgos/templeamer ica, 2000-09-14; cf. Cornell & Ekelund 2003). The extent of such cults outside the web is also dubious, and must be corroborated (Cowan 2005). The latter cults often have more or less explicit political content, and may have racist overtones.

The non-official altars are not supported by an explicit dogma, and have not aroused from any such dogma. It is a social practice with only secondary expressions in writing or systematic oral rhetoric. It is not, thus, any explicit cosmology or system. Similar altars can be found elsewhere. In the Andean world they are quite common, related to more or less officialised saints, and often to completely different traditions, like that of *pachamama, apachetas* (piles of stone with special values), or *alasitas* (miniature figures used for making wishes) etc. which may be linked, partially, to pre-Hispanic traditions. In the Mediterranean world, it is also quite common to find small altars, on the spot of a car crash for example. However, the Argentinean altars cannot be reduced to a mere pre-Hispanic tradition, still less a catholic practice. It is a distinct social innovation.

There are some discussions among scholars on non-official altars in the 1960's, but only recently have they received more systematic attention (cf. for example; Coluccio 1995; Delgado, Mercado & Rodríguez 2004). Since they are non-official they have not been registered by any church in any systematic form. Still, most published texts are very general, and no detailed study of their distribution and character exists, not even for any smaller area. No systematic archaeological analysis has been made. What we are discussing is social practice maintained over several decades, by large segments of the Argentinean population, but in relation to which there is no "canon", "holy text", or state-administrative document regulating or organising it. It is quite probable that municipal governments have been forced to deal with this phenomenon, since their physical form does utilize space, often situated at public terrain. But there is not much of officiality about these altars and instalments. There are some few cases of direct criticism directed at these practices, notably by some priests, condemning them for being non-authorized saints (cf. a Miami based catholic site, www.corazones.org/santos/santos_temas/falsos_santos.ht m, 2001-07-10, article by Padre Jordi Rivero, addressing Argentinean "false saints").

Thus, these materialities are linked to human activity, but no so much to written rules or recommendations. In this sense, the material remains are unique evidence. Important oral history could be made on these practices, but such studies have only been initiated recently. The material evidence is important attesting for an important part of human social practice which could easily be forgotten and remain in oblivion. Making an archaeological documentation and register should at least give some sort of memory over this social practice. Since most "information" has a commercial or state-administrative origin, social practice occurring outside of this orbit receive very little attention, unless it openly run counter to the interests of commerce or state.

Popular Saints

The practice of giving small offerings at these altars is a common enough practice in Argentina, but there have been no written instructions and there is no canon linked to it. So this social practice (involving human beings of blood and bone, besides different kinds of materialities) cannot be explained only by reference to written legal, religious or cultural instructions. It is a social practice only traceable in traditional written form to a limited extent. This is an important observation. Still, these altars are generally referred to in terms of saints. The practice involves, most certainly, conscious intentional human action, but also semi-conscious routine, based on the repetition of observed and/or experienced actions. It could also be argued that it includes unconscious and subconscious elements.

Evidently, elements of these actions are directly inspired by the cult of the Roman Catholic Church. The idea of sainthood itself has such an origin. In Latin America, there are several old well established popular virgins and saints, with a semi-official status, such as figures with strong elements from Virgin Maria. As examples can be mentioned the Virgin of Guadalupe in México (Wolf 1958), the Virgin of Urkupiña in Bolivia, or La Tirana in Chile. In all of these cases, various cultural traditions have contributed, including elements from pre-Hispanic time, and different catholic traditions.

The Argentinean saints are, in several cases, not of ancient age, but rather from the 19th century, or even more recent times. There are so many different ones, el gaucho Cobillos, Pancho Sierra, La Telesita, Difunta Teresa, El Taxista Caputo, Gaucho Gil (a popular 19th century "bandido", cf. Coluccio 1995), and many others.

The woman in the desert: Difunta Correa

Difunta Correa dates to the 19th century. Difunta means "the deceased" and Correa is a family name. The tale has many versions, some collected in summary form by state commissions on folklore in the 1920's (Chertudi & Newbery 1978). One of them (as described by Buntig, 1970) says that a woman in northern Argentina, in 1829, walked through the desert with her new-born child, in search of her husband, drafted for military service. Finally, she died from exhaustion, heat, and – above all -, lack of water. Only a couple of days later some people came to cross the place of her death. Miraculously, the baby had survived, since the breasts had not turned dry.

Altars dedicated to *Difunta Correa* can be found in many parts of Argentina. There is a somewhat larger place of cult at Vallecito, in the province of San Juan. At this spot, people thank her by putting up written plates of copper or other metals. But, and perhaps more interestingly, there is an almost incredible amount of local small sanctuaries spread over the countryside in several provinces. They are frequent along major roads, and it is common to see large trucks close to these altars. But they can also be found along small paths, even up in mountainous sub-Andean zones far away from roads. Repeated elements at these spots include used tires, small altars, usually by simple construction, flowers, small mirrors, and bottles with liquid, generally water. At times, the words "Difunta Correa" have been scribbled on some tire, on a stone, or in other ways. Along major routes, municipalities occasionally put up road signs indicating the presence of a "Difunta Correa" site. The persistence of the practice of offerings to the Difunta Correa is remarkable. Individual sites may be abandoned, but the general practice survives. Along the major road from the capital of the Province of Tucuman to the capital of the Province of Salta, I have observed a Difunta Correa site which recently have received "competition": on the opposite side of the road, there is a "Gaucho Gil" altar. While Difunta Correa is persistent, the popularity is not at a rise. At the moment of writing these lines (2004), Gaucho Gil is perhaps more frequent in the north of Argentina.

Figure 7.1 Altar dedicated to Gilda, a popular saint in rural Argentina, close to Villa Paranacito, km 129 Route 12 . Photo by Hanna Skartveit.

The *cumbia* singer: Santa Gilda

Altars dedicated to *Santa Gilda* are not as common as those previously mentioned. There is an important node of Gilda adoration at the spot of her death in a tragic bus-crash, and at the cemetery. Gilda is a recent saint. Her popularity was at its peak in the 1990's, but she is still very much adored, and has many followers. Her image is at sale among street-vendors in many parts of Argentina. The tale about her runs as follows, and I will take the risk to expand here (cf. for example www.geocities.com/Eureka/3353/gilda.html, 2001-07-03 (Ahora Gilda) and other web sites).

The parents of Myriám Alejandra Bianchi (1961-1996) originally wanted to call their daughter Gilda, after the famous Hollywood movie, starring Rita Hayworth, but they were not allowed to do so by part of the authorities. She came to use the name Gilda all her life, however. As a young woman she was made to work along with nuns, attending children at pre-scholar level. She married at the age of 18 and had a daughter and a son. The rules of the establishment were strict, and when she started to perform and sing publicly in 1987, she was fired. Her singing career brought about the separation from her husband, and she decided to go and live with a popular singer. A new life started, during which Gilda travelled with her new male friend all over Argentina. In the beginning, the concerts were held in areas struck with poverty, and her life had nothing to do with that of famous rock stars. She sang "cumbia", a style of music increasingly popular in Argentina from the 1980's onwards. The rhythm is simple and repetitive. This music was popular in the areas called "Villa Miseria", the "slum". Gilda used a somewhat transformed type of Cumbia, a little more close to pop and rock. Slowly her fame grew. Her concerts became increasingly popular, and she produced some discs for the commercial market. Finally, she also appeared at the big arenas, even in the federal capital, Buenos Aires. She became famous not only as a singer. People started to ask her touch sick children, believing she had special powers to cure. She became, under her own protests, a *curandera.* Her life ended tragically and violently. The tour bus crashed with a truck. She was buried in niche 3535, gallery 24, at the Chacarita cemetery in Buenos Aires (the traditional "popular" cemetery).

Her popularity rose markedly after her death. People came forward, claiming to have been cured after visiting Gilda sites. The Analia Balbi internet site says, I quote: "it is the new Saint of the poor, the new Argentinean myth" (translation by the author, cf. www.members.nbci.com/_XMCM/nesedco/historia/gild ahistoria.htm, 2001-06-29,).

There have been some strange incidents. A young boy, supposedly cured from an incurable disease by visiting a Gilda site, made a political intervention, defending the rights of schoolteachers in public schools, claiming that Gilda had asked him to say these things. Carlos Menem, at that time president of the Argentinean Republic responded, according to newspapers, stating that Gilda was a bad person. Interestingly, he thus accepted what the young boy had said, that Gilda (deceased), has spoken to him. This is a curious incident. It demonstrates, however, the importance of local saints in social and political rhetoric and discourse.

The popularity of Gilda has been remarkable. At Internet there are several sites dedicated to her. In Argentina, there are several Gilda sites, and her image is for sale among many street vendors, and also in shops. She is not among the most common saints at present, but her presence is strong.

Argentina is very much dominated by the Roman Catholic Church, and according to the constitution, the president must be of catholic faith. Sainthood itself is very much catholic. The church has been quite silent in relation to popular, non-official saints, and generally prefers to say nothing. However, there are exceptions. There are some Argentinean "popular saint" hate pages at the net, stressing the fact that these saints are non-official, not "true".

Still, the popular altars are important elements in Argentinean social life, and among those of Gilda. The popularity of Gilda is, perhaps, of particular interest. Gilda herself came from a sort of middle class background. But her frequent appearance in poor areas, together with her life-style (living with a musician, all the time touring and the fact that she was rejected by nuns), give to her a very special position. She is generally represented as a saint in images, and has

nothing of "monster" about her. Her attraction is not at all in being a monstrous creature (the real sensu Lacan, cf. Zizek 1989, 1992: the horrors of the times, only seen in bits and pieces, when uncovered under layers of social imagery); rather she is presented in more "saintly" terms in the imagery.

Most of her songs have very general lyrics about love and deceit. Some of her last lyrics stand out however, and it may be of interest to quote some of them at length. These are only small passages, but these lines often appear in remixed short versions (cf for example at CDformat *Por siempre Gilda,* Universal Music SA, 1997). The content of these songs is remarkable. The first one ("Nos iremos los tres") is about a woman and two men.

> And we three go together
> And we three go together
> And at the end of month
>
> You /two/ cover the expenses
>
> And we three go together
> And we three go together
> And then we'll see
> Who will stay with the dishes

These lines seem to conform to patterns of living not all too infrequent, though not very much accepted officially. More importantly, the lyrics directly mock men, pointing at chores often made by women, cleaning up after dinner etc., and, in general terms, insists on the power and status women *ought to* have. In other parts of this song, there is a reference to "the postmodern", which is a word infrequent in cumbia songs. The second example ("La Cosita") is about a man running after girls, leaving them behind after his personal immediate sexual satisfaction.

> They cut the thing, ay ay ay
> They cut the little thing, ay ay ay
>
> They cut the thing, ay ay ay
> They cut the little thing, ay ay ay
>
> Now he cannot run after girls
> Now he cannot go partying
> Now he cannot put it straight
> He is getting bad, ay man

These lines are indeed even more provocative. The general popularity of these songs is interesting. Their content is, in relation to daily life social practice, directly explosive. Gilda uses the form of Saint to bring special messages, questioning the male patriarchal world, and the religious establishment. Her name Gilda is also of great interest, alluding to popular cinema and a special sort of transgressing female figure.

Figure 7.2 Altar dedicated to Gilda, a popular saint in rural Argentina, close to Villa Paranacito, km 129 Route 12 . Photo by Hanna Skartveit.

Figure 7.3 Altar dedicated to Gaucho Gil, a popular saint in rural Argentina, Route Tucuman - Salta. Photo byPer Cornell.

Saints and the variability in social practice

Regarding saints, their cults often relate to questions of human survival, e.g. sickness, lack of rain, or similar dramatic incidents (Turner 1997). At the same time, it can be said to be linked to desire, and the workings of desire (Acuña 1994). But it is, above all, a social practice. Most of the writing on this cultic tradition has centred on the origin of the cult. Much less has been written about the actual use of altars, about the offerings and the practice of cult and its variability.

Several feminist writers (cf. Vuola 1993; Schussler Fiorenza 1989; Acuña 1994, 1997, 1998) have discussed the multivocality of the cult to Maria, Virgins and Saints. Official Roman Catholic dogma relates these cultic traditions to key values, particularly to motherhood and virginity. This may be interpreted as patriarchal ideology, a means by men to control women, to control sex, biological reproduction, and children; in other words, the control of desire. However, the cultic practice often demonstrates aspects far beyond such conceptions. In the case discussed here, Difunta Correa could possible fit in to the traditional model, but Gilda

certainly does not. Gilda transgresses basic Roman Catholic values. While Difunta Correa in theory could have entered the path to beatification and eventual canonization, Gilda could hardly have done that in the 19th or 20th centuries.

A particularly interesting aspect of the Argentinean non-official altars is that they are used by people of different "ethnic" ascription. People of Italian or Spanish descent participate in this tradition, along with people of Indian descent. In a sense, these cults are highly innovative, thus, crossing traditional cultural barriers. Terms like syncretism (Steward 1995), acculturation (Rouse 1986), or hybridisation (García Canclini 1990) seems of little help in this connection. The discussion of Bonfil Battala (1992) on the creation of the "Indian", after the arrival of the Spaniard, is perhaps more relevant, but must be elaborated and adjusted to the cases under discussion. In the case under discussion, participation in the "non-official altar" cults does not seem to interfere or obstruct cultural variability in other types of social practice among the practitioners.

Figure 7.4 Altar dedicated to Difunta Correa, a popular saint in rural Argentina, Tafí del Valle. Photo by Per Cornell.

And, finally, summing up, bringing us back to materialities...

The popularity of Gilda, seen in the face of the above cited information, is indeed remarkable and interesting. It could be used as material for interesting sociological and anthropological analysis and interpretation.

But what about the materialities? There has been no systematic study of this, and it is, thus, impossible to make more extensive comments. Personal observations by the author, collected on several visits to Argentina from 1987 to 2004, will be the source for reflection here. The first observation is that these saints have a life as materiality. And there are *different sets* of materialities present at the places dedicated to *different popular saints*. Further, their spatial distribution is not identical. In some cases, as in the case of Difunta Correa and Gaucho Gil, they occur close to each other. However, in general, they interfere little to each other in space.

It would be of greatest interest to make a systematic study of these altars and related social practice, integrating archaeology, sociology, social anthropology, and ethnology, comparing different types of datasets, approaching questions of practice, differences in social class, and questions of identity. I hope such a project will be created eventually.

The offerings given to Gilda differ from those given to Difunta Correa. The latter receives, as discussed above, water, tyres and mirrors. Gilda receives many different things. But, in particular, water and other liquids but also toys for children, and nursery bottles, are deposited. Objects, thus, related to children. The patterning here is not evident. Difunta Correa is directly related to the life of a newborn child. Gilda only indirectly relates to children.

Perhaps an anthropologist may come up with a nice "cultural" explanation or interpretation to this phenomenon. But, from the point of view of the archaeologist, it could well be that the rhetorical version, that of the words, does not correspond to that of the world of the materialities. They may, in a sense, be about different "things". It is not necessary, always, to seek the perfect fit. It may well be that it is not there. They may even have different social effects. As materialities, Gilda is about the children and Difunta Correa about the need for water for all humans everywhere. As a social material practice Gilda will, then, never receive the same general application as Difunta Correa. At the same time, Gilda has established a new material social practice, one which may come to open new social fields.

Then, what about time? The differential persistence of altars and saints is indeed a big and interesting topic, and must be addressed in depth. There are, probably, social patterns in these variations. Now, Gilda may come to persist less than Difunta Correa, but, who knows? The contemporaneous gives us no answer.

Acknowledgements

Though this is a very small and short article, many people have been involved in its production. Anthropologist Maria Elena Acuña in Santiago de Chile helped with important comments at an early stage. Sociologist Ulf Borelius, Gothenburg, followed the work from the early beginning. Historian Maria Clara Medina, Gothenburg, helped with much discussion, and helped with translation of lyrics. Thanks also to anthropologist Hanna Skartveit, Bergen for valuable help in several ways, to anthropologist Patricia Arenas, Tucuman, Argentina for discussion, to archaeologist Fredrik Fahlander, Gothenburg for comments, to archaeologist/garbologist William Rathje, Stanford for help with the title, and to Ricardo Kaliman, Tucuman, specialist on popular culture and folklore, for being angry and for many other things. Thanks also to all the participants of the Haina workshop on Latinamerican gender issues in Bergen, Norway, in 2001, at which another, more extensive, related paper was presented (authored by Cornell, Acuña & Borelius). Finally, thanks to Tove Hjørungdal for accepting my paper at her Gender session at EAA in Thessaloniki, and for insisting on me transforming it to written form. I remain responsible, of course, for all flaws and errors.

References

Acuña, M. E. 1994. *Santa Rosa, el soldado y el campesino : género y religión : estudio antropológico sobre el culto a Santa Rosa de lima en la zona de Pelequén.* Facultad de Ciencias Sociales, Departamento de Antropólogía, Universidad de Chile, Tesis (Antropólogía).

Acuña, M. E. 1997. Genero e identidad: algunos elementos de discusión del culto a Santa Rosa de Lima en la zona de Pelequén. *Actas del Segundo Congreso Chileno de Antropología,* Santiago, 1997, pp. 8-14.

Acuña, M. E. 1998. Aproximaciones a la devoción a Santa Rosa de Lima en la zona de Pelequen. *Identidades e ideologías de género.* Santiago: PIEG, pp. 21-33.

Anderson, B. 1983. *Imagined Communities: reflections on the origin and spread of nationalism.* London: Verso.

Andrén, A. 1997. *Between Artefacts and Texts: historical archaeology in global perspective.* New York: Plenum Press.

Binford, L. R. 1978. *Nunamiut Ethnoarchaeology.* New York: Academic Press.

Bonfil, B. G. 1992. *Identidad y pluralismo cultural en Amércia Latina.* Buenos Aires: Fondo editorial del CEHASS/ San Juan: Editorial de la Universidad de Puerto Rico.

Boudewijnse, B., A. Droogers & Kamsteeg, F. 1998. *More than Opium. An anthropological approach to Latin American and Carribean Pentecostal Praxis.* Lanham & London: The Scarecrow Press.

Buntig, A. 1970. *Magia, religion, o cristianismo?* Buenos Aires: Bonum.

Chertudi, S. & Newbery, S. 1978. *La Difunta Correa.* Buenos Aires: Huemul.

Coluccio, F. 1995. *Las Devociones Populares Argentinas.* Buenos Aires: Nuevo Siglo.

Cornell, P. & Ekelund, A. 2001. Vikingar och raspolitik. *Fornvännen 96,* pp. 99-101.

Cornell, P. & Fahlander, F. 2002a. *social praktik och stumma monument. introduktion till mikroarkeologi.* Göteborg: Gotarc C: 46, Department of Archaeology, Gothenburg university.

Cornell, P. & Fahlander, F. 2002b. Microarchaeology, Materiality and Social Practice. *Current Swedish Archaeology,* vol. 10, pp. 21-38.

Cowan, D. E. 2005. *Cyberhenge. Modern pagans on the Internet.* New York & London: Routledge.

Dant, T. (ed.), 1999. *Material Culture in the Social World. Values, activities, lifestyles* Buckingham/Philadelphia: Open University Press.

Delgado, E. J., R. Mercado & Rodríguez, O. 2004. Cultos populares en la Argentina. *Todo es Historia.* Buenos Aires, pp. 6-20.

Derrida, J. 1967. *De la grammatologie.* Paris: Minuit.

Fabian, J. 1983. *Time and the Other. How anthropology makes its object.* New York: Columbia University Press.

García Canclini, N. 1990. *Culturas hibridas: estrategias para entrar y Salir de la modernidad.* México D.F.: Grijalbo.

Gosden, C. 1999. *Anthropology and Archaeology. A changing relationship.* London & New York: Routledge.

Graves-Brown, P. M. 2000, *Matter, Materiality and Modern Culture.* London: Routledge.

Latour, B. 1999. *Pandoras Hope. Essays on the reality of science studies.* Cambridge, Mass.: Harvard University Press.

Leroi-Gourhan, A. 1964/1965. *Le geste et la parole, 1-2.* Paris: Michel.

Lubbock, J. 1872. *Prehistoric Time, as illustrated by ancient remains, and the mores and customs of modern savages.* Third edition. London: Williams & Norgale.

McDannell, C. 1995. *Material Christianity. Religion and popular culture in America.* New Haven: Yale University Press.

Parsons, T. 1951. *The Social System.* London: The Free Press.

Rathje, W. L. & Cullen, M. 1992. *Rubbish!: the archaeology of garbage.* New York: Harper Collins.

Riggins, H. 1994. *The Socialness of Things: essays on the socio-semiotics of objects.* Berlin: Mouton de Gruyer.

Rouse, I. 1986. *Migrations in Prehistory. Inferring population movement from cultural remains.* New Haven: Yale University Press.

Santamaría, Daniel J, S. Bianchi, R. S. Aruj, R. M. Georges, M. C. Leone & Bjerg, M. M.1992. *Ocultismo y espiritismo en la Argentina.* Buenos Aires: Centro editor de America Latina.

Sartre, J.-P. 1960. *Critique de la raison dialectique (précédè de Question de methode). Tome 1: Theorie des ensembles pratiques.* Paris: Gallimard.

Schussler, F. 1989. *En memoria de ella. Una reconstrucción teólogico-feminista de los orígenes del cristianismo.* Bilbao: Desclée de Brouwer.

Steward, C. 1995. Relocating Syncretism in Social Science Discourse. In. Aijmer, G. ed. 1995 *Syncretism and the commerce of symbols.* The Institute for advanced studies in social anthropology (IASSA), Gothenburg university, pp. 13-37.

Turner, B. 1997. *Religion and social theory.* London: SAGE.

Wolf, E. J. 1958. The Virgin of Guadalupe: A Mexican national symbol. *Journal of American Folklore,* vol. 71, pp. 34-39.

Vuola, E. 1993. La Virgen María como ideal feminina, su critica feminista y nuevas interpretaciones. *Revista Pasos.* San José, pp. 11-20.

Zizek, S. 1989. *The Sublime Object of Ideology.* London: Verso.

Zizek, S. ed. 1992. *Everything You Wanted to Know about Lacan: (but were afraid to ask Hitchcock).* London: Verso.

Disseminating the Herding teaching:
How do students grow into explorers of knowledge; and how do teachers grow into facilitators of learning?

Linda Lövkvist & Tove Hjørungdal

Department of Archaeology, Gothenburg University

> If our conception of learning is transformed by new knowledge, then our conception of teaching must also undergo metamorphosis (Hounsell 1997:239).

Abstract

The issue of this paper is the question of how students develop from receivers of knowledge into becoming explorers of knowledge, and how teachers grow into facilitators of this process. Ideas from alternative perspectives on learning are considered in relation to our own context, and are thought to proliferate with successful methods already at work. As a result we suggest a sketch of a possible introductory course in archaeology. Our concept builds on ideas developed within critical and feminist pedagogy, and from feminist practices in the classroom. Other elements are chosen from Problem Based Learning and from Coaching. The aim of alternative pedagogies is to permit students to grow into explorers of knowledge, to find a voice, and in the long run to grow into confident professionals. To put the sketched ideas into practice may however be a challenge with the present instrumentalist culture of tertiary education, along with a subsequent unstable economic situation. In spite of the hindrances there are some strategies which can help us to move in the direction aimed at. Thus the paper also contributes a case study in criticism against the commercialist paradigm in tertiary education.

Focusing learning – an introduction

> What we do in the classroom is our politics. (Tompkins 1991:27)

This paper deals with approaches to processes of learning, in relation to aspects of teaching. The background to our involvement with this issue is first and foremost a general interest in how university teachers influence the students' learning, and as such their development into professionals. In order to discuss this, we shall reflect upon the changes in students' and teacher's roles and positions, which necessarily would be a consequence of changes in teaching and learning methods, as well as of changes in academic conditions. The bottom line of the discussion is on the one hand how students grow from passive receivers of knowledge into active explorers of knowledge. On the other hand it is how teachers grow from authoritarian givers of knowledge into facilitators of the students' own learning process. In close relation to this, we shall present an enlargement of some of the issues in a previous article, where we have called for attention towards educational matters and for a "hopefully forthcoming, more lively debate on gender, pedagogy and teaching" (Lövkvist & Hjørungdal 2000:157; see also Lövkvist 2004:8).

As in our previous article, the discussion is focussed on the question of *how to develop and use alternative,* gender informed, teaching and learning practices in undergraduate archaeology courses. The background to our interest in exploring the issues of gender critical teaching and learning practices is manifold. Most of the topics raised in this article reflect aspects of our own experiences and thoughts, as well as of the current general discourse on education in the humanities in our vicinity. It is the *learning approaches and their practice,* which will be of focal interest in the examination to follow. As such, some methods presented by colleagues, as well as by educationists, are discussed. In general we consider the practices of the methods of Problem Based Learning (PBL), and the methods of Coaching, and ask some questions of where to go from there. We take this issue into account through bringing feminist pedagogy into our discussion. In order to bring the discussion forward, we therefore present suggestions of how one could alter an educational programme in order to organise a class of gender informed explorers of knowledge.

Aspects of Learning

> To learn is to strive for meaning, and to have learned something is to have grasped its meaning. (Dahlgren 1997:27)

To capture the character of learning, one must know what knowledge is, and that in turn is something that philosophers have discussed for almost two and a half millennia – yet without a unanimous consensus. However, with the development of pedagogy as a discipline with an origin in philosophy (via psychology), the complex of learning has become focus within a discourse in its own right. Theories on learning and how it is best achieved have succeeded and replaced each other.

Some important pedagogical influences

The ideas most influential to the Swedish educational system are the ideas of the Swiss philosopher, psychologist and educationist Jean Piaget (Säljö 2000:49ff). Piaget advocates educational *cognitivism*, the philosophical contradiction to behaviourism. In general terms the cognitivist theory implies that the psychological focus of interest is how people think. This tradition is a modern cousin to the Cartesian rationalism, which in turn has its roots in the Classic old Greek dualism, with the characteristic split between body and mind. The theoretical family of cognitivism appeared during the 50s and 60s and it grew very influential in American behavioural science. With the computer as a model of the mind, its central point of departure was that the mind has a basic and more or less static core mechanism that could be studied as a separate phenomenon (op.cit:55). Contextual perspectives such as social and cultural ones were totally absent in favour of more technical aspects. Although no particular pedagogical thoughts on learning were developed within the 'cognitivisms', one of its branches put into focus the view on learning as a person's active process of interpreting and construing understanding, of the world. This branch was called *constructivism*, which viewed humans more like active and creative beings that can interpret and make sense of the world, instead of just being passive receivers of information.

One of the most well-known advocates of constructivism was, yet again, Jean Piaget. In spite of his popularity as a pedagogue, he was first and foremost interested in how knowledge is *established*, and did not want to give any detailed directives to how teaching should be done (Säljö 2000:57ff). Some of his basic ideas have parallels in the views on education with historical pedagogues. So, for example, do they correspond with Aristotle, Sophocles, Jean-Jacques Rousseau and John Dewey in what the latter labelled 'learning by doing' (Kugel 1993:323; Rousseau 1977, 1978; Svedberg 2000:263). Piaget's ideas also match well with ideas claimed by Socrates and Rousseau concerning the role of the teacher, which in their opinion should be more of a stimulating guide than a preaching lecturer. Learning in this perspective demands an active pupil/student, and Piaget advocated that he/she should have to learn by own experience – that is the only way to achieve a complete understanding. This stance was in accordance with his conviction that knowledge was something that the pupil constructed from experiencing relations between various learning materials. An improved teaching would therefore require insight into how pupils think the way they do, their cognition.

Piaget viewed cognitive development as processes towards environmental adaptation. To achieve this adaptation our cognitive structures must be changed according to our perception of the world. At first we *assimilate* new information and perceptions of the world according to our previous patterns of understanding and interpreting the world, as long as we experience it as 'more of the same' (see also Svedberg 2000:255f). However, gradually there will be an increasing amount of cognitive conflicts and analogies to contradict our former cognitive understanding of the world. With this conflict will also a need for *accommodation* occur, i e a need to acquire a new and further developed pattern of understanding. Piaget treated human thinking as a homogeneous phenomenon and considered changes in patterns of cognitive structures as stages of development from concrete simplicity to more complex abstraction. Nevertheless, these stages were later heavily criticised, since children's results in cognitive experiments gave a spectrum of variety in developmental stages. Piaget's ideas proved to be both too much focused on rational thinking and hopelessly ethnocentric.

After this backdrop the educational pendulum seems to be swinging back to more contextual ideas, which, however, were put forward already during the 20s and 30s by the Russian psychologist Lev S. Vygotsky. Many decades before either the cognitivism or constructivism entered the arena his ideas lay in many respects close in line with both the constructivism and Piaget's standpoints. So, for instance, did Vygotsky also consider knowledge as a creative and constructive process and that teaching should be formed so as to urge and inspire pupils to actively finding knowledge themselves (Säljö 2000:65ff). However, instead of regarding pupils as just being active, Vygotsky considered them also being *interactive*. The pupils are not just 'islands of learning', but parts in their environment as well. This means that they are influenced and affected by the context they are a part of, which implies historically, culturally as well as socially influences. Such a perspective gives communication and language a prominent role. Among researchers working according to this socio-cultural theoretical tradition, communication is considered prior to thinking, since socialisation into certain ways of thinking is itself mediated through communication. This contextually contingent interaction is what constitutes development, in that the person is socialised into society through action, through sharing conceptions and social life. And since cultures are different in different parts of the world, their view of knowledge and its aims may also be different.

Central in both Piaget's and Vygotsky's theories, is the dualistic perspective. Learning is conceived of as internalising knowledge (with information as the external factor) into the mind (as the internal factor). Furthermore, learning also implies a division between intellectual thinking (internal) and social interaction (external) as well as between body and mind (Säljö 2000:68, 151).

Figure 8.1 This illustration aims at highlighting the point of view of development/change as psychosomatic, where both mind and body are involved. Both drawings were made by Linda at the age of 11, with only one month in between. The background to this change in perception and ability to picture the perceived was a move of home, school, and teacher at the same time. The new teacher had the same competence as the former and the only difference was that she happened to house a burning interest for various aesthetic creativity and expression. Experiencing that the own drawing performance could result in something more look-alike than before, having stretched the visual perception and conception as well as the internal eye-hand communication resulting in change of expressive ability, gave a satisfactory feeling of astonishment and joy: "Could I do that?!" Learning involves moving forward one's limits of personal understanding and (cap)ability; of expanding and fusing intellect and physical and somatic experiences and skills as well as mental achievements; it involves widening one's concepts of the world as well as one's own possibilities and changing relation to it. Learning can be fun and interesting, though the process of learning also involves a lot of practice, hard work and sometime the feeling of failure and disappointment. This illustration could serve as an (analogical) example with parallels to both education, research and field archaeology. As a beginner in a field of activity we perceive the world in another way than professionals do. After being socialised into a new epistemology and having trained and practised eyes, intellect as well as our motor skills we usually have developed a more complex multi-facetted and nuanced view of the world. It also reflects what effect a teacher's own interest for the subject may have on the pupil/student, a topic which we will return to in the text to follow. However, one could of course question the premise that 'development' always leads to a higher and better level of perceiving, interpreting and understanding the world; a more fruitful attitude would perhaps be to consider it a process of exploring new perspectives and achieving new nuanced and critical stances through analytical understanding – and a lot of work and practice. This is why we believe a reflective stance concerning teaching and learning is important.

Our pedagogical stance

Our own standpoint concerning learning is similar to these educational ideas in some ways, but differs in others. As will be clear in the text to follow, we do, for instance, agree to the idea that learning is an active and constructive phenomenon and that the role of the teacher should be the one of guiding, or coaching. However, we disagree to the dualistic stance of learning described above, and would rather consider learning as a psychosomatic process; as a both intellectual and corporeal move of epistemological horizons (see *Figure 8.1*) (see also Lövkvist & Hjørungdal 2000:167f). We agree with the socio-cultural educationists in their

contextual approach, but we would also like to highlight aspects on gender and psychological factors, which they seem to have overlooked (see also Lövkvist & Hjørungdal 2000; compare Lövkvist forthcoming).

Thus, learning as well as knowledge is situated. In a situated context we consider learning to be about reflection and critical thinking, that leads to a change in thought and understanding of epistemes. In the long run it could even lead to an ontological change. The adventure of learning is about changing the perspectives on the world, on various topics as well as the disciplinary discourse. Learning is for us about understanding, where memorising 'facts' is only a small part. It is about making experiences, taking part of knowledge and information and bringing them into creative use in new contexts and enterprises. This also means being able to identify structures of form as well as of content, of what is to be learned. Teaching then, is the art of assisting the learners, which acquires both interest and patience for the task (see also Lauvås & Handal 2001:16, 21). Students in pedagogical surveys have even commented that the teachers' attitude towards the students is much more important than lecturing techniques and other teaching methods (Hodgson 1997:161). This is our very point of departure in our further discussion about learning and teaching (archaeology).

Meaning and understanding

An essential condition for the process of learning and memorising is that the stuff to be learned has some kind of immanent order and that it makes sense; it has to be understandable in one way or another (Allwood 1992a: 4, 1992b:19; Dahlgren 1997: 37; Svensson 1997: 60ff). However, according to some educationalists, 'sense', or meaningfulness is nothing immanent in either nature or culture (Dahlgren 1997: 37). They claim that understanding or accepting the more shallow character of a phenomenon like shape is a process different from the process of understanding its contextual nature or structure. Hence, there are more factors than external or concrete characters of the object at stake involved in the foundation for understanding. Everything has a meaning beyond itself, since it embraces something more, or is part of something greater. Making connections from/between smaller entities into a greater entity is a mental activity. In this sense of the word, meaningfulness derives from the human mind, which is always in motion. However, motion implies a direction, and we would like to add that the understanding in this sense might not always have the same direction as the educational aims. We understand this definition of 'meaningfulness' to be true for the mind also in its 'learning motion'. Thus texts, lectures etc would be meaningful in their educational aims only by means of the students' degree of active learning. This is an important aspect in this article, to which we will return later on.

The importance of meaning in a learning context has been illustrated in educational research studies. Results showed that even combinations of signs or figures seem easier to learn if they are presented in a way that can bring order and sense to them, where for instance the relation between the whole and the details are important components in the conception. Contextualising this experience into an educational situation, we have come to the conclusion that *the ideal curriculum has clear and explicit bonds between the different courses*. This is an idea that we will develop in a paragraph below.

Another central aspect of learning is the level of pre-understanding and previous knowledge. It has been shown that more and 'tighter' previous knowledge on a field of study means that the 'free' mental resources may be activated to get deeper into the problem than just to understand the more shallow structure of the problem (Allwood 1988:21ff; Hodgson 1997:167f). However, the difference between understanding and learning is that learning is what is new in the understanding (Svensson 1997:68). Thus, in that sense learning could only be considered in relation to *previous* knowledge and understanding. An interesting connection made by some educationalist researchers is that it is possible in many cases to *compensate lack of previous knowledge, by understanding the organising structure* of the information at stake (Svensson 1997:63f). Hence, important skills to obtain in order to understand and learn information, is to grasp the "organising principle and the referential meaning", how to realise how to sift, analyse, interpret, organise and use relevant information; to extend meaning and exceed previous knowledge (Svensson 1997:63f, 68). This is what could be called *'to learn to learn'*.

Some problematic fields for closer scrutiny

Some vital questions for a change of the educational strategy will, for instance, consider the content of and reason why teachers teach what they do, as well as what and why we actually wish our students to learn. Putting such questions to the fore will facilitate to focus on if and how we wish to change direction of the undergraduate education. On the other hand, how can we actually teach students how to learn? Considering that most human beings can, so to speak, 'not not learn' (verbal information from Kroksmark; see also Säljö 2000:12f), our question should be understood as directing interest to the students *approaches* to learning. Examples of this could include getting to know the students' *motives* for learning; their way of *finding* the relevant information; *organising* the pieces of information in a certain way; *processing* data in a scientifically appropriate manner, etc. But to be able to answer these and some closely related questions we would first like to consider some results on students' ways of learning made within professional pedagogy and psychology.

Why[1] do students learn?

> 'Welcome to school, little Pippi. I hope you will be happy here and that you will learn a great deal.'

---

[1] We would like to comment upon the headlines chosen for this and the next paragraph. We have asked questions as to why and how students learn. Our main sources of information have, however, chosen to answer the question of what it implies to be able to learn from a text, or what it implies to be a good teacher/student (Entwistle & Marton 1995:303, note that this is the Swedish edition). The information they have conveyed does, however, also answer the 'why-' and 'how-questions' and we have considered them relevant to reflect upon in our own context. We would also like to add, that we consider the 'what-question' to be highly essential and well integrated within the aspects of 'why' and 'how'.

'To be sure! And I hope that I'll get Christmas holidays', said Pippi. 'Cause that's the reason I have come. Justice above all things!' (In Astrid Lindgren's *Pippi Longstocking,* p. 59)

Learning information not only requires previous knowledge, meaningfulness or understanding structural principles. There must also be a *motivation* for why one would want to invest energy in learning. Four different types of orientations to education studies have been distinguished among students in an English study within a Swedish-English project (Beaty et al 1997:77ff; see also Morgan & Beaty 1997). In these orientations there are two subtypes according to kind of interest/motivation A) internal and B) external:

1. The *academic orientation* is directed towards the academic life. A) Students with an *internal* motivation want to follow up a personal intellectual interest, and the education is seen as a possibility to gain access to interesting lectures etc. They have often had an experience of the disciplinary topic before entering the studies and also want to continue their studies on a higher educational level. They especially appreciate tasks where they are allowed to freely choose their own topic of investigation. B) Students with an *external* interest are driven by a wish to make academic progress to gain high scores and academic qualifications and seem to be quite competitive. Therefore, these students often prefer clear directions that make explicit the examination demands.

2. Students with a *vocational orientation* aim at a job outside the university. A) Vocational orientated students with an *internal* interest for the studies, consider the education important for a coming career. They seem to work harder than other students, since they see the importance of the course for the carrier chosen. B) The aim of most students with an *external* interest to study is to get qualifying merits and acknowledgements.

3. A *personal orientation* has also been distinguished, which aims at personal development. A) Students having an *internal* interest in the studies want to broaden their views or fulfil themselves and consider the studies as a challenge, or simply as interesting. They seek challenge and stimulation and only see to the content of the education, not to a possible future career as a result of their studies. B) Students only driven by *external* force in their personal orientation seem, on the contrary only to be interested in getting compensation for lack of earlier education or to prove their ability. These students are anxious to tackle the course successfully and/or to get something back (as for example response on exams, papers etc, we reckon).

4. Lastly, there is *a social orientation* where the students direct their attention mainly towards the social side of university life. B) Here only students with an *external* interest (though internal the motivation may seem!) have been distinguished, whose main aim is to have fun. The main source of interest for these students is their possibilities to participate in sports or other social activities.

These types of educational orientation should of course be seen as extracted and generalised variables, where one or more orientations interact within each individual student (Beaty et al 1997:76ff). However, it could be relevant to distinguish such orientation attitudes among the students, since the type of orientation, along with the individual interest in education, were found to affect the measure of effort that the students put into their studies.

We have wanted to elucidate this aspect of learning, since many teachers often seem to project their own educational orientation, which usually would fall into an academic orientation (see also Beaty et al 1997:86). This may be one reason why much of the current teaching is directed in an authoritarian way, which may be a benevolent attempt to push the students in the 'right' direction, but usually has the effect of making the students passive instead. The challenge we can see here is to incorporate aspects of teaching that in some aspects could correspond to interest at personal, academic as well as professional levels, although these may, of course, be quite individual. Trying to please many individual interests is of course impossible if one considers this to be of a particular strategy with a certain final result already decided before the teaching starts. We would rather propose that such an attempt should be more open in its character, where one would strive for more engagement, activity and deeper understanding for the topic among the students rather than for a specific result in the content of the task. If done successfully, such a learning milieu will probably gain the results in the end, anyway. This aspect will be regarded in our forthcoming project idea suggested below.

How do students learn?

If they [the students] learn how to learn, they can learn new things and different things that they may need in their lives. That does not mean that students should only learn how to learn. What they learn still matters, but it is not the only thing that matters and, from the view point of this stage, it may not even be what matters most. (Kugel 1993:325)

The previous paragraph has approached interests by means of foundational motivation for orientation in educational studies. However, when dealing with a specific task, there is another aspect of motivation involved, a motivation directed towards the issue at stake.

The relation between learning and study material

In a context of working with a specific task there is a paradox between approach to and motivation for learning when it boils down to the actual studies (Marton & Säljö 1997: 55). An *internal motivation*, in terms of a wish to investigate something, coming from the student her/himself leads the student to a *deeper* understanding of the studied. The student so to speak 'steps into' the content being mediated, absorbs and analyses the central pick of the message (which should be understood as the author's aim and central point of the text and its conclusion). Students with this kind of approach do not try to remember the text, since the text is only a medium to get hold of something *beyond* the text (Marton & Säljö 1997:44f). As a result, they remember the content very well, and retelling the message of the content is thus unproblematic.

If, on the contrary, the interest driving the student to study is solely of an *external* character in terms of pressure due to demands from others, the system, higher scores, or the like, combined with lack of own interest, the learning seems to become more *shallow*[2]. Reading a text, for example, most of these students do not seem to be able to exceed beyond the text 'surface', which means that the content is reduced to text (Marton & Säljö 1997:44). Focusing on the text creates difficulties to remember what is being said; to remember it the student will more or less have to memorise words. In such a situation, the central message is difficult to distinguish, and the chance to get hold of it is more or less caused randomly and by chance. When asked to render the point of the message, get the point of the message did so, simply because *they did not look for it*. We the student retells fragments of the text and has difficulties to render the kernel of the message – in fact, the message can even be totally misunderstood (see also Säljö 1997:103).

The reason for such qualitatively different perceptions of one and the same text have by educationalists been found to be that the students have been looking for different things in the text (Marton & Säljö 1997:43). Students who failed to believe that such a situation might be *avoided by work with groups of students*, since a well performed co-operation works in terms of processing information between the participants. The chance to acknowledge and change direction of shallow learning into deep learning, and thus influence the learning approach could be easier to achieve in contexts of group work. The reason why, is that the learning approach has chances to present itself more explicit in group discussions than in individual work. It has even been said that it is "*/.../ precisely in such encounters between different conceptions of the same phenomenon, or between different 'versions of the world', that new insights may result, i.e. that learning can occur.*" (Säljö 1997:100, emphasis in original) We believe that group works could be one way to achieve learning and avoid so-called *hyper-intention* (i e performance anxiety leading to a shallow approach in order to learn as much as possible) in advantage for a deeper learning.

Returning to the *paradox of learning prerequisites*, it consists of two contradictory elements. Firstly, an inner motivation leads to a deep approach to learning, whereas an external motivation gives a more shallow approach. Secondly, it is difficult to become interested and motivated unless one pays attention to what the text concerns – which is harder to do having a shallow approach. Thus the initial, most crucial but also the most difficult thing to influence, seems to be the one of obtaining curiosity among the disciples for the issues at stake. The question is, however, whose task this is. Is this really the teacher's business, should it not be the students' own responsibility? Why else do they study if they are not interested? Our own personal experiences say that most students are interested in the discipline. However, there is another aspect of the question, and that is the *variation* in content among the courses *within the archaeological programme*. A person may have strong interest and motivation to become an archaeologist, but at the same time consider some courses irrelevant or simply not interesting. Nevertheless, the aim of a multiplicity of courses within an educational programme is to convey the width of the field and hopefully mediate an understanding of the importance and impact of these various areas. For this reason it is important to make efforts to capture the students' curiosity and interest. As Paul Ramsden, English professor in pedagogy, wrote: "lack of interest or motivation can be seen as arising from a context, rather than being fixed attributes which a student brings to a situation – although past experiences (at school, for example) clearly affect current perceptions." (Ramsden 1997:202) Therefore we wish to explore alternative ways of how teachers can affect the students' inner motivation in a positive direction and create contexts for growing curiosity to replace possible lack of interest.

Cognitive organisation

But whereas the above distinction concerns the students' *relation* to the studied in degrees of depth, there are other qualitatively different ways of learning, by means of *cognitively organising* the information (Svensson

---

2   However, students' interpretation of differences in demands and disciplinary nature within art/humanist versus natural science disciplines stimulate aspects of depth versus shallowness respectively. Within the natural sciences a more detailed approach (close to shallow learning) to the topic seems to be needed to enable a gradually deeper insight into the topic. In art/humanist disciplines, on the other hand, this approach could be regarded as a hindering moment in a art/humanist and social science, where a deep approach to the studied is needed from the beginning (Ramsden 1997:209f). Students within humanist disciplines also seem to evaluate the importance of understanding higher, than do students within the hard sciences (Ramsden 1997:201). However, degrees of both learning approaches in combination would probably be most beneficial for art/humanist, social as well as for natural sciences.

1997:65ff)[3]. There is a difference between a more memorising, defining and arranging parts of a material (atomistic approach) on the one hand, and using an organising principal to integrate the parts into a whole (holistic approach) on the other hand.

Within the *holistic approach* to learning various degrees of complexity and completeness have been acknowledged. Each of them corresponds to various ways of relating argument and conclusion. In a holistic approach this is expressed by a differing amount and quality of distinguished aspects and parts as well as the credibility of the content (closeness to data). There are also variations in *the atomistic approach*, concerning differences in integration of details and completeness. *Learning skills could therefore be said to be relational.* The interaction between the active individual and the material to be learned (the content), towards which the act is directed, is what makes up the quality of the learning skill. However, these approaches to learning are not any fixed individual characteristics; they can be used by the same person in different situations depending on the person's aims and intentions for learning. Exactly this openness of interaction, contingent on context, is what is included in the term 'approach', whereas 'strategy' (which we try to avoid in discussions on learning) implies a direction *from* somewhere *to* a certain static and finite goal, according to an already defined plan (Svensson 1997:67).

To return to the difference between atomistic and holistic ways of learning, their qualities also *affect future learning*. As a holistic approach includes the use of an organising principle, which can be used in new contexts, it has quite an important impact on future learning, whereas an atomistic approach reflects a skill which importance is limited in future learning. This is due to the level of detail, where the parts can vary within an entity depending on context without following a certain ordering principal or structure. Learning to organise pieces of information into entities is the biggest difficulty to learn to learn – but once that has been attained, it is the most essential qualitative improvement of all achievements in a learning context (Svensson 1997:67f). *'Learning to learn'* can include distinguishing organising principles both in terms of memorising techniques, but also more complex entities. Learning on such a meta level implies an achieved skill to get to learn other things in future situations regardless of the context where this skill was first obtained. *'Meta learning'*, as we have chosen to call it, is in that sense a far more important a learning than learning other information. The greatest hindrance to meta learning, is when one 'gets stuck' at the level of memorising details instead of lifting oneself up to the level of understanding the entity at stake.

Learning effects from the educational system

Unfortunately, our educational system suffers from yet another considerable paradox. At the same time that there is a lack of explicit aims saying that students are expected to achieve a deep, holistic learning, the system is based on a tradition of examinations as a control of learning. Examinations are traditionally quite limited to their content and extension, and can not reveal the students' understanding of the information to any greater extent (Svensson 1997:69). A successful student not only needs to handle a lot of new information, but also needs to integrate this new knowledge with his or her former epistemology and set of experiences. To obtain this, the student will need...

> /.../ insight, confidence and even independence and stubbornness on the part of the student. This is extremely unlikely to be found among students relying on an atomistic approach and already pressed by the increasing risk of failure. On the other hand, its achievement may in some extreme cases lead to a failure if, in allocating study time, the student places integrated understanding above the requirements to learn a specified range of materials as demanded by the examination system. Here, the paradox is that although in most cases academic failure results from problem with understanding, in some cases it may result from a devotion to thorough understanding. (Svensson 1997:70f)

The relationship between courses and learning will also be touched upon in this context. Once again we have the educational programme in archaeology in mind when quoting what has been said about the impact courses within an educational programme have on learning:

> /.../ the benefits of skilled learning go beyond a better knowledge of a specific body of subject-matter and its long-term retention and application to new material. Ultimately, improvements in skill in learning which stem from any particular course unit are not specific to the content of that unit. They are improvements in the skill of understanding and of learning to learn. The student becomes more skilled at extending his or her understanding through an exploration of new and more complex material. Defined in this way, learning requires a relative absence of stress and a confidence in one's own thinking that are not always fostered in educational systems. (Svensson 1997:71)

Instead such an educational system seems to encourage

---

[3]   The meanings of these concepts are not fixed, but are functions of the content to be learned, "And just as the nature of the learning material may vary, so the meaning of the main difference in approach may vary too." (Svensson 1997:68).

the students to a shallow and atomistic approach to learning. What is interesting is the importance ascribed to the educational programme for 'meta learning'. This is a vital aspect to which we will return later.

The answer to the question of 'How do students learn?' seems to be that there are *various learning approaches*, both concerning the relation to as well as the cognitive organisation of the studied. Gaining a deep and holistic understanding of the studied seems easier when having an internal motivation and the skill in 'meta learning' (i e having learned to learn). Owning that skill of distinguishing the structuring principal of the piece of information is a prerequisite for deeper understanding the core of the message, and that understanding is, in turn, a prerequisite for internal motivation – which is basic for learning... These circular circumstances could be problematic for students who have entered the treadmill in the wrong direction. We believe that this direction can be influenced by external factors to a certain extent (se also Hodgson 1997:170). Although the students have a great responsibility for their own studies, we think it is important for the teachers to show interest in the students' achievements and their study situation, and to try to facilitate to get on well in their task of learning. What we have acknowledged so far, this could be done in terms of alternative tools to *arouse interest and motivation* among the students, as motivation also can be considered as a result of good teaching and not necessarily as a prerequisite for learning only (see also Biggs 1999:61). Motivation could also be altered in terms of arrangement of and between courses as well as other ways of dealing with meta learning. An open mind towards the students and their learning contexts is, however, perhaps the most important thing to have as a teacher and conveyor of information. We will return to these ideas in the chapter on 'Featuring an engendered teaching/learning situation'. But first we will discuss chosen aspects of some common traditional as opposed to alternative ideas on learning and pedagogy.

How do teachers teach?

When the same person is doing the presenting all the time, inevitably one line of approach to the materials is going to dominate. (Tompkins 1991:26)

Leaving for a moment the questions of why and how students learn, we will now turn the focus on the teachers and their participation in the teaching/learning context. Dealing with these conveyors of knowledge, we will change the order of the questions and begin to ask *how* teachers teach, so as to highlight the present traditional way of teaching. Thereafter we ask the question of *why* teachers teach in order to discuss our educational role as teachers and what we might want to reconsider or change. We also consider the ideologies behind some of the alternative teaching strategies which we feel could improve the present situation.

Ideas from alternative learning have been implemented through various methods and practices. We shall give a brief survey of some of these methods and practices, and thus try to emerge some points of value to our own environment and to our own sketch to a possible teaching project in archaeology.

Traditional teaching: "She shall feed her flock..."

But what is traditional teaching then and how is this eventually featured in our experiences? The slightly distorted Biblical quotation, "She shall feed her flock..." would describe the present teaching practice.

So, what do we do actually, as teachers of archaeology? What we give at the moment, are more exactly, brief courses, and there is usually space for traditional lectures and seminars only. What we usually have been able to offer students is restricted to a support for their own self-studies, which is normally given through "cramming" lectures. We can explain the texts to the students, and define and explain the vital notions and terms of archaeology. We can give an overview of main structures in prehistory, as well as of the historical and professional development of archaeology, and we can define where the different edges of research are at the present. The aim of this is to present a structure of prehistory to the student, in order to make their own reading and understanding of texts easier. There is still too much lecturing, and no time for searching for more profound knowledge, or for thinking and maturing knowledge. This would describe an approach still common. Our experiences say that this is a strategy, which makes the students still more dependent on the teacher than they ever used to be, by means of dependency on the university teacher with respect to what they learn, and why they have to learn. That is; instead of encouraging the students to learn how to sift and interpret information, the teacher tells them what they should see as vital – and this is the authoritarian way (See *Figure 8.2*).

Figure 8.2 We conceive a teacher doing 'traditional teaching' – through banking model and/or peak performance – could be compared with a wolf in a shepherds clothes. They both lull their flock into a sense of security, whereas the real outcome could be rather unfortunate...
Drawn by Linda Lövkvist.

This reminds us of what Paulo Freire (1972) once defined as the *banking method* – a teaching method we would see as the arch-enemy of longitudinal learning (a methodology more on terms with gender conscious learning) – as knowledge is not allowed to mature and develop and be connected. In order to visualise the methods most of us want to break with, we shall enlarge on a couple of aspects of them, as the standpoint to leave the methods, also needs clarification and motivation.

What Freire gave the epithet of "banking teaching", is in summary that the Teacher is the Knower, and the Student is the still Ignorant. The teacher shall give her/his knowledge onto the student like a gift, and the student shall store this gift in herself/himself until the moment she/he will need it. A consequence of this says Freire, is that reality will remain in status quo, and this is as well the aim, as the method leaves the student devoid of consciousness about the world, and as such of critical thinking (Freire 1972: 70ff). Nevertheless, behind the times the strategy once criticised by Freire is too familiar to us and still haunts academic creativity.

The performance model

As far as our experience go, we have unfortunately not yet managed to forget this receiving-and-storing-and-reproducing method of teaching and learning in its full consequence. It is therefore refreshing to recognise that there in practice are possible ways of leaving it behind. However, according to Jane Tompkins, professor in English at Duke University, USA, we have much more reason to feel uneasy with another obsolete model of teaching. This model is what Tompkins defines as the Performance model (Tompkins 1991:24). It is very difficult to break with the Performance model, for more than one reason. One of them is the reason that a break would problematize the very role of the traditional teacher. And, not least, it concerns some aspects of education which not many of us might have been able to see through, as it interferes so deeply with our own long process of socialisation (Tompkins op. cit.:25). Seen from a students' horizon, one reason and obstacle, would be that students from the beginning seem to be waiting to be fed. There is already a very strong dependence on authority when the students come to the university, and authority is expected to be shown through the practising of the Performance Model. Another obstacle is that the teacher often thinks she/he must make a good and entertaining lecture. In sum, this model is defined by the expectations (of him/herself, and of others) on the teacher to simply make a good performance out of his/her teaching. She or he has to show the students that she/he is learned, confident and able. The main component behind this model, says Tompkins, is fear – fear not to be good enough (Tompkins loc.cit.).

Taken together, such notions about education must be defined as a substantial part of the root of the problem of how to develop into knowers. In other words; through the act of projecting a notion of absolute ignorance to others, we practice an oppressing ideology and are as well expected to execute this through a peek performance. And what is still worse, through these methods, one is as such bound to negate education and knowledge as processes of investigation (cf. Freire 1972:71).

So far, the discussion of this paragraph has been focused on teacher – student roles and relationships, and on the problems with obsoleteness of the models we have. Another aspect which must be considered in this discussion is the content of existing courses. One important question here is whether we think it is possible to integrate gender conscious teaching and learning into existing courses. It would be quite handy if this was the case, but unfortunately our answer must be 'No'. The reason for this is that by gender conscious teaching and learning, we mean something more than adding a couple of gender informed texts to the existing reading lists. The present context of learning as discussed above is a hindrance to the possibilities to reach the aims of gender conscious education. In other words, our conception of a gender conscious teaching is that the practices of teaching are tightly involved with the contents of education in the process of development. We will return to this aspect later on. However, to be able to do this, we would first like to consider the questions of *why* teachers teach.

Why do university teachers teach?

Good teaching is getting most students to use the higher cognitive level process that the more academic students use spontaneously. Good teaching narrows the gap. (Biggs 1999:58, emphasis in original)

Why do we teach at all, and why do we teach archaeology at the universities? Before giving an adequate and satisfying answer to this awkward question, one has to define the aims as well as the prerequisites of the discipline, and of the education in question. Approaches to and methods of teaching have to suit their aims. The aims of archaeological education in Sweden (and international) must first and foremost be seen as manifold, as there are so many different administrative branches to which archaeology can have relevance. The following aims are among the clearest ones.

An obvious aim of archaeological education is to educate professional and skilled archaeologists. The practice of professional archaeology includes in turn, several areas additional to research and university teaching. The far most extensive one is the profession of field archaeology, which again has more than one aspect. Museums are another area open to archaeologists, as is heritage management. All of these include administration posts as well as scientific and public related ones. It must however be considered, that far from all of those who study an introductory course, and far from all whom graduate in archaeology, aim at becoming an archaeologist. There are for example many school teachers who have a sabbatical leave from their teaching posts to educate themselves in a discipline which they think could complete or extend their knowledge. This concerns not least teachers of history. Another aspect of importance is the international character of archaeology, which also has to be taken into consideration. Lastly, we would like to include another, far from unimportant reason why one should study archaeology. This reason is found in the old humanist tradition of education as an aim by itself. This is a point lately stressed by Dr. Johan Rönnby, one of our colleagues in the University College of Södertörn, south of Stockholm. He states that archaeology as a social and humanist science should not at all need to justify its own existence through reference in the job market and in the extent of rescue excavations. Archaeology is first and foremost a way of broadening one's perspectives on humans and society, and this is also what we should teach our student initially, says Rönnby (2000:1f).

We cannot but agree warmly. This is mainly why we teach. But on the background of the broad aims, prerequisites and possibilities referred to, it is of departure to further studies, and to the development of professionalism. We are here once more at the heart of the matter. In order to be able to work towards the broad and multifaceted aims of archaeology, we have to develop and practice good teaching methods. A general characteristic of what we need is that we have to be very good at teaching students how to learn through their own independent work. Traditional approaches, methods and practices of education, are neither found satisfying nor adequate to the fulfilment of the general and broad tasks we find that we have as university teachers of archaeology. Our next endeavour is therefore to explore some other paths to knowledge.

Some alternative approaches to learning and their aims

> /.../ helping teachers improve their teaching is best done using a theory that helps teachers reflect on what they are doing. For what they need is a framework to aid reflection... (Biggs 199:60)

In this paragraph we will give you a brief presentation of aspects on teaching that we believe could bring new blood and energy into many learning contexts. However, it does not only include experiences of practical and didactic 'know how'. As we believe that attitude precedes methodology, we will first and foremost present some reflective lines on feminist attitudes and approach to one's own role as teacher and what it may do to students and classroom interaction. Secondly, we will comment the usefulness of the methods of Coaching, PBL and Case Methodology. We find that one important point to our own work is how to integrate elements of PBL with gender conscious issues and practices. However, we shall also put both of these schools under some critical scrutiny through questions about how to overcome some critical

aspects of 'survival of the fittest students', as acknowledged by feminists (Hellertz 1999:347, endnote 22; see also the second aim in 'Projected aims' below).

Central to this cross-fertilization of attitude and practice is the role of the teacher and the question of how teaching approaches have been practised and carried out. Hence, to have an opportunity to consider these important aspects, we have taken a look at some examples produced by educators reporting on how they have practised feminist approaches in their teaching.

Feminist pedagogical approach – attitude in practice

Before going into any enterprise one always brings one's attitude and approach into one's action. In order to sincerely mediate our idea of teaching, we want to be straightforward to the reader in our own conception of teaching.

We prefer to consider teaching from a perspective that contributes to make *all* students and their potential visible as unbiased, creative and developing as possible. This approach has been put forward by feminist pedagogues and teachers within other academic disciplines. They are very conscious about what they do in the classroom, which make the ways feminist educators practice in class of vital interest. Although many other teachers may have been aware of various aspects in the classroom, there may be deviations in what is *focused on* for their attention. Feminists have also expressed their *consciousness about action* more explicitly and problematized. Questions occurring to us have thus concerned issues related to actions in the classroom; What do the students do, and what do the teachers do when feminist ways of learning are practiced? These questions have proven to give many answers since scholars stress different points in their own stories of application.

In the following we shall departure in Conkey & Tringham's paper (1997) on the issue of practising feminist learning. From their paper, we will try to pick up some points useful to our own further discussion on learning. Conkey & Tringham (1996), discuss the professors' own recent experiments in their teaching of archaeology – experiments which have been motivated and informed by various aspects of feminist thought. Among their points, is the one of how to scrutinize explicitly the links between their feminist thinking and scholarship and their classroom practices (Conkey & Tringham op.cit. 225ff). On this vital point, they found inspiration in Jane Tompkins' paper, dealing with aspects of the role of the teacher (Tompkins 1991). Central is the focus on the coaching model, besides the point that it is the students who are responsible for presenting the course material to the class (see also Tompkins op.cit.:26). Conkey & Tringham did, like Tompkins, replace the performance model with coaching. Important to this approach, is focus on what the teacher *does* in the classroom, rather than focus on what she *talks* about. The core of Conkey & Tringham's way of practicing coaching was the use of panels.

Their general approach was explicitly, as they themselves put it, "Coaching Archaeology through panels", instead of "Teaching Archaeology through Lectures" (Conkey & Tringham 1996:228ff). A panel is a group of students who teach the class during a series of meetings. The panels did their own planning and preparations ahead of the presentations. Besides the panels, the course learning was as well lectures given by the two professors, and by visitors, and there were as well readings to the course. Another important ingredient in the endeavour of trying to be coaches rather than lecturers was the encouragement of other voices that is the participation of guests from other departments. The idea is to provide alternative approaches and perspectives to an issue (op.cit. 245f).

These were briefly, some aspects of Conkey & Tringham's concept of feminist inspired education. The experiment seems to have been a success for both coaches and students. In their evaluations students held that critical thinking had been encouraged through the coached panels. Although some of the students felt uncertain about the fact that there is no single answer or just one single interpretation, most of them found that the use of various perspectives was a strength (Conkey & Tringham1996:246). The authors also conclude that their coached panels did not only *liberate the classroom*, but as well *themselves as teachers* (op.cit.:226). The latter point is a vital point as well in Tompkins' paper, in her discussion of how she transformed her own role from lecturer to coach (Tompkins 1991).

An important notion is the one of *"coach"* which has been mentioned in both papers (Conkey & Tringham 1996; Tompkins 1991). Coaching is as such a special way of practicing PBL inspired teaching. The difference of coaching in other situations than PBL might just be the lack of the firm structure in the coaching, which is inherent in PBL.

As far as we can see, the most important thing about coaching is the fact that it stresses the role of the teacher as a *facilitator of learning*. This is one of the ingredients we need in order to be able to develop our own plans. However, there are some problematic points in connection to this set of ideas, which are worthy of a further comment: 1) We would like to stress the point that it ought to be possible to use feminist pedagogy in all kind of courses and learning contexts, not only explicitly in feminist or gender-oriented learning (for a similar argument, see Conkey & Tringham 1996:227). 2) Nor should feminist pedagogy be understood as a particular women's way of learning. 3) Another point is the question of how we can define feminist pedagogy. In general we can say that feminist pedagogy in many respects builds on, as well as it represents, a criticism of critical pedagogy (Luke & Gore eds. 1992). Feminist

pedagogues have however more explicitly stressed what they actually do in the classroom. 4) We would also like to add that, to us, feminist pedagogy is as well – very importantly – about attitude and approach towards the students, hence about a *reflecting practice*.

Problem Based Learning and Case Methodology

In methodological issues we have also been influenced by the pedagogical school of Problem Based Learning (PBL) (see for example Berglund 1998; Egidius 1991a, 1999a, 1991b; Flinck & Liljedahl 1997). PBL builds on, and further develops, the premise that human beings are born with an innate urge for learning (see for instance Dahlgren 1987:13f). Its practical implication requires that one applies knowledge and principles in new situations, and thereby one tests and reinforces, the understanding of what is learned. Logically it follows that the interesting part in the learning context is not the result or the solution, but the *process* of getting there.

PBL, as well as Case Method (CM), were developed on principles of learning which can be traced back to antiquity, to the ideas of Socrates and Plato, who focused on learning as a dialogue between teacher and learner (Egidius 1999a:45). The context of modern development of PBL was the one of the student revolt in the 1960s. Criticism was among other things held against universities' isolation from social and political life and against educations' isolation from professional practices. Criticism was also directed against an authoritarian and hierarchical system, of which the teacher lecturing *ex cathedra* came to be the very symbol. Students claimed more influence, democracy, discussions, work in smaller groups instead of attending lectures, and freedom to choose what they themselves found to be of importance and interest to learn (Egidius 1999a:46ff).

Close to PBL is the Case Methodology, and their common bottom line, is that learning is based in work with problems within a subject or a discipline. These problems are examples from real life situations, such as you might meet them within professional work. As educator Henry Egidius put it, the point is, that students practice problem solving already before they receive the knowledge they need (cf. Egidius 1999a:9). PBL and Case Method differ however from each other through the role of the teacher. In case studies the meetings are *lead by a teacher*, whereas the PBL meetings, on the contrary, are *lead by the students themselves*. During PBL meetings, the teacher sits by the students' side as a tutor, or to "lead by the hand" to the sources of knowledge (Egidius 1999a:11; 27ff). This says that the teacher's role is more like the role of an inspiring and responsible leader, or a Coach. Not least, in our eyes this seems to be very far from the role we criticize as being the leader and the spoon feeder, or the shepherd of the flock.

PBL is as such a method of learning once upon a time initiated by students. Later on, the approach has been developed by pedagogues, some of whom were as well among the mentioned students of the 1960s. If you use PBL in its full consequence, there usually is a *seven jump* schedule to be followed. This starts with the introduction of a chosen problem to the basic group, before you go through a closer definition and analysis of the problem, with the testing of alternative hypotheses, until finally the new knowledge you reach is tested again, and evaluated. If you do not follow "The seven jump," Egidius states, you challenge the very working method of PBL (Egidius 1999b:8f).

Despite the fact that we are not professional pedagogues, we think it would be worth challenging the rather rigid structure of original PBL. We think it is possible to make your own way by the aid of chosen ideas as a *source of inspiration*. A vital point with PBL is in our view, that the method has the potential of representing a very broad approach. As such, professionals within several disciplines have already taken up, adapted and developed problem related methods in their own particular contexts (see Flinck & Liljedahl as discussed below). PBL can therefore be seen as a general starting point to our development of more student related methods of learning. It is very much up to us as teachers to consider which issues to focus, and how they could be implemented in our own particular discipline.

Concluding remarks on chosen alternative approaches

Thus, we have found a few good examples of gender- and feminist inspired projects, which already have been carried out with success. Our objective is however not to deal with an already carried out project of learning. Rather, our endeavour is to reflect upon possible methods and approaches in future planning of education. Therefore, we would like to discuss some ideas of special relevance to the future of our own context. We would as well suggest some ideas on how to cope with questions and problems one has to face during a teaching course. The ideas are meant to be a source of inspiration to colleagues finding themselves in the same situation as we are, as non-experts of gender informed teaching and feminist pedagogy. However, we address colleagues who, like us, share a lively interest in questions of gender informed learning approaches in university education in general. The surveyed methods and practices underpinning our project are, most importantly, in stark contrast to what usually is characterised as traditional teaching.

Some needs and suggestions for an engendered teaching/learning situation

> The classroom is a microcosm of the world; it is the chance we have to practice whatever ideals we may cherish. (Tompkins 1991:26)

So far we have considered various aspects on the teaching/learning context, and we have arrived at the point where we would like to present some alternative ideas. Learning contexts are influenced by different factors and they affect the learning ability. Experiences from a research project carried out by professional pedagogues indicate that:

> In any particular learning situation there may be a complex interplay between two groups of elements. On the one hand, there is the content of the task and its organisation. On the other hand, there is the student's previous knowledge and his or her approach to the task, where the approach encompasses a particular intention, a way of thinking about the treatment of the task and an attempt to organise the material. (Svensson 1997:68)

To have a deep, holistic and complete understanding and approach to learning is to be well skilled in the art of learning (ibid). So what does it take in an educational context to achieve the prerequisites needed for this desirable condition? We consider this question particularly important to answer, since pedagogues have found that the relation between teachers' explicit aims and their execution are often not coherent (Entwistle 1997:6).

Our ambition is to present a course issue that is practically possible to 'launch' and carry through. Our first step towards an answer to the question asked above will be to consider the comprehensive frames of the pedagogical context. Instead of reproducing a traditional teaching with the teacher as the 'flock leader', we would like to propose a teaching situation where the students in the herder's 'flock' will be given chances to find their own ways of exploring knowledge and, in a sense, be their own teachers. By this, we do not mean that trained teachers will be needless and redundant – in fact, quite on the contrary. The teaching role will be transformed in a way that will increase its importance to the students rather than decrease it, at the same time as the students, while working together in groups, learn important aspects of meta learning in co-working with their peers. In the quest for new information to learn and integrate with their previous knowledge the students will be more active and independent and have greater possibility to influence the direction of what they will learn. *A situation with chances to influence the own situation has possibility to create a learning context that the student could find more meaningful. This may in turn lead to a positive atmosphere around the topic being studied and wake curiosity and inner motivation in the student, which is exactly what professional pedagogues consider important prerequisites for a deep and holistic learning.*

However, an important note to make before starting a process like this is that it will need much initial work from the teachers involved and, most of all, a well prepared and co-ordinated teaching team. It demands quite a long time of planning and preparation, for instance in order to rearrange the courses. However, once the planning is done, the students work more independently, and the teacher is relieved from great parts of the traditional assignments like some of the lecturing and most of the marking of students' papers. Still, more money put into teaching resources is yet on our want list.

As our sketch could be seen as an alternative to the existing syllabus on the introductory course of the archaeological education, we would like to give a brief description of the present syllabus. Minor changes in courses' organisation and content have appeared continually throughout a range of years. We will therefore also present some positive experiences from ongoing experiments before moving on to the aims of alternative teaching strategies.

The students' present initial encounter with archaeological studies

The Introductory Course is the traditional name of the first term of studying within a university department, and this course runs all through the first term. A term at a Swedish university lasts 20 weeks, and the academic year has two terms, the autumn term (primo September–medio January) and the spring term (medio January–primo June). One term is 20 Swedish credits (30 ECTS). The aim of this Introductory Course in archaeology, as it is designed at the Gothenburg department, is to give a first orientation of the archaeological issue. This means conveying archaeology as a discipline focusing on humanity during long historical sequences, through the interpretations of remains from human life and enterprise. It also includes introducing theories and methods of archaeology. The teaching of the Introductory Course is traditionally done through lectures, group discussions, short excursions, and a field section. The students' level of obtained knowledge is tested through home examinations in the reading sections, besides their compulsory participation in the field-related sections of the course.

Students applying for this course do not have to have any specific previous knowledge except for the demands for University studies in general, which mostly mean a completed College with at least medium grades in Swedish, English and Maths. The archaeology course is so called 'detached', which implies that it can be taken by students either without further studies in archaeology, or as an introduction to coming, extensive studies within the field. However, getting a BA or MA in Sweden takes three and four years respectively and will include a combination of disciplinary topics, with main focus on two of them. These disciplines are usually studied one at a time, where each course will take one term of full time studies to complete. Aiming at their BA or MA, many students chose to continue their studies within archaeology. Nevertheless, they may take other courses in between the terms of archaeological studies.

At the present the Introductory Course is organised into four smaller, partial courses, or sections:

Issues of course sections	Length of sections
General Prehistory I (Global prehistory)	6 weeks
General Prehistory II (Nordic prehistory)	6 weeks
Teories & Methods (including History of Archaeology)	6 weeks
Field section (including survey and recognition)	2 weeks
	20 weeks
	=20 weeks (30 ECTS)

General Prehistory I and II aim at presenting an inauguration to the variation of current central archaeological problems. These sections also include studies on local conditions and processes. The teaching methods of these courses usually have included literature studies, lectures and encounters with original prehistoric finds at the department and in museums. The section of Theories and Methods includes lectures and literature. The fourth section is devoted to acquaintances with cultural landscapes with visible remains above the earth and professional ways of describing them. The students will also accomplish terrain recognition and survey of prehistoric sites. Each section of the Introductory Course is usually followed by an evaluation from the students. This is an opportunity to present their opinions on various aspects of the course, as well as it will provide the teaching staff with feed back on course organisation and teaching as well.

The disadvantages with such a course organisation are in our opinion, at least threefold:

1) The organisation *splits up* the various themes, or sections, instead of connecting them. We believe that linking the various sections of the Introductory Course more explicitly into a wider context would be a better alternative. This would make easier a more profound understanding of phenomena such as long time processes and the importance of theory and method to the interpretation of these processes, including gender aspects etc.

2) The schedule with a 'split' programme of clearly separated sections is inclined to create a *rushed atmosphere* for students and for teacher as well; if you miss something, you will easily get behind very quickly. In this perspective, working with group projects will give the students possibilities of creating a plan of their own, that suits them better. We also would like to try the alternative of lecturing two parallel issues at a time. We simply imagine that this is a method which will give a more relaxed atmosphere, since it leaves room for a more flexible solution to the present problem of catching up with the missed information.

3) Also leaning heavily on lectures, i.e. traditional teaching does, as already mentioned, *make the students very passive* – a situation we would like to change, not least from the point of view of our own experiences.

Lately, however, some changes in teaching methods have been developed and practiced in our Gothenburg department with positive results, which shall be acknowledged below.

The present introductory course in archaeology is to most students their initial encounter with archaeological studies. However, all the more often it is their initial encounter with university studies in general. This is why we think it is as crucial to introduce them to good policies on how university studies are expected to work. The notion of giving the teaching for first time students a special design has also been presented by Ramsden (1993:67). The reason for giving extra attention to these students is that it has been found that students continue their study approach, which they have learned through previous education. Since the system of most elementary schools and higher education usually seem to have encouraged a shallow approach, this is also what these students bring to their university studies. Therefore, it is of extra importance to find ways of quickly guiding the students into a deep and more holistic study approach. This is why we suggest that the students already during their first term of archaeological studies should be introduced to the importance of *co-operation between peers* and of *actively taking part in finding information themselves*. Another aspect that we consider important to introduce to these students is to highlight an awareness of *their political and democratic rights, responsibilities and their ability to influence*. These aspects are highly relevant also after graduation, when they for example as scholars are expected to be able to handle these practices and ethics professionally. This actually marks a central point of departure to our educational prospect.

There are, however already some pedagogical strategies which have been tried within our department in Gothenburg, and which actually correspond to some of our aims. The strategies in mind represent changes of importance, if not heavy in extent, and they have been practised at our department for a couple of years, and since the autumn term in 2000 respectively. The working methods in question constitute a creative way of dealing with educational matters. Therefore they deserve some attention also in this context, and will be considered as a possible and welcome 'ingredient' with a potential for development.

Positive experiences from ongoing teaching approaches in Gothenburg

There are indeed as well positive experiences to take into consideration, and they shall be enlarged upon in some aspects here as they should be taken care of in an endeavour of development.

To give a background, we can first take a look back to the beginning of the 1990s. Then, the syllabus was still arranged so as to present and teach about prehistoric artefacts from all periods, all in a special section at the end of the Introductory Course. This course section had of course been preceded by a course in general Nordic prehistory, so there were evidently possibilities for the students to return to the literature of that section. However, this organisation with a separate artefact section, created an artificial learning situation all the same. The students had to virtually memorise design, function and period for every artefact without any greater *pedagogical* connection to the artefacts' cultural and historical context. As we have learned from the previous chapter 'Aspects of learning', learning under such conditions is very difficult. It creates a situation where the students do their best to learn the artefacts by heart, just to be able to achieve the scores needed to pass the course, instead of learning for understanding aspects of the artefacts in a wider context. In all probability this was a matter of Freire's classic "banking teaching". This course arrangement was, however, given up some years ago in favour for a more integrated version, where the artefacts are being considered in connection to the courses presenting *each prehistoric period respectively*. The advantage of integrating the artefact course into the courses dealing with the Nordic prehistoric narratives is the inverted value of the case referred to above.

A further change in educational direction actually concerns the approach to *how* artefacts are learnt, too. During the autumn of 2000 Tove Hjørungdal, Elisabeth Arwill-Nordbladh and Håkan Petersson started to integrate small cases of investigation for the students to execute, similar to PBL, but on a smaller scale. The students were put in a situation where they had to *interpret the contexts of various artefacts themselves*. The aim of the second course moment 'General prehistory II' in which the task is integrated, is twofold. Firstly, it is to study central aspects of processes in Nordic prehistory. Secondly, it aims at giving an insight into the plurality of prehistoric material remains. In the particular task in mind, the students worked in groups and got to choose an artefact to investigate by means of description of type, its local topographical context, dating and its cultural/societal context. They were told that they (fictively) were expected to hold a seminar for an archaeological student organisation to inform its members about their interpretation of their 'find'. In reality, of course, they made a brief presentation of their conclusions to their class. This teaching strategy has many advantages. It not only presents the material in a pedagogical manner, which may establish a base for aroused interest and creativity, as well as it 'engenders' the artefacts through the interpretations. It also encounters the students to a situation, which they as graduated archaeologists will meet in their future job. This will give the students some archaeological practice in a more professionally related sense and could thereby make the interpreting issue less deterrent a moment. Such a situation might make the students feel confirmed and more comfortable in their future professional role, which could contribute to an increased self-confidence.

Since the autumn of 2000 Tove used yet another moment for the students to present their conclusions of team work in the introductory course, where the results of a minor task was arranged by the students and put up as a small *poster exhibition* at the department. The task was a part of the section on archaeological theory and method. The students also held a short public analysis, or 'vernissage', of the content and their conclusions. The idea was very positively received by the students, who in their own course evaluations about this specific course moment used epithets like 'good and fun', 'good with group work to learn to co-operate', 'good way of accounting for our results' and 'different'. As we pointed out earlier, *having fun 'doing' the learning is a promising entrance to a 'deep' and 'holistic' learning, as well as for 'meta learning'*. Tove's own reflections on the course section was that it gave a professional dimension to the issue, which will give the students more insight into difficulties and possibilities with these theoretical and methodological aspects, as well as into social realities within the group. Except from a couple of slightly negative voices, the students were very devoted to the task and they read more extra curricular literature, information that they had searched and found themselves from various resources.

Lastly, we would like to consider the Gothenburg experiences of *home examinations* for all undergraduate levels of the archaeological education. Some ten years ago the teachers introduced the 'home examination', where the questions asked were adjusted to the new examination context. Instead of giving questions that implied expectations of relatively short – and rather shallow – answers, the questions were changed into the design of an investigating character. As the students have to work themselves through the texts in order to understand, and to be able to write their own texts, these small intellectual quests demand a deeper understanding of the studied and a taking of stances to the studied contexts. The majority of the students prefer this kind of examination, although a few students think it implies too much effort and rather prefer traditional examinations. Instead of getting nervous and anxious for having to memorise a considerable amount of literature the students now have more time for reflecting upon the content and developing an own point of view. Although the teachers get longer papers to mark, sometimes even delayed, they find them much more interesting to read and they can also see more of individual development in the students' attitudes related to the educational issues. The experiences from the home examinations were so positive, that the teachers decided to change all the previous traditional examinations into home examinations and this have worked out well.

The experiences presented in this paragraph have given very positive effects and impacts on the teaching/learning situation during different parts of the course. We consider them, with preference, useful in a course of the kind we suggest in this paper and which we soon will present.

Finding our way. Approaches suited for archaeology

Didactics and educational methods are of course context based in their practical needs and designs according to discipline, topics, amount of students, etc. We therefore think it appropriate to comment upon the alternative methods introduced earlier in an archaeological context.

PBL is, for a start, not a wholesale method for teaching and learning. Above all, PBL is developed within medical and nursing training, which do as well have different aims and different professional working methods compared to those archaeologists in general have (cf. Silén 1996). Out of the approaches surveyed, we think we have to pick up a choice of issues, and try to adjust the ideas to our own context and discipline. In order to discuss how to make a selection of issues and ideas, we shall take a look at a teaching project undertaken at the Department of Education at the University of Lund (Flinck & Liljedahl 1997). These educationists have made their own way, guided by chosen aspects of PBL. Their aim was to help their students to reach profound learning, and their point of departure was the question of whether PBL with its specific structure can be a possible way of reaching profound learning (Flinck & Liljedahl op.cit.:5).

One important difference between medical training and the discipline of education, is that the students might choose to stay at the Department of education just for one term i.e. 20 weeks, whereas in medical training the students following each other throughout their entire education. To have PBL suit their own discipline, Flinck & Liljedahl altered the following issues. *First*, the cases presented to the students in Education studies in Lund, are much wider, and have to be given much more time than they are given within medicine. *Second*, concerning the roles of lectures, the educationists chose to plan lectures from the beginning, and not just give them on request of the students, which is more usual according to original PBL. *Third*, the number of students in each basic group is in Flinck & Liljedahl's department 8-10, as compared to 6 or 7 in original PBL. It should also be stressed, that the roles of the lectures, and the size of basic groups, are as well very much related to resources, and not to character of the discipline alone. To the experiences and results conveyed by the educationists in Lund, the high quality of the course is the aspect they stress. To explain this more extensively, this means that most students thought they learned better and more, and that the relationship between student and teacher was much better and more democratic. Central to the learning process is that students learned quickly to problematize a case, and start the self-studies. Another positive result of the project, was that the lecturers involved worked as a team, which lead to better co-operation, as compared to former traditional teaching when a lecturer planned and executed the course by herself (Flinck & Liljedahl op.cit.:6ff).

It seems very clear as well to us, that original PBL in its full consequence, would not suit our introductory courses in archaeology. This seems as well to be the experience made by some of our colleagues in the Department of Archaeology, University of Uppsala, where PBL seems to be tested on a more systematic level than in other departments of archaeology in the country. From here it was stated that despite its positive aspects, PBL was very time consuming, for teachers and for students (Häggström 2001). This makes us think it through once more. Most important, the notion of the time variable relates to aspects of what Flinck & Liljedahl put forward. As far as we can see in this respect, we share some vital conditions with the Education department, not least because the term lasts for 20 weeks as well for us. Many students stay with us for one term only, usually because they do not plan to be professional archaeologists.

Another aspect of importance, and which we also share with Education, is the wide limits and the many approaches within our subjects. Neither of them is just a discipline of a specific vocational field (as compared to e.g. nurse training). This makes also Flinck & Liljedahl's ways of designing and approaching the processes of cases in PBL, of relevance to us. In conclusion, we simply have to do like our teaching colleagues in the Education department in Lund, i.e. try to find our own way by the aid of fruitful ideas from PBL.

We have been considering some alternative general approaches to how archaeology could be taught and learnt. They are also commensurable with a lot of specific working methods that should be given as good alternatives to traditional lecturing, and that focus on the students. There are several methods additional to those we already have touched upon.

In this vein should briefly be mentioned a method of potentials in the most positive. This is the method of working with students' journals on which we are developing at the moment (Hjørungdal et al 2004). Related methods are to be found among what educationists name portfolio, or learning portfolio (Biggs 1999:72). We were therefore happy to find a comparable concept of working methods in archaeology through Yannis Hamilakis' example with student-centred journals. Hamilakis poses the question why there is so little discussion of pedagogy in archaeology? Current strategies for university studies are all through instrumental, and bring no space for pedagogical issues such as critical reflection. One method of bringing reflection into learning was done by the introduction of students' journals. In Swedish archaeology similar ideas have been discussed for an introduction (Lövkvist 2004: 74ff). The results and effects of the use of the journals were complex, but did not suit all students (Hamilakis 2004).

We have as such seen some glimpses of alternative ways of learning in academic contexts. Some of them are more successful than others, and could have been adjusted to context, to level of education and maturity of learning ability.

Strengthened by many of these insights and by the fact that it should be possible to make further issues and designs specific to archaeology, we shall continue our discussion by announcing our ideas to an alternative syllabus for the 'Introductory Course'.

Featuring some suggestions to disseminate the 'Hearding Teaching'

Knowledge is a social phenomenon in the sense that we mostly use it in intercourse with other people. Therefore it is a reasonable idea that knowledge should be acquired in similar circumstances, ie in interplay with others. (Dahlgren, Dahle, Ludvigsson 1987:22)

In this chapter we will first explain the aims behind our wishes to disseminate the herding teaching. This is followed by a more thorough presentation of their practical implications and some related problems. They consider changes both in course content and disposition, aspects of group works as well as examination forms and some further reflections on a future Introductory Course. But first, the very aims of the concept we started to discuss some years ago.

Aims

Our idea of an alternative teaching approach in archaeology (ie considering our current context) is to give the students an opportunity to get a better grip of various (engendered) contexts during long terms, and to better understand backgrounds to continuity and change. Our theoretical base for its execution is influenced by ideas on engendering and coaching teaching based on PBL from a feminist pedagogical standpoint. In this proceeding, we will also take the previously presented aspects of students' learning into account. Practical means for realising their aims could, in our case, be listed as the following (but note that this is not a hierarchical order):

1) Promoting a *clear connection and 'fluidity' between the various courses and course sections* within the educational programme would make more sense to different aspects of archaeological matters, for instance between issues like great prehistoric processes and local traditions, theory and archaeological data. This would make an understanding of the various aspects of prehistory easier, and might hopefully arouse the students' curiosity, and thereby affect their inner motivation for learning. A project of this kind would therefore be one of co-teaching, co-operation and intermediation between different course sections, preferably running through a whole term.

2) Another aim is to *make the students more active* in

their own *learning* process and in *democratic issues and practices*, but also to *co-operate and learn from others*. This would affect their sense of possibilities for influence in their work as well as their meta learning. According to feminist pedagogues, it is important to help students develop a voice of their own. An own voice is a necessary instrument in the development of democratic approaches to learning, as well as in the development of democratic professional practices. The other aspects of the idea of "A voice of one's own," ought thus to be the idea of developing "A sensitive ear". Learning to listen to your colleagues is for many students and scholars as least as important as is working on developing a personal voice. We would like to add this aspect just in order to stress the point that the coin has two sides.

3) A third aim, which goes hand in hand with the second aim, is to *loosen the authoritarian role of the teacher*. An important idea in the plan to follow is that this could be solved by making the students work in small groups[4]. Here the students would benefit from 'flocking' around themes of investigations and take part of each other's results. This will also contribute to the process of making them more active, as well as promoting their meta learning when they have to take into account the various ways of which different individuals reflect upon the same piece of information.

4) A fourth aim is to *incorporate gender* to a greater extent than is the case today. Although conceptional changes in attitudes towards the studies in individual students have been difficult to trace, pedagogues have found that the education does affect the structure of their opinions of phenomena on a more general level (Dahlgren 1997:36 and cited literature). We hold the opinion, that gender issues and perspectives are important for many reasons through their critical approaches. Gender critical approaches are important to interpretations of prehistoric contexts as well as in the analyses of current social and professional structure within the archaeological enterprises. We consider it therefore essential to convey a gendered consciousness to the students, which they can reflect upon and develop further in their own archaeological adventure. Gender approaches like masculinity, life cycle, feminist perspectives, queer theory, as well as ethnicity etc could be integrated into lectures, and would also constitute themes for the student groups to work with. Tasks referring to students' own positions in academy along with their life history and education could be integrated in these themes, as well as could

reflections on other archaeologists' positions and biographies. This topic would correspond to the section, which is scheduled as "History of Archaeology" in the syllabus of our present Introductory Course.

5) A fifth important aim is the one of making the *students acquainted with various aspects of the research agenda*. Through this, they will get a closer look into ongoing research as well as of experience of co-operation, which is a way to prepare them for future projects. Not least, this represents a method of co-operation of which we, most probably, will see more in and between universities, museums and so called 'rescue' excavations. The working approach also has the potential of giving the students more experience for their forthcoming extensive essay, which is a major task of the later, third term studies in Sweden.

Changes in course content and disposition

The teaching prospect we were discussing, was planned to run over a whole term (20 weeks), and as such it needs some considerable planning and reflection in advance. Therefore, we shall present some suggestions to possible ways of carrying our aims through. A short summary will be supplied as we extend on our suggested ideas in the text. Some initial questions to ask oneself and the rest of our teaching team would, of course, be what and why changes are wished for, and what educational direction the course should take. Our main concerns are how students grow into explorers of knowledge and how teachers grow into facilitators of learning.

So how would one go about making the present, different course sections more 'connected'? As presented in the paragraph on the Introductory Course, the various sections of this course consider 'General prehistory' by means of first, global and second, Nordic conditions, followed by the sections 'Theory and Method' and 'Field Section'. In order to *prosecute our first aim* to make the various course contents more integrated and 'fluid', our initial suggestion would be that the wide and enormous scope of the global prehistory and development of humanity ought to be narrowed down, both in time and space. An alternative to the present outline approach to global prehistory would be a choice of global topics. However, in order to live up to chosen PBL ideas on the organisation of courses (see for instance Egidius 1991:8) we would like to *get away from the very division between each teaching topic*. Our frame idea of doing this is to *let the course sections run parallel to each other* during the whole term (i e the entire Introductory Course).

A rough suggestion of how to implement this would be the following;

> The teachers of the course could give initial introductory lectures as well as complementary lectures throughout the

---

[4]   We are well aware of the fact that groups have their own dynamics, and that they imply difficulties as well as advantages. The field of group dynamics is, however, a huge topic and quite a lot of research is done (see for example Egidius 1991:23ff). However, we have chosen not to go any deeper into these questions in this article.

course. The lecture topics should be chosen and planned from the beginning by the teachers involved[5]. Students' projects, which will concern a) a global perspective, little by little narrowing down to b) Nordic prehistory, will be considered from theoretical and methodological perspectives. Field descriptions as well as terrain recognition and survey concerning the prehistoric cultural landscape will be included in the course sections dealing with Nordic prehistory.

Our second aim to consider would be how to get the students *more active* in their own learning, in co-operation with their peers, but also to *incorporate democratic issues*. It should be noted in this context, that a new paragraph in the Swedish University and College Law says that the student shall have the right to influence the education at the universities and colleges (Högskolelagen 1 kap. 4a§, Lag 2000: 260 – this law came into force 01-07-2000). This second aim would in practice also coincide with *the third aim* of *loosening the authoritarian role of the teacher*. In cohesion with these aims we wish the students to make *group projects* to co-operate more, which will also increase their possibilities of considering each other as a source of knowledge and creativity.

According to the PBL ideas presented earlier, the cases, or 'problems' should be *suggested and led by the students* themselves – which would also leave the *teacher as a coach* and release her/him from the more authoritarian teacher's role. The students, according to our project, would themselves suggest/choose the problem area to investigate, as well as they would plan the work, collect literature and other material needed. We suggest that the group should have working sessions in the form of organised, democratic meetings. Ten meetings during the whole term should be a minimum. Every 'session' should be documented by meeting protocols, including a list of meeting attendants (which should change functional roles from meeting to meeting), names of chairperson and secretary, and meeting issues. The latter should contain issues like the progress of the work, discussions and results concerning the individual students' contribution, as well as what needs to be done until the next meeting.

The 'coach' teacher of the group should attend at least 30 % of the meeting occasions to be able to tutor the students and notice the progress of their work. The protocols will, after each meeting, be handed over to the supervisor. This strategy is supposed to make the students co-operate, to become more active as well as responsible for their own part of the project, and give them an opportunity of practising the art of democratic influence.

A comprised practical outline of the second and third aim would hence be:

> The students will meet regularly during the term under democratic forms, where problems will be defined, discussed and planned by the students themselves. The meetings will be documented by proper protocols, which will be reported to the supervisor. Some 30 % of the meetings will be attended also by the teacher/coach.

The *fourth aim* would be to involve gender conscious issues to a greater extent than is the case today. Within each of the suggested themes there are possibilities to apply one or more gender perspectives. The idea is to give the students an opportunity to get a better grip of various (engendered) contexts on a longitudinal base, and to better understand reasons for continuity and change. Our conception of a 'gendered' teaching is that it should incorporate gender issues and approaches in every level of the project. This means that we integrate gender issues to a higher extent (wherever this is not already done) in a) literature, b) lectures, c) group discussions, and d) in thematic PBL quests, both individually and in group. This might still be a tricky aspect of the project, as most gender conscious research so far concerns Bronze Age, and especially the periods of the Iron Age. Stone Age, specifically the Mesolithic era suffers from lack of basic research with gender perspectives, although more research has been published since the 1990s (Arwill-Nordbladh & Hjørungdal 1999:452ff). There is however good and gender critical scrutiny on the issue of the development of early humanity (cf. Sørensen 2000:182ff. for an overview of engendered Palaeolithic studies). Concerning countries with which the western part of the world has rather limited contact, like countries in the former Soviet Union, Asia, and the whole Middle East new gender informed knowledge is hard to get hold of at all. Recently a book on gender and Chinese archaeology has appeared (Linduff & Sun eds. 2004), and could make an excellent contribution to a global perspective on the subject.

When it comes to literature, we would change and integrate gendered texts so as to cover for approximately 50 % of the literature list wherever this is possible. The current situation in our own department is that the amount of gender conscious literature varies from term to term. However, like Spector and Whelan we think it is good to keep some of the traditional androcentric texts to give a historical frame and explanation to the need of gender

---

[5]   This brings us into a situation where the individual teaching team will have to make a choice. We have suggested that this kind of teaching approach would imply a shift in teaching resources, implying that some of the lecturing time could be disposed on 'coaching' the students. If such a choice is to be done, one would also need to consider how and what one would prefer to keep among the existing lectures. One could either prefer to give priority only to some of the lecturing themes, or try to compress them all into the smaller number of lectures. Maybe there are those who have thought of other ways of dealing with the problem too. Flinck & Liljedahl at the Education department, University of Lund, decided to plan from the start which and how many lectures they should include in a course (Flinck & Liljedahl op.cit.).

aspects in research and education (Spector & Whelan 1988). Where gender conscious literature is still absent, the working methods will be lectures and group discussions, both with an attempt to put traditional (androcentric) texts under gender critical light. When the group projects scrutinise topics of investigation, they could therefore, additional to a traditional perspective, also choose to focus a specific gender approach on the same issue. Working with two alternative theories will give the students an insight into the issue of the interpreter's relation to her result.

By now our comprised idea of the project could be summarised all together to the following sentences:

> The teachers of the course could give initial introductory lectures as well as complementary lectures throughout the course. The lecture topics should be chosen and planned from the beginning, and by the teachers involved. Students' projects, which will concern a) a global perspective, little by little narrowing down to b) Nordic prehistory, will be considered from theoretical and methodological perspectives. Field descriptions as well as terrain recognition and survey concerning the prehistoric cultural landscape will be included in the course sections dealing with Nordic prehistory. The students will meet regularly during the term under democratic forms, where problems will be defined, discussed and planned by the students themselves. The meetings will be documented by proper protocols, which will be reported to the supervisor. Some 30 % of the meetings will be attended also by the teacher/coach. Gender issues will permeate all levels of the project, i e in literature, lectures, group discussions and thematic PBL quests. The latter should be chosen by the group members, but the teacher will create a tableau of choices that could be combined in terms of processes of prehistoric themes over time; gendered approach; and an alternative, additional theory for the sake of comparison of results.

By now we have arrived at the *fifth, and final presented aim*, namely to enable the students to get acquainted with various aspects of the research agenda. This is actually performed through the very group project itself. More and more often research is involved in projects of various kinds, where the group works could be seen as a way of students getting used to co-operation. Another aspect of the research agenda could be to briefly present recently published reports from locally ongoing research projects. If possible, representatives from these local research projects could be invited to tell the students about their project, while the students have possibilities to ask questions which may even relate to their own project in terms of scientific or social 'problems'.

One of the results we hope for from the group project, is that it will enable 'meta learning'. In a context like the one presented, aspects of meta learning could be considered in terms of deeper insight into how projects work from the inside out, by means of, for instance, putting up – as well as following up – aims and goals, and methods of gaining and presenting information. Social aspects in this context are the insight into the different individual wills, pre-understandings, and previous knowledge, usually present among the various participants. Most students have probably been involved in traditional group works during their time at compulsory school and during college years, but at the time of their university studies, they have been able to gain more experiences both personal, professional and/or different disciplinary issues that they can bring into and enrich their group work.

Since the meta learning is integrated in the practical implications of the previously presented aims, no further aspects in our comprised alternative suggestion for teaching needs to be added for this fifth aim. It is already there, omnipresent.

Aspects on student quests in groups or individual

Instead we will turn to some suggestions on how the content of the themes for the group works could be arranged. Considering our five aims and the design of the group projects, examples of problems, or PBL quests, could be organised in sections. From a tableau, such as the one suggested below, each group will have to choose one theme from every section to consider and integrate in their project:

Prehistoric themes	**Theories & Methods**	**Gender aspects**
Settlements	Structuralism	Queer theory
Burials	Processualism	Ethnicity
Landscapes	Post-processualism	Age and lifecycle
Rock carvings	Marxism	Gender
Sacrifices	Theory of practice	Feminism
	Phenomenology	Masculinism

There are, of course other aspects to consider. We would like to mention especially the aspects of time span and geographical context, as they so obviously illustrate the formerly discussed extension and wide limits of the discipline of archaeology.

Smaller individual projects or tasks, running parallel to these group projects could also be possible. This could activate the students in another, more individual way, leaving them on their own to consider all the aspects needed to complete their task. However, this might encourage them and confirm their own capability of succeeding in various situations. These individual projects could then be reported to the teacher and conveyed to the other students. The problems defined by the students could be of a kind, whose results could be incorporated into the group project, for example one specific aspect of their chosen prehistoric theme. However, also the group works will have to be reported in one way or another. This is what we will consider next.

Final reports

To integrate a professional dimension to the conveyance of information, one way is to let the students arrange an *exhibition* on their project results. This exhibition could also encompass a 'vernissage', where the students present their results to a group of visitors. Another exercise, which could be integrated into this exhibition, is that each group could be 'exhibition critics' with the task to review another group's result. This way of reporting would, apart from being a fun alternative to exams, be professionally related, since it integrates a whole research process. It would range from searching, deriving, processing as well as integrating and interpreting information; it also includes reporting the results from this process in a way that makes it comprehensive and available for others. By the way, making and presenting exhibitions is a fully realistic future professional job for many educated within archaeology. Another scenario could be that the results from the work might be accounted for in written text in a *paper* which, after the supervisors' acknowledgements, could be included in the compulsory course literature. A verbal presentation to co-students could be expected as well, where also the actual co-operation and the development of the group projects would have an opportunity to be commented on. Presenting their results according to these suggested alternatives, the students will take the role of informants, where they have something to contribute – in short, a *disseminated* teaching. Having various methods for reporting will promote various qualities and skills in the students.

The 20 week term could be finished off by a written *home examination*, which may be divided into two parts. One part could be more traditionally organised with all-embracing questions on the literature. The other part could embrace a quest, where the work/s done by one or two other groups will have to be discussed or commented on, in the light of curricular literature. This strategy will make it important to the students to take part in the other groups' results, which will be included in the assessments for their examination marks. The final phase is also a good time to *evaluate the project*, both for students and teachers.

Reflections on a future Introductory Course

It is our firm belief, that a working method in this vein has the potentials for a more profound learning maturity to the individual students. We would however, finally, like to pay attention to a few things worth considering before one initiates a course of this character.

Planning changes in teaching methods and in course content may take quite a while to do, so a good idea would probably be to start the planning at least one term in advance. How long time the students' group works will take, depends on what the teacher puts most emphasis on, how the research cases are constructed, as well as on how many scheduled hours there are to one's disposal (cf. Flinck & Liljedahl op.cit.). One has to be realistic in both aims and arrangements, but also get the students to understand their own responsibility when it comes to planning their time and work in the group. Proposing one way of dealing with the frequent problem of getting started with their work, one could schedule for a couple of seminars along the term. These seminars could be regarded as a forum for the students, where the groups could present their aims, how far they have come in their work, as well as deal with their difficulties (if they have any) etc. Students could thus spend these seminars as a way of discussing and helping each other through mutual information on their own solution to problems that might have arisen, and such pep each other.

One difficulty with a concept like this could be the fact that many students are very dependent on the teacher. However, we propose liberation of teaching resources from lectures to supervision of groups. The students will have a better chance to ask questions to the supervisor and get personal guidance in their research. We are aware of the fact that there sometimes are problems getting the students to attend, since some students may just not turn up at lectures, group sessions etc. Either those students could make up a group themselves, if they have come up with alternative meeting occasions that suit them better, or the existing groups will have to agree to meeting occasions that suit most of the group members. The individual contributions within the group could be done whatever time that suits the students the best. Hence, complaints that the scheduled time for the task does not suit them would be no excuse for not completing the task.

Another obstructing factor could be ambitious students' fixed ideas about graduation marks and their 'hunt' for higher marks. This phenomenon is not least an effect of political structures, and is unfortunately nothing we could change with this project. The suggested final written examination will contribute to make the students (externally, nota bene) motivated to make their best in the group projects and also actively take part of the others' results. However, regardless of examinations, and although the group project is expected to close up in a report of some kind, one could keep in mind that according to the idea of PBL, the *process* is more important than the final result. The results may not always reflect the actual learning achievements, which could be more complex and longitudinal than what is mirrored in a final report.

Despite our ambitions of developing alternative teaching, we are well aware of how the reality looks like to many teachers. Many other factors than those directly associated with the teachers affect the possibilities of changing form and content in higher education. The universities in Sweden have an obligation to the state to provide the people with higher education of excellent quality. However, the societal frames within which the universities are situated are all but realistic with respect to how this should be implemented. In the next chapter of this text we shall look closer at some aspects of this reality. We have chosen to approach some aspects of this harsh reality by the means of a fairy tale.

Education in Wonderland – a bizarre fairy tale

For, you see, so many out-of the-way things had happened lately, that Alice had begun to think that very few things indeed were really impossible. (In Lewis Carroll 1984 (1865) *Alice's Adventures in Wonderland*, p. 29)

> *"Can you please tell me a crazy story?" asked Alice pleadingly while placing herself next to the White Rabbit. "Mm... Oh dear, oh dear, what should that be? I'm afraid I have run out of stories..." muttered the Rabbit thoughtfully to himself, scratching his chin as he scanned his rather good-to-be-a-rabbit-memory. "But wait a minute — Yes, I know a story, and it's the craziest of them all! It's your lucky day, Alice!" said the Rabbit finally, very delighted and pleased with himself.*

> *"Once upon a time, as good stories always tend to begin, there was a Wonderland" began the Rabbit. "It was called so because the inhabitants were given expectations that a Wonder would happen thanks to their Fair(y) Rulers. However, since the Wonder kept on being conspicuous by its absence, the people were kept waiting in wonder why the Wonder did not appear, and what had really gone wrong with their Rulers. But as with the rulers people have on their desks, the Rulers were*

> *both flat (as a bad joke) and rather single-tracked (as a straight line never sliding aside or being flexible), just sticking stubbornly on to its own ruled aim. Once they had made a decision, however mad or proven misleading, they continued along the same track. The wonder-full people in the Wonder-less Wonderland became more and more overloaded with work, since the promised Wonder 1) did not appear; 2) was not of the kind that was really needed and; 3) took resources from the measures that actually <u>were</u> needed. This unfortunate backward strategy was a result of the Rulers' aim to create what proved to be the non-realistic never appearing Wonder."*

> *The Rabbit laughed amusingly. "Was this not a crazy story?" he asked, very content with himself to have been able to make the long story very short. "Yes, indeed" nodded Alice approvingly. "But tell me more – do I know this Wonderland?" The Rabbit frowned and his whiskers vibrated along with a sneaking feeling that this story would most certainly be a longer version than he had initially intended. "How should I know?" he said rather irritated, but finally agreed to continue the story.*

> *"The Wonderland was called 'Sweden' in the Real World. Its political Rulers at the time considered Higher Education, especially Arts and Humanities as something that was good to have every now and then, for instance to contribute to new knowledge and perspectives on their cultural National Heritage. Nevertheless, the Rulers did not want it to cost anything, so they continued to give less and less money to the Arts and Humanities and still expecting more outcome!" Alice and the Rabbit laughed in chorus for a good couple of minutes to the wonderfully awkward equation, and the Rabbit started to feel better about the storytelling.*

> *"Wow" said Alice finally "yes, that was really a crazy story. But what did the people working in these fields think about that?" she urged, thirsty for some more information on this fantastically odd story. The Rabbit sighed, since he realised that his afternoon nap would be a history too, if he would give in to the girl's wish. But since he was as good-hearted as he was white-furred, he decided to continue. "Well, I happened to get some information from two she-human archaeologists from that Swedish Wonderland when I visited the Real World. This is their version of their reality:"*

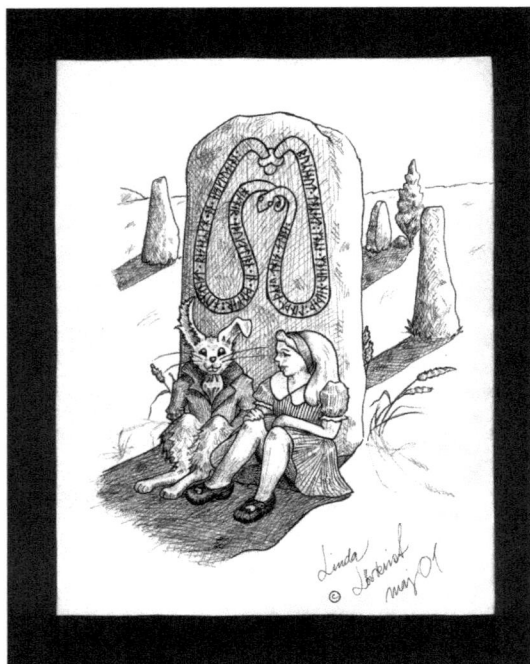

Figure 8.3 Alice with the Rabbit in the Classic Wonderland picturing an illusory idyll. Telling a story is not always a pleasant quest... For those of the readers who cannot decode the runes (so called 'stung runes'), they inform us on the following: 'Higher education in danger. Humanist research on exclusion. Burnout threat. More money needed. Linda drew this stone.'

Illustration by Linda Lövkvist

The Emperor's New Clothes – a too stripped an economical outfit

The current political perspective on higher education has given some important economic effects on university research, especially within the humanities. Some years ago the Swedish social democratic government decided to decentralise higher education. Some of the intentions aimed at were to create centres for higher education closer to people in the countryside as well as to create more opportunities for higher education among the Swedish people. Another aim concerned the idea of increasing the number of research milieus in the country. The strategy was to promote former university colleges and increase their status to that of the older, traditional universities.

One of the effects of this political act was to let the new as well as the 'old' Universities share the same economic cake. However, building up a new university takes a long time, plenty of hard work and quite a lot of money. As the Swedish universities are free from charge, all their money comes from governmental funds. Although having an ideological idea of creating more equal possibilities for people to study closer to their home, regardless of whether they are urban or rural citizens, the Swedish

politicians did overlook some side effects of their plan. Splitting the money on more hands does not exactly increase the possibilities for each individual university to promote either teaching or research. To 'starve' the undergraduate education is not a particularly wise strategy in a nation that wants to produce high quality and keep pace with the international market. Research is, as most academics know, quite economically demanding, and time consuming, and whatever is taken away of economic resources will show off later, in terms of lower quality and burned out personnel. In a small country like Sweden, one will also have to account for a realistic view on the recruit foundation – among the 9 million citizens, there will have to be enough interested people to fill up all universities. Some of the new universities have already had problems filling their education programmes with undergraduates. Postgraduate education as well as other research needs a creative milieu to flower. Multidimensional discussions have need of many academic voices to bring the research horizon forward. Creating such a climate will need many people on each level of the academic enterprise *within the same* educational/research centre.

"But that almost sounds like another story I have heard", interrupted Alice. She hesitated a little and added "well, at least it reminds me of the story of the Emperor's New Clothes. There too something was taken away and pretended to be something else than it proved to be in the end... The emperor expected ovations from the people for his new outfit that was supposed to be very avant-garde, but ended up very embarrassed for the mistake he made when people saw it through! And in this story the economical outfit is split between too many hands, undressing vital parts of higher education from resources. That sounds rather naked too..." She wanted to make herself a bit clearer, and so reviewed the story to the Rabbit: "Once upon a time – at least according to the famous 19th century Danish author H C Andersen – there was an Emperor. He enjoyed spending much money on exclusive clothes, and so it happened that he employed two men who claimed to be weavers. They convinced the Emperor that they could produce a beautiful material including the special effect of seeming invisible only to incompetent public and government officers. "Great", thought the Emperor, who now thought he could at last spot those among his employees who were clearly incompetent. Hence, when the cheating 'weavers' arrived with the new 'clothes', the Emperor tried them on, admired himself in the mirror and went out on a grand procession to meet the people. Walking out in the nude, he made a fool not only of himself, but also of the rest of the court. "

Figure 8.4 What is happening to higher education in Sweden, and especially within the arts/humanist disciplines, is that its government is stripping it from resources, with the same ridiculed effect as the naked Emperor. The cheating weavers would in a travesty on the Swedish situation symbolise the government, while the Emperor would be higher education. However, who the incompetent public government officers would symbolise is a question we leave to the reader to decide... The signals from the Swedish government could be interpreted like they would claim that only the good researchers could survive the cuts in resources and that others need not bother. Sadly, however, the situation is rather the opposite; good research does – and must be allowed to – demand high costs. If the economic situation for higher education and research will not improve soon, the Swedish nation will jeopardise the international credibility of its research. Illustration by Linda Lövkvist.

The Rabbit took no notice of Alice's comment, but continued his bizarre fairy tale from the Real World Swedish Wonderland.

So far only the situation for universities in general has been pointed out. Swedish politicians have an enormous faith in the 'hard sciences', in terms of medical research, technical achievements etc. Gaining more knowledge within and around various fields of humanities does not seem to score as high marks as the 'hard sciences', and hence less money have been invested in human sciences than on the 'hard sciences' the last few years. This was earlier quite a hard blow for many departments at, for example, the Gothenburg University. The Gothenburg Faculty of Arts, holding approximately 30 departments, lost 3-4 % of their economic appropriations from the state between 1995 and 1996 (verbal information from Edvardsson; see also Lövkvist 2004). This resulted in 400 educational places less at the undergraduate level, implicating less teaching hours, which means that the Faculty has had to cut in the 'human resources'. This did in turn imply that quite a few teachers' posts have been abolished, and hence the remaining teachers at the departments had to take over much of the duties connected to these posts. To take a look back, in 1999 the effect of the economic governmental appropriations was

20% less for the Gothenburg Faculty of Arts compared to the 1993-1994 'educational year'. The teaching hours were 12 hours less per student and term in 1999 than 5-6 years before. These are just a few examples describing the situation, and presented here to reflect some of the economic problems that the Swedish higher education of the humanities is struggling with. The general message was, in conclusion, "Higher quality with more scarce resources." Rather much like the Emperor's New Clothes – stripped and vulnerable, leaving the Emperor balancing on the edge of Embarrassment.

There was a still moment of reflection before Alice broke the silence: "But what happened to the research?" she asked, thoughtfully. "Yepp! That is a very good and highly relevant question indeed!" the Rabbit admitted. "This is what I heard:"

Research on exclusion

Having these economical frameworks in mind, the reader may already have anticipated the fact that the research situation for the teachers is not of any luxurious calibre. Since the early 2000s saw a slight economical input into the humanities, teachers' research hour per week were increased from 10% to 15% or from 4 hours to 6 hours a week, and in the Spring of 2005 the rate will be lowered again to 10%.

The amount of time that each teacher has for own research can however vary slightly between the Swedish universities. There is no natural connection between teaching and research in Swedish universities – research is on exclusion among teachers, and you also usually teach issues on which you never have done any research. There is however a silent demand on you, that with your four or six weekly hours of research, you should be able to manage to write at least some papers, as well as to contribute a couple of conference papers each year. The old saying, "Publish or perish" is still operative among us, and makes up a silent threat.

Considering the situation where the teachers have to take over some of the duties from the previously liquidated teachers, the time for own research is leading an insecure existence in the risk zone of extinction. Questions repeatedly posed are; How will Swedish researchers be able to keep pace with the international research front? And how will this affect the teaching situation for present and future students? Own research makes the interest and engagement grow in the researchers, which also will affect their teaching (Berglund et al 1998:32). Students with enthusiastic teachers get enthusiastic themselves and their learning will have good prerequisites to prosper (see for instance Hodgson 1997). This is a vital aspect of the background on which we must discuss Swedish University teaching in the humanities. If the situation does not improve, we can only see two remaining alternatives. Either research, along with the undergraduate education, within the Swedish humanities will be watered down and lose importance on many levels, both internationally and nationally; or the teachers/researchers will be burned out in their attempts to make up for the lost economical resources. Burned out people do not have any energy left to be creative until the situation improves and the research will be watered down anyway. Hence, the only thing that the burnout case can bring is personal as well as scientific loss.

"That was really sad", said Alice. "I wonder what the people within Higher Education felt like..." The Rabbit continued patiently his report from the Real World.

The Burnout threat

Some years ago attention was directed against the so-called Burnout Threat. Thus, in the June 2000 issue of the staff newspaper at Gothenburg University, we could read that ill vacancies increased among teachers and postgraduate students (Eriksson 2000:3). In one of the union journals for Swedish archaeologists, the DIK-forum[6], there is another article on stress and burnout published in December, where Töres Theorell, Professor at the Karolinska Institute and head of the Institute for Psychosocial Medicine, is interviewed (Rågvik 2000:8f). The Swedish research Counsil (FRN) has as well edited a book on the issue, with Professor Theorell as one of the contributors. He describes what happens biologically in the body due to stress and how it makes us react depending on if we can influence our situation or not. Stress is not necessarily a bad thing; if we have a combination of high demands and good possibilities of control of the situation, our work will be active and progressive, and we will increase our ability to handle stress. If the situation is the opposite, with few possibilities of influencing a demanding situation, the risk of illness will follow as a result of long lasting physical tensions. This kind of stress situation is the initial symptom for many diseases, like infections, high blood pressure, chronic fatigue, depressions as well as heart and vascular disorders, just to mention a few examples (Theorell 2000).

To speak on behalf of the university teachers in our surroundings, they seem to have too much to do, and live under a strong pressure of expectations on them to make still better performances, and to work still more. All this is supposed to work out smoothly in spite of scarcer resources, as there is a cut in educational budgets in the humanities at the moment. A situation, which could help, would be to put more human resources into the educational system, but that would bring also an increase of economical costs, which will not be accepted by the authorities. The teachers' situation would therefore seem to be of a kind of stress

due to external reasons, which they can not influence. Many people seem to have reacted negatively on this stress by means of burnout. Theorell has seen an interesting *political connection between economy and human burnout* (Rågvik 2000:8f). He notes that *economical cuts* in society were the recurrent headlines in the *beginning of the 90s*, whereas *burnout* was the main focus in the *end of the decade*. Burnout is obviously an accelerating problem, and the teaching policies and the possibilities for change, have to be regarded against aspects of this background as well. There are certainly reasons for feeling uneasy about how stress and the burnout threat generally are coped with. People who cannot keep it up, are (indirectly, though) told that they are awkward, and not really wanted here.

"Well", said the White Rabbit "this is really not The End from what I have understood, but it is as far as I heard from my last visit in the Real World. At least it will give you an idea of the most important background to the upside-down Educational Wonderland – or Sweden if you like. And maybe one day when I have done some more Real World recognition, I will be able to tell you what happened next. I hope you have enjoyed yourself so far. "Oh yes", said Alice, "thank you so much for telling me this story! It was really a crazy one, and very tiresome at that!" She yawned widely and fell fast asleep. The Rabbit was not late to see the chance to get his delayed, and very much longed for afternoon nap. He made himself comfortable, let his long ears fall down to cover his eyes, and soon he was heavily asleep too.

The present situation in conclusion

The above sketched economic, pedagogical and general academic situation not only cuts the shorten the economic means for existing activity, it also marginalises the possibilities for changes in teaching practices that may be needed to improve the quality of the education. This is the (un)economical spin-off effect of the situation, since it tires teachers and students, and preserves the level and character of knowledge. What needs to be highlighted in this context is that people, who feel good and happy in their situation, have more to give. Or, as Tompkins put it:

"/.../ the politics of the classroom begins with the teacher's treatment of and regard for him or her self." (Tompkins 1991:27)

Taken together, the current and future situation could, by far, be light-years better. We would also like to add, that the circumstances described here are important ingredients in the present reality, which makes our suggested, otherwise practically feasible, project run the risk of turning into a visionary ideal in an ineffable

---

6   DIK is short for Dokumentation Information Kultur (Documentation Information Culture).

Academic Dreamland. This really makes one wish to be in Alice's clothes instead, waking up among the kittens, just to realise that all the crazy stuff was just a dream.

The challenge

We have now presented two problematic areas in the field of academic creativity and improvement in learning facilities. Hence the challenge could be seen as twofold.

One part concerns how to break the earlier presented dependence on authorities in learning and to inspire students to a growing interest in the discipline, hence increase their approach for deep learning. We are convinced that this problem cannot be solved through technical improvements in terms of better lectures, better picture shows or the like. As Paul Ramsden put it: "A good performance is not necessarily good teaching. In fact, an entertaining lecturer may leave students with a sense of having been entertained, but with little advancement of their learning." (Ramsden 1993:74). Thus, that would only encourage the students to absorb and pass on the performance model, which according to Jane Tompkins is based in fear of being exposed and evaluated in negative terms. As fear is no good breeding ground for learning, we rather believe that educational ameliorations are to be found by means of qualitative measures. Teaching issues should first of all put the *students and their learning approach in focus*, but also present an explicit and critically conscious *approach* towards the disciplinary topics and learning context as well as the *content* of the teaching/learning situation.

The other part of the challenge is connected with the present prerequisites for academic teaching and learning. In order to keep the level up, the economic situation has to be improved, and to stabilise. This point was as well stressed at an Archaeologists' Attendance in Uppsala in January 2001, which among other issues had the cut in educational resources on the agenda, as the cut in resources reached the extreme bottom at that time (Häggström 2001).

Summary

In this paper we have focused on aspects of learning, including a survey and reflection on approaches to learning in archaeological education. It has been vital to see learning approaches on the background of aspects of current academic, pedagogical, economical and social conditions of learning. The scope has been to take a closer look at methods and practices of learning, which seem possible to integrate with a gender conscious perspective on the discipline and on scholarship in general. The aim of gender conscious approaches to the processes of learning is in general to permit students to grow into independent and confident explorers of knowledge with a voice of their own. Thus, we have considered some alternative methods of learning as developed and practised by professional pedagogues and by our own colleagues, and tried to integrate them.

The question of exactly how students grow from being receivers of the teacher's knowledge, into becoming independent and confident explorers of knowledge should be seen as an exciting challenge. There are many approaches to this process, and there are many alternative ways of organising and practising teaching and learning in order to reach such an aim. What critical methods of learning hold in common, however, is that students should have a *more active* role in their own learning process into becoming more independent and self-governed knowers. Our own suggestion is just one among several possible ones to a Disseminated Herding Teaching concept, which deals with ways of trying to get to terms with the situations for both teachers and students.

Hence, we have regarded our issue in relation to general circumstances as they appear today, and over the last few years. We preferred to use an allusion of Alice in Wonderland to consider the general situation from a somewhat more ironic and distancing perspective. The present problem of urgency is represented by a general instable situation, with sudden and unforeseen cut in resources that will have various consequences for both teachers and students. We have considered some of these consequences, as presently debated in our context, such as lack of time for thinking and planning, or for development of education on behalf of the teachers' situation. Other obstacles for the teachers are the lack of scheduled hours for own research as well as the ever present threat of burnout. The students, on the other hand, do not get enough time for thinking and maturing in their learning process, such as we believe would be possible to enable with a change of teaching practices and in course organisation. Students also run the risk of being passive receivers of knowledge as they just absorb information presented from the teacher, instead of taking a more active part in their learning.

The problematization and discussion of the context of tertiary education developed here can be seen in the light of a similar discourse as explicated by Hamilakis (2004). Vital aspects of the discussion focus on pedagogical solutions to the restricting circumstances of the instrumentalist politics, on an economical as well as a pedagogical level.

Last but not least, we hope for a *response* from other university teachers with visions, to see *other possible alternatives* for educational change. Although there are many constraining facts in our daily educational practice, we would like to stress the fact that we have to focus on possibilities and actively try to find them in various ways. We also wish that, by and by, there will be a following visible – and published – interest and discussion on this issue. Closing this paper, we would therefore like to pass on two important issues to discuss concerning aspects on how to manage to include *all* students in the ambition of a more active learning in the classroom as well as in group projects. Whose voices are heard in the group discussions – how do one involve the inaudible others? Whose interest is governing the group and hence also the processes of the other students' growth into explorers of new knowledge?

Concluding remarks

The initial draft of this paper was written already in 2001, based on a paper we presented at EAA in Lissbon in 2000. Since then it has undergone substantial revisions. When the first sketch was about to be written, the most urgent problem to good teaching and learning, was the Universities' lack of money, and the paper started out on this vital problem. Due to the instrumentalist and economist perspective on students and learning, the general economic situation in tertiary education finds itself in a permanent instable situation.

During the last few years, the problem has sharpened its focus very much on the relationships between education and research, and on university teachers' lack of time for development and research.

We try to see education and learning in Archaeology in a local Gothenburgian perspective, as well as in a Swedish national, and a general European perspective.

Presently the money in our own everyday context is not so scarce any more, mostly according to our Department's running of a developmental project in pedagogy, *"From Receiving to Performing: Learning Field Archaeology"* financed by the Swedish Council for the Renewal of Higher Education during the period of 2003-2005. This project focuses on the development of alternative working strategies and methods, which make it possible to integrate students more actively in their learning and their education at large. Starting with the methods of the field courses, any good working methods developed are expected to be transmittable to other, more theoretical courses, and even to other disciplines.

We are working with different aspects of peer related learning, and with students' diaries (Hjørungdal et al 2004). The working processes and the results of this project will be presented extensively in other contexts.

An important result already to be considered is that we due to the developmental project and its input in resources are able to work on a full scale change of the undergraduate education in Archaeology given at the Department of Archaeology, Gothenburg University.

Through Yannis Hamilakis' recently published paper on archaeology and pedagogy, we were able to see still more dimensions as well as possibilities in our context of education. Among other things we find it hopeful that we already share the method of student-centred journals with the University of Southampton UK. Last but not least, Hamilakis' paper makes coherence and context to the discussion of the current politics of pedagogy in tertiary education at large, in whatever European country and at whatever of its universities we find ourselves. Feminist and related pedagogies have the potentials of a critical voice in this context.

Note

The teaching- and learning developmental project *"From Receiving to Performing: Learning Field Archaeology"* is financed by the Swedish Council for the Renewal of Higher Education, during the period of 2003-2005. The project is run by the Department of Archaeology, Gothenburg University with the aim to develop the field courses. Project manager is Tove Hjørungdal, and project collaborators are Åsa Gillberg, Per Cornell, Håkan Karlsson, Anders Gustafsson, and Roger Nyqvist. There also is a collaborating students' group, at the moment made up of four students from different levels of the undergraduate education in archaeology.

The project was designed, and an application made, through a cooperative effort by a number of the teachers at the department. Methods of, and attitudes to learning developed through this project, also smooth the progress of an all through revision of the undergraduate education at our department (Hjørungdal, T.; Gillberg, Å., Cornell, P., Karlsson, H., Gustafsson, A, Nyqvist, R. & Bille, U.: forthcoming).

Acknowledgements

We wish to thank Professor Lise Bender Jørgensen, UNIT University of Trondheim, Norway, for her most thorough and helpful comments on an initial draft of this paper. Many thanks to Mats Edvardsson, former educational leader at the Chancellery of the Faculty of Arts, University of Gothenburg, for providing us with information. Linda is the resource behind the adaptation of the fairy tale into our context.

References

Verbal information
Edvardsson, Mats, former educational leader at the chancellery of the Faculty of Arts at the University of Gothenburg, information by telephone March 13th 2000 and, January 24th 2001.
Kroksmark, Tomas, Professor in Didactics at the University of Gothenburg. Lecture given October 5th 2000.

Unpublished
Häggström, L. 2001. *Ämneskonferens i Uppsala 29-30 januari 2001*. Unpublished report, Department of Archaeology, University of Gothenburg.

Literature:

Allwood, C. M. 1988. Skolans inverkan på tänkandet. In: Strömqvist, S. & Strömqvist, G. (eds). *Kulturmöten, kommunikation, skola.* Norstedts. Stockholm, pp. 18-32.

Allwood, C. M. 1992a. Vad är kunskapsantropologi? In: *VEST* 2/1992, pp. 3-13.

Allwood, C. M. 1992b. On the anthropology of knowledge. In: *Proceedings from the 1992 4S/EASST Conference,* pp. 9-21.

Arwill-Nordbladh, E. & Hjørungdal, T. 1999. Genusperspektiv i nordisk arkeologi. In: Burenhult, G. (ed). *Arkeologi i Norden 2.* Bokförlaget Natur & Kultur, Stockholm, pp. 452-455.

Beaty, L., Gibbs, G. and Morgan, A. 1997 (1984). Learning Orientations and Study Contracts. In: Marton, F., Hounsell, D. and Entwistle, D. (eds). *The Experience of Learning. Implications for Teaching and Studying in Higher Education.* 2nd edition. Scottish Academic Press, Edinburgh, pp. 72-86.

Berglund, B. Morsing et al. (eds). 1998. *Jämställdhet, ett gemensamt ansvar. Slutrapport från ett samverkansprojekt i lärarutbildningen.* Pedagogisk kommunikation. Nr 5,

Berglund, B. Morsing et al. (eds). 1998. Högskolan i Växjö, Institutionen för pedagogik.

Biggs, J. 1999. What the Student Does. In: *Higher Education Research & Development.* Vol. 18, No. 1, pp. 57-75.

Carroll, L. 1984 (1865). *Alice's Adventure in Wonderland and Through the Looking Glass.* Puffin Books, Penguin Books Ltd.

Conkey, M. & Tringham, R. 1996. Cultivating Thinking/Challenging Authority: Some Experiments in Feminist Pedagogy in Archaeology. In: Wright, R. P. (ed). *Gender and Archaeology.* PENN. University of Pennsylvania Press. Philadelphia. Ch. 8.

Dahlgren, L. O. 1995 (1986). Learning Conceptions and Outcomes. In: Marton, F., Hounsell, D. & Entwistle, N. (eds). *The Experience of Learning. Implications for Teaching and Studying in Higher Education.* 2nd edition. Scottish Academic Press Edinburgh, pp. 23-38.

Dahlgren, L. O., Dahle, L. O. & J. Ludvigsson 1987. Varför PBI? In: Dahlgren, L. O. & Kellgren, K. (red). *Problembaserad inlärning.* Studentlitteratur, Lund, pp. 13-27.

Egidius, H. 1991. *Problembaserad inlärning – en introduktion.* Studentlitteratur, Lund.

Egidius, H. 1999a. *PBL och casemetodik. Hur man gör och varför.* Studentlitteratur, Lund.

Egidius, H. 1999b. *Problembaserat lärande – en introduktion för lärare och lärande.* Studentlitteratur, Lund.

Entwistle, N. 1997 (1984). Contrasting Perspectives on Learning. In: Marton, F., Hounsell, D., & Entwistle, N. (eds). *The Experience of Learning. Implications for Teaching and Studying in Higher Education.* 2nd edition. Scottish Academic Press Edinburgh, pp. 3-22.

Entwistle, N. & Marton, F. 1995 (1986). Att förändra uppfattningar av inlärning och forskning. In: Marton, F., Hounsell, D. & Entwistle, N. (eds). *Hur vi lär.* (Swedish edition of *The Experience of Learning*) Tema Nova, Rabén Prisma, pp. 285-308.

Eriksson, A. 2000. Drastisk ökning av antalet långtidssjuka. *GU Journalen,* juni, 5/2000, p. 3.

Flinck, A. W & Liljedahl, K. 1997. *Experiences of Alternative use of Problem Based Learning (PBL) in a Theoretical Context.* Paper presented at "International Conference on project Work in University Studies" Roskilde 15-17 Sept 1997.

Freire, P. 1970. *Pedagogy of the Oppressed.* Herder & Herder. New York. (Swedish translation by Fredrik, Gustaf and Sten Rohde 1972: *Pedagogik för förtryckta.* Gummessons Kursiv. Stockholm).

Hamilakis, Y. 2004. Archaeology and the politics of pedagogy. *World Archaeology Vol. 36(2),* pp. 287-309.

Hellertz, P. Westin 1999. *Kvinnors kunskapssyn och lärandestrategier? – En studie av tjugosju kvinnliga socionomstuderande.* Akademisk avhandling. Örebro Studies 17. Örebro universitet, universitetsbiblioteket.

Hjørungdal, T.; Gillberg, Å., Cornell, C., Karlsson, H., Gustafsson, A, Nyqvist, R. & Bille, U. (forthcoming). *Paper presented at the 10th Annual Meeting of the European Association of Archaeologists.* Lyon 2004.

Hodgson, V. 1997 (1984). Lectures and the Experience of Relevance. In: Marton, F., Hounsell, D. & Entwistle, N. (eds). *The Experience of Learning. Implications for Teaching and Studying in Higher Education.* 2nd edition. Scottish Academic Press Edinburgh, pp. 159-171.

Hounsell, D. 1997 (1984). Understanding Teaching and Teaching for Understanding. In: Marton, F., Hounsell, D. & Entwistle, N. (eds). *The Experience of Learning. Implications for Teaching and Studying in Higher Education.* 2nd edition. Scottish Academic Press Edinburgh, pp. 238-257.

Högskolelagen 1 kap. 4a§, Lag 2000:260.

Kugel, P. 1993. How Professors Develop as Teachers. *Studies in Higher Education. Volume 18, No. 3 1993,* pp. 315-328.

Lauvås, P. & Handal, G. 2001. *Handledning och praktisk yrkesteori.* 2:a upplagan. Studentlitteratur, Lund.

Lindgren, A. 1976 (1945). *Pippi Longstocking.* First published 1945 by Rabén & Sjögren. First translated by Oxford University Press 1954. Published in Puffin Books, in the Penguin Group 1976.

Linduff, K. M. & Y. Sun eds. 2004. *Gender and Chinese Archaeology.* Walnut Creek, CA: Altamira Press.

Luke, C. & Gore, J. eds. 1992. *Feminism and Critical Pedagogy.* Routledge.

Lövkvist, L. 2004. Utbildning i förklädnad. Om

jämställdhet, genus och annat smått och gott. In: Hjørungdal, T. (red). *Dialog med de sega strukturerna. Om arkeologisk utbildning och genusperspektiv.* Gotarc Serie C. Arkeologiska Skrifter No 55. Göteborgs universitet, Institutionen för arkeologi, pp. 49-88.

Lövkvist, L. & Hjørungdal, T. 2000. Voices from an Educational World. Some issues of gender-conscious teaching and learning. In *Current Swedish Archaeology*, Vol 8, 2000, pp. 157-178.

Marton, F. & Säljö, R. 1997 (1984). Approaches to learning. In: Marton, F., Hounsell, F. & Entwistle, N. (eds). *The Experience of Learning. Implications for Teaching and Studying in Higher Education.* 2nd edition. Scottish Academic Press Edinburgh, pp. 39-58.

Morgan, A. & Beaty, L. 1997 (1984): The World of the Learner. In: Marton, F., Hounsell, D. & Entwistle, N. (eds). *The Experience of Learning. Implications for Teaching and Studying in Higher Education.* 2nd edition. Scottish Academic Press Edinburgh, pp. 217-237.

Ramsden, P. 1997 (1984). The Context of Learning in Academic Departments. In: Marton, F., Hounsell, D. & Entwistle, N. (eds) *The Experience of Learning. Implications for Teaching and Studying in Higher Education.* 2nd edition. Scottish Academic Press Edinburgh, pp. 198-216.

Rousseau, J.J. 1977: *Emile, eller om uppfostran.* Första delen. Stegelands.

Rousseau, J.J. 1978: *Emile, eller om uppfostran.* Andra delen. Stegelands.

Rågvik, H. 2000. Stora förändringar i arbetslivet har lett till ökad stress. I *DIK-forum* No. 18, 2000, pp. 8-9.

Rönnby, J. 2000. Visst skall vi utbilda i arkeologi! *Gjallarhornet.* Utges av Svenska Arkeologiska Samfundet. Årgång 20, Nr. 4, 2000, pp. 1- 2.

Silén, Ch. 1996. *Ledsaga lärande – om handledarfunktionen i PBI.* Linköpings universitet: Institutionen för pedagogik och psykologi.

Spector, J. & Whelan, M. 1988. Incorporating Gender Into Archaeolgy Courses. A Curriculum Guide for Introductory Human Evolution and Archaeology Classes. *KAN,* No 7, pp. 79-94.

Svedberg, L. 2000. *Gruppsykologi. Om grupper, organisationer och ledarskap.* Andra upplagan. Studentlitteratur, Lund, pp. 250-270.

Svensson, L. 1997 (1984). Skill in Learning and Organising Knowledge. In: Marton, F.,Hounsell, D. & Entwistle, N. (eds) *The Experience of Learning. Implications for Teaching and Studying in Higher Education.* 2nd edition. Scottish Academic Press Edinburgh, pp. 59-71.*S veriges Rikes Lag. Högskolelagen* 1 kap, 4a§.

Säljö, R. 1997. Reading and Everyday Conceptions of Knowledge. In: Marton, F.,Hounsell, D. & Entwistle, N. (eds.). *The Experience of Learning. Implications for Teaching and Studying in Higher Education.* 2nd edition. Scottish Academic Press Edinburgh, pp. 89-105.

Säljö, R. 2000. *Lärande i praktiken. Ett sociokulturellt perspektiv.* Prisma, Stockholm.

Sørensen, M. L. S. 2000. *Gender Archaeology.* Polity Press.

Theorell, Th. 2000. Stress – en vetenskaplig utmaning. In *Jäktad, pressad – utbränd? Forskare diskuterar strategier mot skadlig stress.* Källa/52. Utgiven av (edited by) Forskningsrådsnämnden augusti 2000, pp. 10-25.

Tompkins, J. 1991. Teaching like it matters. A modest proposal for revolutionizing the classroom. In: *Lingua franca: the review of academic life,* pp. 24-27.

www.ingramcontent.com/pod-product-compliance
Lightning Source LLC
Chambersburg PA
CBHW061000030426
42334CB00033B/3304